ARCHITECTURE AND MODERN LIFE

OTHER BOOKS BY BAKER BROWNELL

THE NEW UNIVERSE
EARTH IS ENOUGH

OTHER BOOKS BY FRANK LLOYD WRIGHT

AN INTERPRETATION OF JAPANESE PRINTS
IN THE CAUSE OF ARCHITECTURE
EXPERIMENTING WITH HUMAN LIVES
AUSGEFÜHRTE BAUTEN UND ENTWÜRFE
SONDERHEIT
WENDINGEN
MODERN ARCHITECTURE
THE NATURE OF MATERIALS
AN AUTOBIOGRAPHY
THE DISAPPEARING CITY

THE MING JAR AT TALIESIN

Spring Green, Wisconsin

ARCHITECTURE AND MODERN LIFE

BY BAKER BROWNELL AND FRANK LLOYD WRIGHT

ILLUSTRATED

HARPER & BROTHERS PUBLISHERS
NEW YORK AND LONDON MCMXXXVIII

ARCHITECTURE AND MODERN LIFE

CONTENTS

ILLUSTRATIONS

ARCHITECTURE AND MODERN LIFE

I. Architecture and Social Life

THE Hudson river tunnel is a glistening conduit through which a large amount of mankind is piped to New York in the morning and piped back to Jersey in the afternoon. It is smooth and looks aseptic. Its sides slide by in long motion, rhythms of light, the rustling of wheels. It delivers fifty thousand people every few hours silently, precisely, and with as much comfort as city people are permitted to have. What the railroad tunnels do as the climax of much contrivance and effort this vehicular tunnel does casually, as if it were the natural thing to slide under the Hudson river to New York.

Man is a fluid in metropolitan regions. He flows through the rush hours, rolls along the bank-full streets. The tunnel is built for that fluidity. It is a homoduct, if God and the Oxford dictionary will permit the word, that interprets to some extent the social character of the times. It is architecturally the pressure to and fro of people, a structure of society worked out in the rock of the river bed. The violent ebb and flow of modern city life is here made smooth in a habit of concrete and steel. Does this distort the meaning of the word "architecture"? Not as this book means it. Architecture is

1

architecture, not merely building, because it does interpret the structure of the society to which it belongs and in which it flourishes. Architecture makes social life articulate, tells its meaning, and is a chief fruit of culture. Mere building records the necessities of existence, but architecture is creative. It is itself a flux. It is the flow of human life in the channels cut by civilization in the rock face of earth.

But architecture not only interprets the nature of social structures; it may create them in the present and prophesy them in the future. In this respect architecture, an art, is different from engineering, a science. The engineer—at least as he is now trained—is responsible only for the physical character of the job to which he is assigned, regardless of other consequences, but the architect must have wider vision. As a creative artist he must consider the nature of human expression and the sensuous effects of his work. He must build into his structures the good life as a new kind of beauty. Like the engineer he will master materials and the activity of building, but he goes further. The engineer is responsible for facts: the architect is responsible for values too. His work is not so much *for* men as it *is* men.

A stainless, light-filled tower might rise above the city. It is clear and hard like a pinnacle of ice. It has left stone and its mass behind, as well as brick, tile, and other opaque earthenware. Only glass and stainless metal belong here above the jungle of the streets. It is some fabrication of thought and of things, of new materials and fresh values, as complex in the making as it is delicate and simple in result. It stands alone,

2

like a virgin above the soiled frumperies of her older sisters below. It is expressive, timely, and a creation, no doubt, as well as an interpretation of human and aesthetic values. But creation is complex. Involved in this case there are not only new methods of engineering that eventuate in new forms of visual beauty; there are new accessories of convenience, new lighting patterns, new habits of office work and daily routine that amount to invention. There are new restaurants, perhaps, above the city, new patterns of eating, new dancing, new music. It is a more intrinsic recreation, if architecture is what it should be. In all this and more, the prophetic stainless building is involved.

The virgin stands icily above the city. She is remote and beautiful. But those who live and work on the streets below must pay a penalty for her purity. She is aristocratically apart, she breathes a better air, but her beauty and isolation must be rooted in the jungle below. She must feed on its darkness and congestion. Her presence in part, as things are, must create them. The physical building may be partly cause, partly consequence or condition in a much entangled pattern that includes both good and bad. It is creative. The tall, pure tower looks forward and backward; it is good, bad, but the quality of thought that can give such integrity to the building can and does work constructively in the social life of the times.

The stainless tower, like the great city itself, must be indeed a monument to the extreme concentrations of power, population, wealth, deadly facilities, that mark the modern era. It is tense and shining, but the instability of a people that knows

3

no rest shows there. On streets laid out for a three-story town, an eighteen-story town must operate with a corresponding increase in velocity and interference. On human beings built for a slower pace of spasmodic action and repose the city lays a driving pressure and urgency. It seeks experiments and expedients in the emergency. It fails in sincere courage and vision. The natural integrity of life is broken down into intense activities each in its special compartment having little or nothing of the whole. The stainless tower is a part of this confusion but, though in it, is not of it. The internal integrity of its natural character that might be a factor in better social life seems of little avail for the moment. Architecture has hitherto made the structure of a society more fixed and more elaborate. Then excess brings inevitable change. An organic architecture such as this not only embodies social structures but suggests other and better structures. Seeking an architecture more free in relation to change, more independent of the fixed symmetries imposed on life, organic architecture keeps itself free to continually begin at the beginning and continually live anew.

Architecture thus embodies social structures and suggests others when free to create them. When free it is organic, growing. Organic architecture continuously arises from within. It continuously begins at the beginning instead of growing more static as it grows older. Organic architecture alone has this power of growth in form.

This creativeness of organic architecture reaches out from life and back into life, in and out of varied parts of living. It

4

means not merely the looks of buildings or the number of rooms, the size, the materials: it means also the effect that architectural forms have on people's action. For the lives of people take architectural forms that in turn affect the ideals of people and their action. As a house is built so the pattern of activity of those will be who live in it. Organic architecture controls their movement, their comings and goings. It clarifies and cultivates their sense of form in space, in color, in mass, and in action. Shall the housewife turn right or left after four steps, shall she move about with grace and ease, or shall she climb up and down from one floor to another floor or otherwise waste her steps in needless to and fro? Shall the child pause at the window for the view before he climbs fifteen steps to his play room? Shall confinement mark his life at home or shall his life be characterized by a sense of free action, spaciousness, and innate harmony? To these modest questions the house says "Yes" or "No." Many other questions it answers. Separately they are small matters, but together the very texture of living. The routines of life have their rhythms. They are a varied but eternal dance for which architecture provides a score. The kinaesthetic or muscular implications of architecture are an important though rarely recognized aspect of the art's creativeness. The rectangle, for example, was never well adapted to human movement. The hexagon is better. The folkways and habits of living, from the most lowly to the sublime, are the ways of architecture. If architecture is empty, there is proof enough that life is empty.

The humble privy has become in recent years another example of what architecture may do as a creative social influence. This refers not so much to the aesthetic studies by Chic Sale, as to widespread work through the southern mountains and elsewhere generally in the improvement of public health and private decency by means of standardized designs for sanitation. Where conditions permit, the privy has come indoors as an integral part of any good building. Elsewhere, throughout wide regions, privies have been made safe to health and better looking by means of new design. Rebuilding, with public help, has created new folkways in this respect. The new designs reflect into the structure of society, and better health and more decent ways of living are the consequence. It is a lowly example and obvious enough, though to some it will seem beneath the dignity of architecture. But to those who believe with the modern poet that all significant experience may be the subject of art, even the building of a privy may involve architectural values. These human necessities are as legitimately involved in architectural values as eating or sleeping or dreaming.

Just as interpretation emerges as creation, so creation is prophecy. Architecture which is a genuine interpretation of the present is a prophecy of social structure yet to come. Unless architecture is this prophetic interpretation, we may still call it building but we may not call it architecture. For architecture is no mere reflection but as true interpretation of the present is naturally prophetic. It takes divine initiative, as it were, for in the old Biblical way it not merely foretells the future but, in embodying the advanced thought of its time,

Photo by Edmund Teske

THE ARCHITECTURE OF THE LANDSCAPE

About Taliesin

Photo by Karl Tens

INTEGRAL DECORATION IN NATURE

IN THE LOGGIA AT TALIESIN

is a power that actually moves the world towards a better state. If Radio City is a symbol of the good and evil of the present, Broadacre City envisions that way to life and beauty implicit in the future as the present: that future is always now. If Radio City is the man of today tipped up edgewise so that all may see his cellular imprisonment in the system that he serves, Broadacre City emphasizes the fact that the horizontal line of human movement on the ground is more important to man than the verticality of floor above floor. Without losing the elemental human virtues of the day of our forefathers, it avails itself of the inventions of the present, and offers a way to use them for humanity. Architecture is unique among the arts and professions in its ability to give to the present the possibilities of the future. It can make the future move. It can force tomorrow into the concrete realm of things touched and seen. It shows a complete cross section of our civilization in terms of this future within the present.

In a larger and perhaps more mystical sense of the word, architecture is itself whatever is organic. It is the organic pattern of all things. This remains the hidden mystery of creation until the architect has grasped and revealed it. We have said that architecture interprets structure and through structure creates form, prophesies new form: now we say that architecture in a more philosophical sense is whatever significance structure itself possesses. It is the significant structure of all created things as the mind may know them. It is at least the geometric pattern of things, of life, of the human and social world. It is at best that magic framework of reality that we sometimes touch upon when we use the word *order*. Architecture is this aura (or "oversoul" as Emerson might say) of structure. It is a true expression of the life of the human and social world. Buildings, merely, know nothing of it. Buildings are only material projects in some medium. In other media there are collateral projects and many illustrations. Music, economic activity, statesmanship, the dance, poetry are a few of the media in which other illustrations of this structure may occur. Only when buildings illustrate this structural integrity of all things are they architecturally expressive and good.

A battleship and a powerful newspaper, for example, are a good deal alike. They are parallel illustrations of a structural character that has great emphasis in modern society. They are timely, if time bound. They are angular, jut out boldly. They incorporate power and skill. Like airplanes, automobiles, electrification they are forms of the new world. Though our sentiments towards battleships may vary from dislike to admiration, it is true that the battleship in any case is expressive. It expresses the structure and purpose of society, or at least one aspect of it, and punctuates our power.

In this billion horse-power America, to continue the illustration, social structures are designed primarily to encourage action and to do work. In the entire western world, indeed, machine power is about the only mark of distinction. Other societies may rightly claim higher morality, more cleanliness, more religion, better art, more love, more wisdom and happiness: we are superior in power. We have more energy. We can do more work. America alone exploits more energy and uses more per capita than any people in human history. The

8

battleship is an expression of that power. So is the big business newspaper. In a society where power and skill have so great a structural importance they are illustrations in different media of the same thing. They are forms identified with the structure of society. In this internal sense, too, is architecture structure.

The foregoing paragraphs have said that architecture interprets the structure of the society in which it is and as prophecy must create the future. These aspects of architecture will be developed by illustration and discussion through the first part of this book. In another and more metaphysical sense, architecture is itself the structure in all things. This will be considered throughout the book. The second part of the book will deal with the dominant characteristics of architecture in the past and present; the third part with the characteristics of the modern social world so far as they influence expression; the fourth part with the architecture of the future; the fifth part with society and the future; the sixth part with the nature of a balanced society; and the seventh part with the philosophy of society as architecture and of architecture as society.

Thus the following chapters are devoted to the theme that a natural architecture is not only the concrete expression of the life and structure of society but is social creation emerging as master building. It belongs to the materials used, and to the men who use them. It participates in their nature and their inherent patterns of relationship, but in turn it transmutes that nature and those structures from the realm of the potential into the realm of created things. It is not only part of their action, it is a bridge over which the past reached the present and the present will reach the future. For us in America, it is a new reality.

In the western world were three great architectures, the Greek, Roman, the Gothic, and now it will recognize another, the "Modern," or Organic. Each one begins in the basic act of building. The development of each one, to some extent, is responsible to the materials used, to the men who build, and to the society in which the building takes place. If the architecture of Egypt was an interpretation of flesh and death eternal, the architecture of Greece, earliest among western peoples, was a celebration of the sureness and immediacy of life, but with little or no sense of its organic character. If Gothic architecture was an expression of straining dreams, phantasy, escape from the ruthless life of that time, modern organic architecture, our theme, comes to mark again belief in life as a whole. It accepts, gratefully, its achievements. It goes along with the restless, seeking powers of man. It moves toward a more faithful reality than Realism or Romanticism could ever be.

Very different are the modes and men and materials of these architectures, as different as their varied expressions. In

10

Egypt, for example, building belonged to stone. In Greece, building belonged to wood imitated in stone. And yet they both belong to stone in their physical antiquity. This is true although Greek buildings in their day were in spirit still gorgeously painted wooden buildings done in stone with little sense of the organic. As the Gothic towers of the builders of the thirteenth century tortured stone into forms that stone never should have, so they tortured life into unworldly aspirations. They not only emulated the forest in stone, but to escape the rough realism of the time, made stone soar in most incongruous flights. Modern builders may, and sometimes do, leave stone behind for lighter, tensile or more plastic stuff —steel, glass, and what we call synthetics. Forms today must be immeasurably changed by steel and glass. Modern organic architecture accepts and trusts the modern achievements of this world and regardless of old forms goes along with them to forms more faithful, not to realism or romanticism, but to reality.

The three great western architectures were embodied in stone. Now organic architecture is first to become independent of it—which is but one example of the difference today. In many other ways modern work might be an original and primary synthesis of the materials, the social interests, the technologies and power of the modern age instead of the confusion of all of them owing to the substitution of academic standards for the nature of growth and of organic change. Little of the work of this time is organic or even "modern," as we have here for the moment used the word.

11

The earth teems with tawdry buildings, cheap fashions, eclectic "styles," for the eclectics we have always with us. Eclectics are our characteristic mass product. Meantime American skyscrapers continue to imitate in steel the earlier forms in stone. They are nondescript, usually alien to the nature of their materials and the new reality that is organic. With their range immeasurably widened by steel and glass, modern buildings might achieve a new integrity, an organic architecture fearlessly accepting the laws of change inherent in all nature, including human nature. But few of them do. They are a babel of styles. Facility outruns thought and feeling. Intricate confusions surround the few examples of organic work. These examples are hard to find. All kinds of work are done today, both good and bad, to make a complex, contradictory world, and all of it is clearly modern, or at least contemporary. But we shall ignore the bad, for the purposes of this work, and use the word "modern" as referring to the great work that can be done and has been done in terms of modern values and conditions.

It is sunset and the dying sun spreads its last glory over the gas tanks—or are they oil tanks?—that mark the northern waters of San Francisco Bay. The air is misty rose, the water calm, as the sun leaves the darkening continent and sinks into the sea. To the north white forms arise—vague, bulbous, rose touched by the sun. Mist obscures their base. They float like great birds, balloons, the domes of Venice over the sea. They ride upon the air like escaped domes by Michelangelo, without distance seemingly, both near and far. Are they that soap

12

bubble, named St. Peter's, repeated here in flocks upon a western shore? No, they are the gas tanks. Their aluminum painted sides glow with rose fire. They stand in vague rows and ranges off towards El Cerrito.

These gas tanks are features of a kind of world that neither Greek nor Gothic, Egyptian, Renaissance nor any other older style could comprehend. Simple as they look there, rosy across the water, they are commands of steel, coal, petroleum, of railway men and miners, of new-found technics in a new kind of struggle to live. Their structure is the structure of that world. Their function is bound closely within that modern world's social pattern. These bland, unconscious gas tanks cannot be called art or works of art. If form follows function, however, and if expressiveness and plastic form are the ways of art, they well may stand ready to enter that portal by way of architecture. They are now the concern of architecture. They are deeply identified, like many other modern necessitous works, with such skill and power as we have today.

Modern organic architecture—to apply the term again to great work in the present and future—is not only comparable, then, to the other great architectures of the western world; in its expressiveness and its plasticity it must rise superior to them. It not only gives form or expression to the society from which it emerges; it plastically and rhythmically adjusts its structures to that contour, the contour of need. It has flow and continuity like movements in music or of a strong graceful person walking, for this is the meaning of plasticity; it intelligently serves, as Louis Sullivan has said; it does not suppress.

13

Modern organic architecture, in a word, is expressive and plastic because it begins with an integration of modern life. It gives when it accepts. It accepts when it gives. It formulates from within. It does not reformulate. The nature of this integration with modern life is identified with its nature. Why is this integrity new to America?

As architecture is integrated with modern life, so first it will appear as economy. It is clean. Nothing is stuck on. Nothing is present that does not contribute.

It has, second, honesty. Brick is brick and looks like it, feels like it, serves like it. So does iron, glass, wood, or steel. Pretense and fake, false fronts, loafing columns, false plaster of Paris echoes of honest craft from days gone by, are not present. Things not only are what they seem: they reveal more than they ever seemed.

Architecture, third, is functional. Its working parts are revealed as expressive features. It is never ashamed to confess its purpose. Purpose is exhibited. At its least, architecture is chaste and exact like a good machine: it is direct. But it is not a machine any more than a man's heart is a suction pump. Only when it is more than a machine is any building architecture.

It is, fourth, organic. Form and function are one. More than any appearance, or comment, or any mere convenience, it is something that is. It issues proudly from the practical nature of the thing as an entity. It has, by right, individuality. The complexities of materials and men, of social patterns and activity, have been organized within its frame, and it is responsible to their natures. It is a finer order than men could

14

otherwise know or have dreamed. It reduces them to simples. They have informed it. And it is responsible to life alone for whatever life it has.

It has, fifth, such beauty as it knows inherent in its structure, and it has the magic of expression. It says something by way of itself that it alone may say. It has significance, and having significance has the countenance of truth.

These few truths of form and feature that we have called modern—although the word means only *à la mode*—are not so much modern in themselves as they are modern where architecture is concerned. They are eternal. They assume that architecture is a plastic part of living in the present and all its works. They are fused with the moral and social implications of life, in contrast to current aesthetic eclecticism. Though this "organic" point of view is not, of course, a unique discovery of this age, it is a point of view that results always in freshness, vitality, and consequence. Though Lao Tze, the old Chinese philosopher, was aware of it, though Walt Whitman sensed it, the practice of the thought involved has, in architecture, been rare. It has still to grow up. The thought now penetrates to the basis of building in the nature of materials, methods and men and their human situation. Architecture may now safely abandon forms and their reforms held through habit or traditions: it creates forms anew out of the living reality of today. Or better, perhaps, it enters that reality and with both feeling and science imbues it with form and structure. It goes to the roots. That is its logic. It is radical. That also is its poetry.

The towers of America rise from the western plains and

15

prairies as well as from the larger towns. In Wasco, Illinois, or Lily Lake, on Simpson's farm west of Clinton, Iowa, above the valley floor at Black Earth, Wisconsin, they may be seen. Towers mark the countryside. For three thousand miles from east to west and a thousand miles from north to south, are towers. Tower after tower pins down the continent on its base of soil and rock. From above they look like smoothed stakes driven there. They are the grain elevators of concrete and their smaller colleagues, the silos. If the towers of great cities and their imitators in smaller towns are restless fingers reaching towards God knows what, the gray grain elevators and farm silos are towers with more repose and at least some genuine significance. They stand along the waterfronts and the railroad sidings. They are simply built to contain, to hold in safety, the grain stores of a nation, with no thought of beauty or other consequence. They are, so to speak, merely the nation's granary. But they stand clean, reticent, secure, examples of firm orderliness, of refreshing simplicity. In this they belong to the new architecture that we have called organic. Man has taken many liberties with his towers. These, almost alone among them, have something of the significance and inevitable rhythm of a naturally created thing that is the basis of organic architecture. They stand, not classic certainly, nor as yet historic tradition. They are a wholesome negative. They have yet to make the affirmation that must be the substance of an indigenous American architecture.—B. B. and F. Ll. W.

16

II. Some Aspects of the Past and Present of Architecture

THE land is the simplest form of architecture.

Building upon the land is as natural to man as to other animals, birds or insects. In so far as he was more than an animal his buildings became what we call architecture.

In ancient times his limitations served to keep his buildings architecture. Splendid examples: Mayan, Egyptian, Greek, Byzantine, Persian, Gothic, Indian, Chinese, Japanese.

Looking back at these, what then is architecture?

It is man and more.

It is man in possession of his earth. It is the only true record of him where his possession of earth is concerned.

While he was true to earth his architecture was creative.

The time comes when he is no longer inspired by the nature of earth. His pagan philosophy is breaking down, owing to changing social conditions, to new science, new facilities, easy riches. The social world begins to turn upside down. Science takes the place of art. Things serve the man better than thoughts.

Nothing in his experience enables him to resist the disintegrating effect of money and machines. An enemy to his

17

nature, likely to emasculate or destroy him, is embraced by him.

His creative faculties (art) are conditioned upon this earth. His possession of earth in this sense grows dim as his intellect (science and invention) discovers ways to beat work. Money shows him new ways to cheat life. Power becomes exterior instead of interior. His own acts—which are vicarious—are no longer inherent.

In these circumstances architecture becomes too difficult, building too easy. New facilities are here for which he has no corresponding forms. He seems for the moment powerless to make them. He is lost to the source of inspiration, the ground. He takes any substitute. Neither the pagan ideal nor its counterpart, Christianity, longer lead him.

In the stress of circumstance a new ideal appears capable of leading him out of bondage into life again. Again the ground comes into the light as a brighter sense of reality dawns. It is the sense and nature of that which is within—integrity.

The room or space within the building is man's reality instead of his exterior circumstance. Though as old as philosophy, the new ideal takes on fresh significance in the ideal of architecture as organic. It must be integral to a life lived as organic.

New sense of the whole enters the life of man to bring order out of chaos. The old—"classic," eclecticism—is chaos, restlessness.

The new—"integral," organic—is order, repose.

18

All materials lie piled in masses or float as gases in the landscape of this planet much as the cataclysms of creation left them.

At the mercy of the cosmic elements, these materials have been disintegrated by temperatures, ground down by glaciers, eroded by wind and sea, sculptured by tireless forces qualifying each other. They are all externally modified by time as they modify this earth in a ceaseless procession of change.

Stone is the basic material of our planet. It is continually changed by cosmic forces, themselves a form of change. Contrasted with these great mineral masses of earth structure—this titanic wreckage—are placid depths and planes of mutable water or the vast depth-plane of the immutable sky hung with evanescent clouds. And this creeping ground-cover of vegetable life, more inexorable than death, is rising from it all, over all, against all, texturing with pattern, infinite in resource, and inexhaustible in variety of effect. This is the earthly abode of the buildings man has built to work, dwell, worship, dance and breed in.

Change is the one immutable circumstance found in landscape. But the changes all speak or sing in unison of cosmic law, itself a nobler form of change. These cosmic laws are the physical laws of all man-built structures as well as the laws of landscape.

Man takes a positive hand in creation whenever he puts a building upon the earth beneath the sun. If he has birthright at all, it must consist in this: that he, too, is no less a feature

19

of the landscape than the rocks, trees, bears or bees of that nature to which he owes his being.

Continuously nature shows him the science of her remarkable economy of structure in mineral and vegetable constructions to go with the unspoiled character everywhere apparent in her forms.

The long, low lines of colorful, windswept terrain, the ineffable dotted line, the richly textured plain, great striated, stratified masses lying noble and quiet or rising with majesty above the vegetation of the desert floor: nature-masonry is piled up into ranges upon ranges of mountains that seem to utter a form-language of their own.

Earth is prostrate, prostitute to the sun. All life we may know is sun life, dies sun death, as shadow, only to be born again. Evidence is everywhere.

Material forms are manifest in one phase today, to be found in another tomorrow. Everywhere around us creeps the eternally mysterious purpose of this inexorable ground-cover of growth. It is mysterious purpose, desperately determined, devouring or being devoured in due course upon this titanic battlefield. Growth seeks conquest by way of death.

To what end is all in pattern?

Always—eternally—pattern? Why?

Why this intrigue of eye-music to go with sensuous ear-music?

What is this inner realm of rhythm that dances in sentient beings and lies quiescent but no less sentient in pattern?

There seems to be no mortal escape, least of all in death,

20

from this earth-principle which is again the sun-principle of growth. Earth becomes more and more the creative creature of the sun. It is a womb quickened by the passions of the master sun.

Nevertheless, every line and the substance of earth's rockbound structure speak of violence. All is scarred by warring forces seeking reconciliation, still marred by conflict and conquest. But in our era violence has subsided, is giving way to comparative repose. Streamlines of the mountain ranges come down more gently to the plains. Geological cataclysm is subsiding or becoming subservient. Divine order creeps out and rises superior to chaos. Pattern asserts itself. Once more, triumph.

Ceaselessly, the rock masses are made by fire, are laid low by water, are sculptured by wind and stream. They take on the streamlines characteristic of the sweeping forces that change them.

Already matter lies quieted, and with it violence and discord. It is bathed in light that so far as man can see is eternal. Penetrating all, itself penetrated by itself, is mysterious eye-music: pattern.

Meantime in all this lesser building within greater building there is other animation, still another kind of building: these are creatures of creation patterned upon similar patterns until plant, animal creature and earth and man resemble each other for purpose malign or beneficent. Insect, reptile, fish, animal and bird are there in all the elements using gifts of life in this mysterious yet strangely familiar resemblance that we call

21

our world. The seemingly senseless destruction g.. ... each.

Some law of laws seems to keep in full effect ... change in this world-workshop. The crevices and se... of earth, shadows of the great underneath are swarming ...... fantastic insects, also singing, working, dancing and breeding.

But with this singular creature, man? Gaining dominion over all, what will he do to maintain his dominion? What will be his essential "pattern"? What does the vulnerable master of cause and effect know of instrumental cosmic law? What may he create?

Man by nature desired to build as the birds were meantime building their nests, as insects were building their cities, and as animals were seeking their dens, making their lairs, or burrowing into the ground. And architecture became by way of this desire the greatest proof on earth of man's greatness, his right to be born, to inherit the earth.

If the man was poor and mean by nature he built that way. If he was noble and richly endowed then he built grandly, like a noble man. But high or low it was his instinct to build on this earth.

By innate animal instinct he got his first lessons. He got

22

WISCONSIN FARM BUILDINGS

ideas of form from those nature-forms about him, native to the place where he lived. Consciously or unconsciously he was taught by birds and animals. Inspired by the way rock ledges were massed up against sky on the hills, he was taught by the stratified masses of the rock itself. Trees must have awakened his sense of form. The pagodas of China and Japan definitely resemble the pines with which they were associated. The constructions of the Incas married earth itself.

Man's faithful companion, the tree, lived by light. The building, man's own tree, lived by shadows. Therefore, early building masses naturally belonged to the sunlit landscape in which they stood. The stone constructions of the Incas belonged there. Those of the African, of the sea-islanders and of the cliff-dwellers belonged there. The more developed buildings of Persia, China, and Japan belonged there. Later a building had become consciously no less a child of the sun than trees themselves always were.

Probably man first lived in stone caves, when he did not live in trees, using selected sticks and seeking appropriate stones for tools. Concerning this point it is perhaps better to say he first lived sometimes in trees and sometimes in stone caves. As he moved north or south his type of dwelling changed with the climate. The north always demanded most from him in the way of building, if he was to preserve himself. And the Esquimaux learned to build their igloos of blocks of snow cemented with ice.

Farther south the builder was satisfied with some grass and leaves raised up on a platform of sticks, or with some kind of tent that he might fold up and take with him on his horse as he rode away. While still dwelling in caves the man perhaps learned to make utensils out of wet clay. He burned them hard for use. These utensils he seems to have made with a higher faculty. His instinct became an aesthetic sense of environment. It taught him something of form. He learned from the animals, the serpents, the plants that he knew. Except for this faculty he was no more than another animal.

Still clinging to the cliffs, he made whole caves out of wet clay and let the sun bake the cave hard. He made them just as he had made the vessels that he had previously put into fire to bake and had used in the cave in the rocks. And so, once upon a time, man moved into his first earth-built house, of *earth*.

This large clay cave or pot of the cliff-dwellers, with a lid on it, was among the first man-made houses. The lid was troublesome to him then and has always been so to subsequent builders. But previously better forms of houses had come from the sticks that had been conferred upon him by his friendly companion, the tree. The lighter, more scientific house-shapes were at first conical, made so by leaning upright sticks together at the top. And the builder covered the sticks with skins of the animals he had eaten. But later man made more roomy houses by squaring the interior space and framing the walls upright. To make the walls he put sticks upright and crossed them at intervals with other horizontal sticks firmly lashed to the vertical sticks, finally covering all with various forms of mats woven of tall dried grasses or grasses lashed directly to the framework. Some forms of these earlier houses in certain parts of Africa and of the South Sea Islands are beautiful architecture to this day.

Then the builder had to contrive the lid—by now it may be called a roof—by framing much heavier sticks together, sloping the sticks across the interior spaces from wall to wall to carry overhead masses of tall dried grasses laid on smaller cross sticks in such a way as to run the water off. He covered this overhead wood framing in the manner of a thatch. The shape of this cover (or roof) was what most affected the general aspect of his building. Sometimes the roof stood up tall within the walls. Sometimes in shape it was a low protective mound. Sometimes it projected boldly. But it always showed its wood construction beneath the final covering.

Walls at first of earth, stone or wood stood up and out heavily as most important. The roof was seldom visible, especially where war was in man's mind, as it usually was. Later the sense of roof as shelter overcame the sense of walls, and great roofs were to be seen with the walls standing back in under them. Man soon came to feel that, if he had no roof in this sense, he had no house.

Later he came to speak of his house as "his roof" and was fond of inviting strangers to come and sit or stay "under his roof." If other men displeased him he drove them "from beneath his roof." His roof was not only his shelter, it was his dignity, as well as his sense of home.

Civilization proceeded. Unless man had war in mind (as he usually did) the roof-shelter became the most important factor in the making of the house. It became the ultimate feature of his building. This remains true to this late day when changes of circumstances have made it the roof that he needs to fortify instead of the walls. The real menace of attack is now from the air.

The real science of structure entered into building with this sense of the roof and of wood, or "the stick," because every roof had to be framed strongly enough to span the interior space from wall to wall. Sometimes, as a confession of inability, perhaps, or a forced economy, the roof had to be supported on interior posts or partitions. Various picturesque roof forms arose as different materials were used to span the space below. More pains had to be taken with these spans than with anything else about the building. Although stone was used to imitate wood construction, the dome, the perfect masonry roof, soon arose among the myriad roofs of the world.

In all this work the principal tools in human hands were fire, the simple lever, and the wheel. But, in human hands, these soon grew into the might of the machine. Explosives soon came along to multiply the force of lever and wheel.

Early masonry buildings were mostly the work of men employing the simple leverage of inclined ways or using the bar as direct lever in human hands. The lever in some form (the wheel is the lever also) was used to make these early buildings.

Materials in primitive architecture were always most important. The character of all the earlier buildings was determined more by the materials available for construction than by any other one thing. Wood, brick, and stone always said "wood," "brick," or "stone," and acted it. Later the builder

26

lost sight of nature in this integral sense. But these good limitations held until the so-called "Renaissance" or "Rebirth" of architecture.

Being craftsmen, because taught by experience with materials in actual construction, the early builders could find a right way to work whatever materials they found. They were ways that were best suited to the kind of buildings we can call architecture. Now the kind of building that we can call architecture today is the building wherein human thought and feeling enter to create a greater harmony and true significance in the whole structure. Shelter and utility in themselves were never enough. The edifice was the highest product of the human mind. Man always sought reflection in it of his sense of himself as God-like. Man's imagination made the gods, and so he made a God-like building. He dedicated it to the god he had made. His architecture was something out of his practical self to his ideal self.

The gods were various, but as the God he made was high or low, so the buildings he made were noble or relatively mean.

As we view the widely different kinds of buildings built by red, yellow, white, or black men, we see that all were clustered into various aggregations under many different conditions. These aggregations we call cities, towns, and villages. In primitive times these clusters of buildings were occasioned by animal fear and social need of daily human contacts, or by obedience to rule. So we see buildings in clusters great, and clusters small. No doubt the cluster once represented a certain social consensus. The village once satisfied a real human need.

The warlike tribe had its village. The peaceful tribe tilling the ground also went to its village for the night. It was necessary to go for protection on one hand, and offense or defense on the other. And always, for the convenience of the chieftain as well as of his subjects, all was closed in around him. Man, the animal, has always sought safety first. As a man, he continually seeks permanence. As an animal he wishes to endure his life long. As a man he has invented immortality. Nowhere is this yearning for continuity or permanence so evident as in his architecture. Perhaps architecture is man's most obvious realization of this persistent dream he calls immortality.

Animal instinct has reached upward and found a higher satisfaction.

These various clusters of buildings grew from tribal villages into towns, from towns to cities, and from lesser to greater cities until a few cities had something of the might and character of great individual building. Sometimes a city became as various in its parts as any building, and similar in greatness.

But usually the city was an accretion not planned beyond the placing of a few features. These features probably were

28

not designedly placed. The city happened much as any crowd will gather about centers of interest wherever the centers of interest happen to be. Sometimes a circumstance of transport or historical consideration changed this center.

And, usually, there was a difference in degree only between the village, town, and great city. The one often grew into the other so that original spacing suitable to the village became a serious fault in the subsequent city. Populous crowding took what places it could find. It often took them by force of circumstance. Real freedom of human life in such circumstances soon became a farce.

In early times cities and towns were surrounded by fortified walls because cities and towns were forts. When might made right, the chieftain, the baron, the pirate and the bandit throve. Often the most successful robber became baron, sometimes monarch. The ruffian could rule in feudal times and often did rule, as he often rules in our own time.

The "divine right of kings" was a relatively modern improvement. It was an assumption that wore itself out by attrition. But meantime, by way of baron and monarch, we see architecture more and more undertaken as the great emprize of the rich and powerful rather than a service to the genius of a whole people or as the expression of race. Architecture became self-conscious. It began to be pretentious, affected and petty. Oftentimes as the robber chieftain became the baron and baron became monarch, the desire to build became vainglorious. It far outran necessity. All the great buildings thus built—many palaces and tombs, even churches, baths, theaters, and stadiums—were built as monuments to the powerful individuals under whose patronage they were erected. But conquering races were always coming down from the north as potentate rose against potentate. While baron contended with baron, neighboring cities were razed or enslaved by vandals, as they were called. This vandalism put new vandals into the places of weaker, older vandals. They called the weaker ones vassals. This is reflected in what remains of the architecture of periods when conquering mainly consisted in tearing down whatever the enemy might have built up. The more laborious and painstaking the building up had been, the more satisfactory was the pulling down.

In time, by way of the popular desperation caused by kingly discord and the baronial jealousies that employed men more for destruction than construction, government gradually became republican in form until in our day the people have subscribed to the idea of democratic government. This shows, at least, that the ultimate rise and progress of the whole people towards self-determination was proceeding, if slowly, through the human wreckage that we are viewing as ancient architecture. And however far away a satisfactory result may be, or however difficult it may be to imagine an indigenous architecture as its own expression, this struggle to rise does still go on among the peoples of the world. It is a seething in the mass. This, too, has affected the spirit that we call architecture. It is about to appear in new and more harmonious ways of building. Because they are more direct and natural, we are learning to call the new ways of building "organic." But to

30

use the term in its biological sense only would be to miss its significance. The word organic should signify architecture as living "entity" and "entity" as individuality.

Let us now go nearer to the grand wreckage left by this tremendous energy poured forth by man in quest of his ideal, these various ruined cities and buildings built by the various races to survive the race. Let us go nearer to see how and why different races built the different buildings and what essential difference the buildings recorded.

Whether yellow, red, black, or white race took precedence in the buildings that followed down the ages is not known. We have many authorities ready in this respect to cancel each other. History, necessarily post mortem, must be some kind of internal evidence discerned within what remains of the building itself. Remains of each separate race have for the most part totally disappeared. Some subsist merely as cuneiform writing on stone or as porcelain tablets. So conjecture has wide limits within which to thrive. But architecture appears, more and more with every fresh discovery, to have had common origin in the civilizations of the past. It seems now to be on the way out rather than on the way in.

In the evolution of the kind of building that we may call architecture, such primitive civilizations as remain have a high place. We may not neglect the contributions from the South Sea Islanders, from far south to the north, or of the Pacific savages who already made their implements look and feel stronger as utensils through the decoration they put upon them. The old Persian, the Dorian, and Ionic, and the old Byzantine all are architectures of vast importance. Their origins are lost to view. And all are tributary in our view of architecture. They proceed from one common human stock. But we begin with those great architectures in view from about 1000 B.C. to 1300 A.D. This is a period of time in which the greatest buildings of the world, traces of which are still visible to us, arose out of the soul and the soil of civilization. Civilizations are original cultural impulses whether they converge on some downward road or not.

Uncertain scholarship places the Mayan civilization centuries later than the height of Egyptian civilization. It was, say, 600 B.C., Germans and others dissenting. However that may be, Mayan and Egyptian both have more in common where elemental greatness is concerned than other cultures, unless we include the great work of the To, Cho, and Han periods of Chinese culture. These we may also place from 600 B.C. to 600 A.D. And as we have seen, architecture was in point of style relative to all that was used in it or in relation to it, that is to say, utensils, clothes, ornaments, arts, literature, life itself. All, manifestly, were of a family. They served a common purpose converging to a common end.

The Egyptian of that period was already more sophisticated than either early Mayan or early Chinese, and so might well have arisen at an earlier period in human development than either. Or, if primitive character is the more ancient, then the Mayan might be the elder. In Maya we see a grand simplicity of concept and form. Probably it is greater elemental architecture than anything remaining on record anywhere else. Next would come the early Chinese, especially their stone and bronze sculptures. In both Mayan and Chinese there was an assertion of form that could only have proceeded from the purest kinship to elemental nature and from nature forms of the materials used by both. Egyptian architecture, pyramid and obelisk excepted (they probably belong to an earlier period), had a sensuous smoothness and comparative elegance inspired by the sensuous human figure. Egyptian architecture was a noble kind of stone *flesh*. In the Egyptian dance, as contrasted with the Greek form of the dance, you may see this verified. The background of the architecture, the Egyptian landscape, was the sweeping simplicity of deserts relieved by greenery of the oasis. By his industry in the agrarian arts the Egyptian grew. He was astrological. He was a God-maker through myth. Egyptian individuality seems rounded. Its reward seems completely recorded by architecture. It is the most sophisticated of survivals from ancient origins.

But the Mayan lived amidst rugged rock formations. He contended with a vast jungle-like growth in which the serpent was a formidable figure. The Mayan grew by war. He was a great ritualist. He was a God-maker through force. Flesh lives in his architecture only as gigantic power. Grasp

33

the simple force of the level grandeur of the primal Mayan sense of form and the Mayan enrichment of it. Grasp the cruel power of his crude Gods (to objectify one, a sculptured granite boulder might suffice), then relate that to the extended plateaux his terraces made and to the mighty scale of his horizontal stone constructions. You will have in these trabeations the sense of might in stone. Even a Mayan "decoration" was mighty. It was mostly stone built.

Yet, both Egyptian and Mayan races seem children of a common motherland. With a broad grasp compare the might and repose of the Mayan outlines with the primitive Egyptian form in its almost human undulations; so rounded and plastic is the Egyptian architecture against the endless levels of the undulating sands surrounding it that it is the pagan song in an architecture of human profiles cut in stone. Though it is modeled in stone like the human nude, it finds great and similar repose in the ultimate mass.

Then compare both Mayan and Egyptian architecture with primal Chinese nature-worship as seen in the outlines of early Chinese forms. They are influences, no doubt, coming in from the mysterious Pacific. A sense of materials is there. It is seeking qualities. It is form qualified always by the profound sense of depth in the chosen substance and in the working of it. You will then see that what the early Chinese made was not so much made to be looked at as it was made to be looked into. In whatever the Chinese made there was profundity of feeling that gave a perfect kinship to the beauty of the natural world as it lived about man, and that was China.

It is an architecture wherein flesh as flesh lives not at all. The early art work of China is ethereal. And yet altogether these architectures seem to acknowledge kinship to each other, whether Mayan, Egyptian, Dorian or Chinese.

Early stone buildings—perhaps earlier than Egyptian or Greek—in the hands of the Byzantines became buildings quite different from Inca, Egyptian, or Chinese stone buildings. The arch was Byzantine and is a sophisticated building act resulting in more sophisticated forms than the lintel of the Mayan, Egyptian or Greek. Yet it is essentially primitive masonry. Byzantine architecture lived anew by the arch. The arch sprung from the caps of stone posts and found its way into roofing by way of the low, heavy, stone dome. Its haunches were well down within heavy walls. It was a flat crown showing above the stone masses punctured below by arches. St. Sophia is a later example. The stone walls of Byzantium often became a heavy mosaic of colored stone. The interiors above, roundabout and below, were encrusted with mosaics of gold, glazed pottery and colored glass. The Byzantines carved stone much in exfoliate forms, but the forms preserved the sense of stone mass in whatever they carved. Heavy wooden beams, painted or carved, rested on carved bolsters of stone or were set into the walls. Roof surfaces were covered with crude tiles. The effect of the whole was robust nature. It was worship by way of heavy material, masterful construction and much color.

The Romanesque proceeded from the Byzantine. And among the many other influences today our own country—so long degenerate where architecture is concerned—in the work of one of its greater architects, Henry Hobson Richardson, shows Romanesque influence.

St. Sophia is probably the greatest remaining, but a late example, of the architecture of Byzantium. In point of scale, at least, it is so. The Byzantine sense of form seems neither East nor West but belongs to both. It is obviously traditional architecture, the origins of which are lost in antiquity. Eventually becoming Christian, the Byzantine building was more nobly stone than any Gothic architecture. It was no less truly stone, though less spiritually so, than Mayan architecture. Into Byzantine buildings went the riches of the East in metals, weaving, images and ritual. Byzantium grew most by merchandising. Notwithstanding the dominance of the merchant class, a robust spirit lived in Byzantine work. It still grappled earth forcefully with simple purpose and complete individuality.

In the domed buildings of Persia we see the Byzantine arch still at work. Their buildings were the work of an enlightened people. Their architecture was probably the pinnacle of the civilizations that proceeded to the valley of the Euphrates and the Tigris from the supposed cradle of the white race. Persian architecture lifted its arches and domes to full height, in full flower, when great medieval Western architecture was beginning to point its arches in stone. The Persian loved masonry. By the most knowing use on record of clay and the kiln he achieved enormous building scale by way of bricks and mortar. He worked out his roof by way of the kiln as a great masonry shell domed and encrusted with extraordinary tile mosaics. He made his brick domes strong by placing their haunches well down into massive brick walls. His masonry dome was erected as an organic part of the whole structure. And lifting this sky-arch high, with gently sensuous, swelling sides, he humanized it completely. The Persian liked his dome so much that he turbaned his head, we may imagine, to match it, and robed himself from shoulders to the ground in keeping with the simple walls to carry the patterned enrichment. As ceramic efflorescence it flowed over his buildings, and as weaving and embroidery it overflowed upon his garments and carpets.

The Persian was born, or had become, a true mystic. And because he was a mystic, this particularly developed man of the white race naturally loved blue. He put blue within blue, blue to play again with blues in a delicate rhythmical pattern displaying divine color in all and all over his wall surfaces. He kept his wall surfaces unbroken, extended, and plain, so that he might enrich them with these sunlit inlays of his spirit evident in glazed colored pottery tile. His jars, less elegant than the Greek, were shapely and large and blue as no blue—

37

not even Ming blue—has ever been blue. His personal adornments and ornaments were blue and gold. Subtle in rhythm and color, indelible in all, were rhythms as varied as those of the flowers themselves. Under his thought, walls became sunlit gardens of poetic thought expressed as geometric forms loving pure color. So also were the woven carpets under his feet with which he covered the red and blue mosaics of his floors.

And then the Persian surrounded his buildings by avenues of cypress trees and acres of living flower gardens. He mirrored his domes and minarets in great, placid, rectangular adjacent pools of fresh water coming flush with the ground and rimmed from the gardens by a narrow rib of stone.

Yes, the Persian liked his domed buildings so well that he not only dressed his head likewise but was continually making out of brass or silver or gold or enamel, similar buildings, in miniature, and he domed them too. Filling their basements with oil he would hang these little buildings by hundreds inside his buildings as lamps to softly light the glowing spaciousness of his wonderfully dignified interiors. His sense of scale was lofty, and he preserved it by never exaggerating the scale of his exquisite details. So these edifices stood out upon the plains, blue-domed against the sky among the rank and file of Persian cities as complete in themselves as the cypress trees around them were complete.

No ruffian ever ruled the Persians, but one did conquer them. His name was Alexander.

In the works of this imaginative race, sensitive to inner

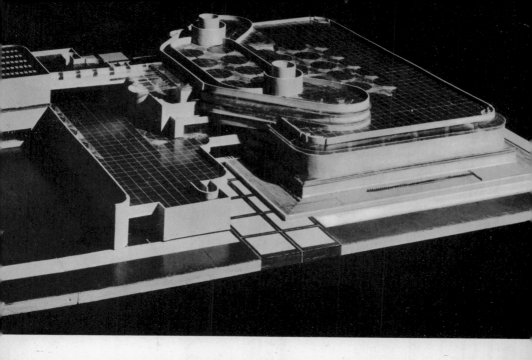

E JOHNSON WAX COMPANY BUILDING

DE VIEW FROM THE REAR

acine, Wisconsin

rank Lloyd Wright, Architect

w form of office building—low and streamlined in appearance, and to be built of brick of a ed color. Two horizontal bands of glass tubing encircle the building—one at a 6-foot level; ther at the angle made by the wall and roof. The main unit of the building is one vast room—130 by 210 feet on the ground, 20 feet high, and large enough to house several red employees.

ination is provided throughout the building in a manner never attempted before. Daylight enter the building through the bands of glass tubing which encircle the building and from ghts of glass tubing overhead. Artificial lighting will emanate from the same source. In this light, whether daylight or artificial, is brought into the building in such a manner as to ice shadowless illumination.

es for department heads and junior executives are located on a mezzanine gallery that girdles reat workroom, while the chief executives and officers are housed in a pent-house structure the main office.

rvices, such as rest rooms, toilets, and lockers, are placed in the basement below the main room, where all workers have direct access to them. Twin elevators serve the mezzanine and tive offices.

the building is to be completely air-conditioned both Summer and Winter none of the used in the circumferential bands is designed to open. Instead the building is equipped with nostrils"—circular shafts reaching from basement to roof—through which the air-condi- g equipment will breathe in its fresh air. The building has no exterior openings except the bered entrance doors. Beneath, a spacious car port where the cars of visitors are parked, e streets. Floor heating in main room.

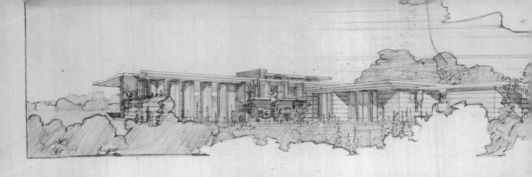

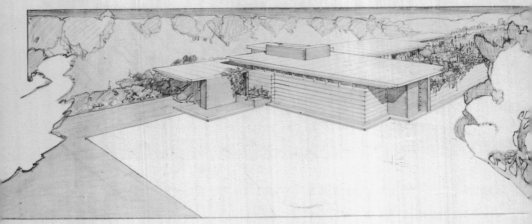

PLANS FOR
H. A. JACOBS HOUSE

Madison, Wisconsin

Frank Lloyd Wright, Architect

Total cost of House $5500 including architect's fee of $450

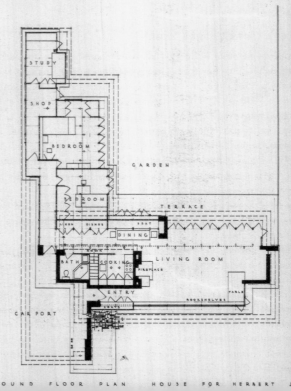

STUDY

SHOP

BEDROOM

GARDEN

BEDROOM

TERRACE

DISHES   SEAT   DINING

BATH   COOKING   FIREPLACE   LIVING ROOM

ENTRY   BOOKSHELVES   TABLE

CAR PORT

GROUND FLOOR PLAN   HOUSE FOR HERBERT

rhythms, superlative craftsmanship by way of the greatest scientific masonry the world has ever seen is yet to be found in the remains of the period ending about the eleventh and thirteenth centuries. The workman was the potential artist. He was not yet the time-bound slave of a wage system. And the architect was grandly and usefully a poet.

The *quality* of a man's work was then still his honor. These noble buildings were made of and made for well-made bodies, tall of stature, fine minds. Black heads and deep dark eyes were the perfect complement for this poetic sense of building and the garden, and of blue. So the Persian of old made his God of Beauty and passionately dreamed his life away godward.

What a romantic of the race was this Persian, what mystic romance this Persia! Aladdin with the wonderful lamp? The wonderful lamp was Persian imagination.

In these creations of Persian life the upward growth of imaginative philosophic building had come far toward us, far beyond primitive walls and roofs of mankind. It came probably as far as it was ever to come with the exterior sense of form. Yet it was much more developed than the pagan sense of mass which preceded it.

The opulent Arabian wandered, striking his splendid, gorgeous tents to roam elsewhere. He learned much from the Persian; the Hindu, learning from the same origins, was himself seemingly more involved. He raised his complex but less spiritual temples to his God in the manifold tiers and terraces and domes of masonry or copper or gold. They even rivaled the Persian in exuberance but seemed to lack the pure and simple synthesis of form and clear pattern and color achieved by the Persian. This architecture traveled South and East, by way of its genius, Buddha. It influenced China, Java, Bhutan, and Thibet.

The Hindu carved and grooved, fluted his groovings with moldings. Then he loaded his architecture with images where the Persian held his surfaces true, as he inlaid them with precious materials to give them sun-glory as strong walls. But a Persian building sang in sunshine as the nightingale sings in shadow.

Perhaps Persian architecture was the end of a quality of the spirit, a feeling for the abstract as form in architecture. Probably it was gradually lost, never to be surpassed unless the ideal of architecture as organic now reaches logical but passionate expression in years to come. These simple masses of noble mind and the exquisite tracery of fine human sensibilities remain in our grand vista to remind us of this phase of human architecture, called Persian. It is the natural dome among the more self-conscious roofs of the world of architecture.

Somber, forest-abstract made in stone, the architecture we call Gothic is much nearer to us and has taken to itself a long course of time in which to die. To the development of architecture in "Le Moyen Age" came stone embodying all earlier wood forms of architecture. The wood forms became more and more implicate and complicated as Gothic masonry perfected its science.

Stone craft as organic structure rose to its highest level. In the beautiful cathedral constructions of the Gothic builders, the "Gothic" of the Teuton, the Frank, the Gaul, the Anglo-Saxon, not only did the architect decorate construction but he constructed decoration. Some of this was not integral to structure. No stone arris was left unmolded. Stone itself had now blossomed into at least an affair of human skill, usually into a thing of the human spirit. The "Gothic" cathedral seems an expiring wave of creative impulse seizing humanity by way of stone. The noble material, becoming mutable as the sea, rose into lines of surge, peaks of foam that were all human symbols. In it images of organic life were caught and held in cosmic urge. It was the final movement in the great song of stone as in ages past we see man singing it in architecture. The human spirit, as organic or living entity, seems here to have triumphed over organic matter.

But this great architecture grew by feudal strength. The spirit called Gothic at this time pervaded the baron, the merchant, the guild, the peasant. In a religious age Mariolatry, the devil and hell became articulate in architecture, a dream of heaven. Flesh remained the rough, salty romance of the people. The merchant rapidly grew in power.

In all these great periods of human history the buildings themselves, in point of style, were related to everything put

41

into them for human use or for beauty. They were related to anything else that was in any way related to them, even clothes and ornaments, the way of wearing them and of wearing the hair, the grooming of eyebrows, even making up the face. We may reasonably see these architectures altogether as having common origin, all flowing in the same direction. The features of all are truly the features of humankind. Human nature is their nature and human limitation their limitation. For, not only were ancient popular customs in perfect harmony with ancient buildings, utensils, and ornaments, but even human personal manners were affected likewise by environment and affected or reflected environment. Better to say that environment and architecture were one with nature in the life of the people at the time, whenever and wherever it existed as architecture.

This is the great fact in this great human-scape called architecture: architecture is simply a higher type and expression of nature by way of human nature where human beings are concerned. The spirit of man enters into all, making of the whole a God-like reflection of himself as creator.

In all buildings that man has built out of earth and upon the earth, his spirit, the pattern of him, rose great or small. It lived in his buildings. It still shows there. But common to all these workmanlike endeavors in buildings great or small, another spirit lived. Let us call this spirit, common to all buildings, the great spirit, architecture. Today we look back upon the endless succession of ruins that are no more than the geological deposits washed into shore formation by the sea, landscape formed by the cosmic elements. These ancient buildings were similarly formed by the human spirit. It is the spirit elemental of architecture. The buildings are now dead to uses of present-day activity. They were sculptured by the spirit of architecture in passing, as inert shapes of the shore were sculptured by cosmic forces. Any building is a by-product of eternal living force, a spiritual force taking forms in time and place appropriate to man. They constitute a record to be interpreted, no letter to be imitated.

We carelessly call these ancient aggregations "architecture." Looking back upon this enormous deposit to man's credit, and keeping in mind that just as man was in his own time and place so was his building in its time and place, we must remember that architecture is not these buildings in themselves but far greater. We must believe architecture to be the living spirit that made buildings what they were. It is a spirit by and for man, a spirit of time and place. And we must perceive architecture, if we are to understand it at all, to be a spirit of the spirit of man that will live as long as man lives. It begins always at the beginning. It continues to bestrew the years with forms destined to change and to be strange to men yet to come.

We are viewing this valid record of the inspired work of the red men, yellow men, black men or white men of the

43

human race in perspective outline. What we see is a vast human expression having a common ground of origin. It is more a part of man himself than the turtle's shell is part of the turtle. A great mass of matter has been eroded by man's spirit. These buildings were wrested by his tireless energy from the earth and erected in the eye of the sun. It was originally the conscious creation, out of man himself, of a higher self. His building, in order to be architecture, was the true spirit of himself made manifest (objective) whereas the turtle had no freedom of choice or any spirit at all in the making of his shell.

Considering this, we may now see wherein architecture is to be distinguished from mere building. Mere building may not know "spirit" at all. And it is well to say that the spirit of the thing is the essential life of that thing because it is truth. Such, in the retrospect, is the only life of architecture.

Architecture is abstract. Abstract form is the pattern of the essential. It is, we may see, spirit in objectified forms. Strictly speaking, abstraction has no reality except as it is embodied in materials. Realization of form is always geometrical. That is to say, it is mathematic. We call it pattern. Geometry is the obvious frame-work upon which nature works to keep her scale in "designing." She relates things to each other and to the whole, while meantime she gives to your eye most subtle,

44

mysterious and apparently spontaneous irregularity in effects. So, it is through the embodied abstract that any true architect, or any true artist, must work to put his inspiration into ideas of form in the realm of created things. To arrive at expressive "form" he, too, must work from within, with the geometry of mathematic pattern. But he so works only as the rug maker weaves the pattern of his rug upon the warp. Music, too, is mathematic. But the mathematician cannot make music for the same reason that no mere builder can make architecture. Music is woven with art, upon this warp that is mathematics. So architecture is woven with a super-sense of building upon this warp that is the science of building. It also is mathematical. But no study of the mathematic can affect it greatly. In architecture, as in life, to separate spirit and matter is to destroy both.

Yet, all architecture must be some formulation of materials in some actually significant pattern. Building is itself only architecture when it is essential pattern significant of purpose.

We may look back now upon the character of the great works of man called architecture and see how, by way of instinctive abstraction, the hut of the African sometimes became in the sun very tree-like or flower-like or much like the more notable animal forms or hill-shapes round about it; how the cliff dwellers raised the clay up from under their feet into great square vessels for the sun to bake; and how they put smaller vessels into them, fire-baked into admirable shapes, for daily use or for fire-worship; how their vessels were marked by imaginative patterns, and how meanwhile they were making small human images to go into them or go along with them. We have seen how the Incas carried along earlier traditions, extending back to lost civilizations, and completed the rock strata of their region by noble structures of stone adorned by crude stone human images, and how they put stone and metal and pottery into them all and shaped them for use. Both buildings and their contents were enriched by adornment. They may be the record of greater, more ancient civilizations from which they were themselves only migrations.

We have seen how the Byzantines lifted stone up into the arch and then on up into the dome, asking their materials, even so, to be no better or worse than they were. We have seen how the Egyptians, another migration, worked stone ledges into buildings, and buildings into stone ledges; how they knew metals, pottery and weaving and adorned their buildings with the human image by way of painting and sculpture. Upon their walls, those pages of stone, were their hieroglyphics. But their buildings were in themselves hieroglyphs of truths coming to them from some ancient source of origin that seems common to all. This feeling seeps through all ancient architecture to us of the present day.

And we see how the later Greeks consciously evolved flower shapes in stone, but worked stone also as wood. After the Dorians and Ionians they seemed to have less sense of materials than other peoples. But the Greeks developed painting far and sculpture still further and put the building into the

46

vase, as into the building they put the vase and the manuscript. The vase was the result of their search for the elegant solution, their supreme contribution to culture.

We have seen how the Persians came from similar distant origins, how they blue-domed their buildings under the canopy of blue and emblazoned them with blue and purple ceramic flower gardens, making their buildings flower gardens within flower gardens, and put into them illuminated enamels, pottery and weaving. They omitted human images except when illustrating their books.

We have seen how, more recently, the cathedral builders put the somber uprising forest into stone, until stone triumphant could endure no more and began to fall. But meantime they had been weaving into their stone forest great glass paintings and wood carvings, and finishing them with pictured woolen and linen textiles, painted wood and stone images, great music, stately ritual and many books.

We have seen how the pagoda of the Orientals grew to resemble the fir trees, and how their shrines harmonized with the pines around them, and how within their buildings was a wealth of nature-worship in gold and painting and sculpture. Writing and myriad crafts were at home among them, and these buildings too were loaded with images.

And now, finally, we may see how all this was man's sense of himself: how it all came to be by the simple way of human use and purpose, but how also, in all ages and all races, it was man's greatest work wherein his five senses were all employed and enjoyed. By way of eye, ear, and finger, by

47

tongue and even by nostril he was creating out of himself greater delights for a super-self, finding deep satisfactions far beyond those he could ever know were he merely a good animal.

But we are compelled to see, looking back upon this vast homogeneous human record, that the human race built most nobly when limitations were greatest and, therefore, when most was required of imagination in order to build at all. Limitations seem to have always been the best friends of architecture. The limitation in itself seems to be the artist's best friend in the sum of all the arts, even now. Later, we must see how subjugation, sophistication, easy affluence and increasing facility of intercourse began to get things all mixed up until nothing great in architecture lived any more. All architecture became bastardized. Finally the great arch of the Persian dome was fatuously invited by a "greatest artist" in the name of art to live up in the air. It was tossed against the sky to stand on top of round columns. Unnecessary columns were placed against sturdy walls for mere appearance' sake. Roofs likewise became more ornamental than useful. Wood got to be used like stone, and stone like wood. Pottery began to be used like anything else but seldom used as itself. In short, mere appearance became enough. Integrity was given no thought. Also we are compelled to see how, when greater facilities of machinery came into use in the nineteenth century, the great art of building soon became utterly confused, degraded by mere facilities. The people began putting into their buildings so much piping and wiring, and so many sanitary appliances of every kind, that architecture of the earlier sort may be said to have died. Building had become so easy that architecture became too difficult.

No stream rises higher than its source. Whatever man might build could never express or reflect more than he was. It was not more than what he felt. He could record neither more nor less than he had learned of life when the buildings were built. His inmost thought lives in them. His philosophy, true or false, is there.

Inevitably, certain races were more developed than others. Some were more favorably situated. And we see that the influence in architecture of certain races profoundly or superficially affected other races. An instance: the artificial cornices and necessary columns of the Greeks still shape our public acts in the useless cornices and unnecessary columns of modern architecture "à la mode." Later work of the middle ages, called Gothic, still shapes our modern educational institutions and churches, and the modern homes of opulent tradesmen. They mark our public money-boxes called banks. It may be that the heights of architecture were reached so long ago that the various subsequent styles we now call "classic" and practice regardless, were already degenerate when they occurred.

Throughout this authentic human record, inscribed in the countless buildings erected by man's labor, now fallen or falling back again upon the earth to become again earth, a definite character may be discerned determining man's true relationship to time and place. The sum of man's creative impulses, we find, took substance in architecture as his creative passion rose and fell within it. It always was creative. We have now reached the point in time when such original impulses subside or cease. Inspiration is no more. Go back 500 years and nothing can be found in architecture worthy to be called creation, as architecture has been creative, except as folklore, folkways, folk building.

The last original impulse, called Gothic, has subsided and the "Renaissance," a period of rebirth of original forms that were also "rebirth" when first born, begins. Creative impulses grow dim, are all but lost. Only rebirth is possible to the culture of the period we are now to consider. It is probably an over-cultured period. Apparently, humanity had gone as far with its pagan ideal of architecture as it could go. The hitherto vast, uninspired merchant class has been gradually gaining the upper hand in society and will soon outbid the higher classes for power. It will then proceed to foreclose upon a decayed, uninspired higher class.

The handmaidens of architecture—music, painting, sculpture—during these 500 years are going on their way. Music, young, healthy, is growing up independently into Mozart, Bach and Beethoven. Painting based upon the work of Giotto and the early Italians begins to set up in this world of the "Reborn" as an art complete in itself. By way of many schools and phases it is to eventuate into the easel picture or the bogus mural. Sculpture begins the struggle for liberation from architecture that began with Buonarotti. Undergoing

50

many transformations it ends in realism or in imitation of the primitive. At this period handicraft, still active and essential, is yet to die because men have found an easier way to accomplish the work of the world. Having found it, it is easier now for them to "immortalize" themselves.

From Italian sources, chiefly gathered together at Florence, where degeneration and regeneration of all arts were interlocked, Italian revivals of ancient Greco-Roman architecture begin to reach the various European capitals as patterns. By importation or export these patterns are later to be exploited among the various Western nations. Ancient Greek, itself a derivation, becomes the standard of a new "low" in Western culture. The artificial cornice, the column and entablature, become the common refuge of a growing impotence.

Derivations of derivations, commercialized as Georgian "Colonial," or what not, are soon exports (or imports) to the new world, America. Later, all styles of all periods of "rebirth" were exported or imported by the Americans, as the Romans imported them and as the Japanese now import them, to be mingled, soon mangled, by the new machinery of endless reproduction. The saws, lathes, planers of modern mills are soon to strew the empty carcasses of these erstwhile styles far and wide until Queen Anne comes in and all sense goes out.

Where the primitive and splendid sense of structure or building construction was going on down the ages, the reality of all buildings for human occupation was found in the enclosing, supporting walls. But a deeper sense of architecture has come to light. This is due to a new philosophy, to the invention of new machines, and to the discovery of new materials. The new architecture finds reality in the space within the walls to be lived in. The new reality of the building is the interior space which roofs and walls only serve to enclose. This reality was not felt by primitive builders. Nor is it yet known to the pseudo-classic members of our academies today. Slowly dawning as the exterior or pagan sense of building dies, this interior ideal, or inner sense of the building as an organic whole, grows. It grows more consistent, carries more genuine culture with it as it develops: culture indigenous.

In modern building this ideal of structural cause as organic effect is destined to be the center line of man's modern culture. An organic architecture will be the consequence.

Ancient builders went to work "lavishly" upon the walls and roofs themselves as though they were the reality of the building, cutting holes in the walls for light and air. In the name of art they made such holes ornamental by putting molded caps over them, or by putting up unnecessary columns beside them, or by working needless moldings and insignificant ornament into or onto the walls. They built cornices. They surrounded all openings with more moldings to heal the breaches that had to be made in the walls to let in light and air, and to get in and out of. An architect worked with his building, then, much as a sculptor would work with his solid mass of clay. He strove to mold and enrich the mass. He

52

tried to give to it some style that he had learned or happened to like. Exterior modeling and featuring thus became, by adoption, the so-called western academic concept of architecture. This academic—"classic"—concept was chiefly based upon Greek and Roman buildings. But meantime the Chinese, Japanese, Persians and the Moors, Orientals all, developed a somewhat different sense of building. Their sense of the building was also the mass of solid matter sculptured from the outside, but the Oriental sense of the building was more plastic, therefore more a thing of the spirit.

Being "plastic," the building was treated more consistently as a unit or consistent whole. It was less an aggregation of many features and parts, all remaining separate features, by, and for, themselves. In organic building nothing is complete in itself but is only complete as the part is merged into the larger expression of the whole. Something of this had begun to find its way into many oriental buildings.

During these later periods of various "renaissances," even the Pope's authority at Rome, the religious capital, has been rivaled by the authority of the Italian artist and workman, as the Italian Renaissance grew upon Europe. And so the remarkable Italian city of Florence grew to be the artist capital if not the cultural capital of a world.

But it became the artist capital of a western world that could only buy or sell. Already it was prostitute to imitation. It was a world prostitute to imitation because, with the exception of music and painting, and always excepting the newly born literature, society was unable to distinguish between birth and rebirth. It was unable to create anything much above the level of technique, scientific process or mechanical invention. The new world was learning to buy and sell its way to whatever it wanted in this matter of culture. By way of commercial reproductions of the styles affected by these European cultures society gratified such creative aspiration as remained.

Upon this prevalent rising tide that is called "commerce" comes the printed page, "letters," the book. Society becomes consciously literate as the printed book absorbs ever more of the cultural energies of mankind. Upon any large scale this scientific art of printing was the first application of the machine to human affairs. It is the machine that brings the book to humanity. And men, by means of the book, grew more literal. Life itself became and continues to grow more and more vicarious.

Human nature always seeks an easier way to do its work, or seeks a substitute. Human effort finds this "easiest way," or a substitute. The nineteenth century, especially, found both in machine development. As a consequence of this easy release all life, therefore all architecture, became less and less from within until society became content that art be something purchasable, something to be applied. The tendency of art in such circumstances is to become uncreative. It appears as some perverted form of literature or at least as no more than something literal. Realistic is the word. Machine power increased the deluge of literature and ready-made European "objets d'art." A newly literalized humanity becomes obvious to commerce as the new facility for exploitation. Yes, "realistic" is the proper word for the art work of the period. It was really no great art at all. Photography could take over the popular "art interest" of the period. It proceeded to do so.

Yet, the machine is to make opportunity new. The science of printing is to make the book a medium for human expression more facile than building and the book is to become a means of recording life perhaps more enduring than the great edifice ever was.

But, meantime, the printed word accelerates. An increasingly vicarious life and servile art is becoming universal in the western world. Foregathering to listen, to stand, to watch, or to ride is now sufficient. Fifty thousand people watch a football game. Ninety thousand watch a prize fight. A remittance man sits at the steering wheel of a hundred and twenty-five horse-power car, with the airs, and sensation, too, that the power is his own—is, in fact, him. Connection with the soil is giving way to machinery. Contacts between men are increasingly had by electrical devices. Intercommunication becomes instantaneous and far reaching, but actual human contacts become fewer and more feeble. Superficial release is provided by literature, now ubiquitous, and new ways and means to beat work are found. Culture as architecture and architecture as culture is on the way down and out. Structure no longer finds beauty by way of integral evolution. Nor does society think to ask for such.

The place where this great integrity was wont to be is fast becoming an empty place.

The machine can exploit externality. But as we have set it up the machine can do nothing nor let much be done from within. The machine reduces and reproduces such forms of old-fashioned representation in art as are most salable. Those most salable are naturally those most realistic or superficially elegant. Grandomania flourishes in consequence. Architecture as something ready-made is in the hand of the highly specialized and speculative salesman. Characteristic of this show-window period, architecture can only be a thing of mixed origins and haphazard applications. We may see it around us everywhere. Styles now abound. But nowhere is there genuine style. These are the days of the General Grant Gothic and the Pseudo-Classic. When Michelangelo piled the Pantheon upon the Parthenon and called it St. Peter's, he, a painter, had committed architectural adultery. It was destined to bring forth a characteristic monstrosity, namely, an arch set up into plain air on posts to shift for itself. It is an imitative anachronism that characterizes our public acts, as illustrated by our capitols, court houses, and town halls. A noble thing, the Persian dome has become ignoble. Now it is base. The same depravity sees a Greek temple as fitting memorial to Abraham Lincoln. He is the Greek antithesis. Nothing is Greek about his life or work or thought. A Gothicized French Chateau, incongruous pattern, is the unsuitable stall for some urban fire engine. Any Roman bath or sarcophagus will do to lend prestige to the sacrosanct bank on any town sidewalk anywhere. A Gothicized cathedral is set up at Yale to throw a glamour over college athletics. Another may serve to memorialize the grandmother of a successful speculator. All serve, unchallenged, this commercialized assumption or provincial gesture that the period calls culture.

In short, in this present time only the bastard survives even as a temple for the work of the Supreme Court of the United States. Stale survivals of every sort are "modern." Business turns to help itself liberally to "the classic." The "classic" goes to market as diamonds go.

Art and religion, in this inversion of human circumstances, lose prestige. Both these resources of the human spirit become purchasable and, as a natural consequence, life itself becomes purchasable. Meantime, science, far more useful to trade than either art or religion, grows in dominion. Neither art nor religion is longer a necessity to the people. The people have sought a replica. They have found and bought a substitute. The merchant has become the ruler for the time being of man's singing, dancing, dwelling and breeding. And the creative individual in the arts must become pauper, at this time when Sir Joseph Duveen is a knight, Andy Mellon a prince, and a Rockefeller, king.

In the preceding era, men of Florence were the guiding spirits and the light on the horizon, such as that light was. So, now in the twentieth century, social, economic, and artistic forms are determined by outward rather than by inner factors. Today the "civilized" world has come to the consequences of "renaissance." It has tried to live on a decadent precedent. Architecture and its kindred, as a matter of course, are divorced from nature in order to make of art the merchantable thing of texts, classroom armchairs and, above all, of speculative "price," that it now is. It is a speculative commodity.

The artist, now no more than the designing partner, the official streamliner, the interior decorator, the industrial designer, is entirely outside. Nothing could be more external than an interior decorator. Nothing could be more irrelevant than the exterior architect. Nothing could be more remote from life at the moment than citizens content to live in what either of them produces. Perspective is in reverse. The cart is before the horse.

A new type of patron of the arts has grown up out of this perversity. He is a Frick, a Widener, a Morgan, a Henry Ford, or a Bendix. Perhaps he is a Hart, Shaffner and Marx or Metro-Goldwyn-Mayer. He is, and he must be, some success in speculation upon some grand scale. Not for nothing is Joseph Duveen a knight.

By money power democracy has been perverted to inverted aristocracy. The new world has made social parasitism and vulgarity academic. What by nature can only be grown, may by such modern improvements be mere artifice freely bought to change hands at a price. Life itself must now be standardized because it is to be prefabricated, show-windowed, and eventually sold. Yes, and sold even now.

Trade and machine production are having their way and their say in the standardizations of our day. How can the young escape? As for the architect, who consents to buy and

58

sell indulgences for his people, indulgences unwittingly provided by the traffic in foreign cultures to which he himself helped educate them: with him standardization has had its way too. Unwittingly, the Cass Gilberts, Ray Hoods, Corbetts and Walkers, the McGonigles and Popes carry on the work of the McKim, Mead and Whites, the D. H. Burnhams, Richard M. Hunts and the Henry Hardenbergs. They are merely useful tools of this devastating power.

The great and liberal arts that man nourished because they nourished him have gone. They have gone by this some route to the mill which is this remorseless standardization for profit. And the tide of literal representation by way of the press, radio and cinema, all rapacious maws for more fodder of the sort, rises unsteadily to new monopolies.

At this moment, 1937 A.D., any ideal at all organic in character becomes impractical if not slightly absurd: shop keepers all. All in all are ruled by the expedient.

Only petty specialists in architecture and the sister arts are needed on the job made by our order of "business." Its wholly artificial power must be maintained upon an artificial basis. It is engendered and kept by indiscriminate use of indiscriminate increment. The whole man can no longer be used. He too is a "job."

Let us frankly admit it:

The universal modern "art" is really salesmanship.

Showmanship is perihelion. Everywhere, it is at a premium.

The show-window is the most important form of all artistry in these United States. Let it stand for the symbol of this era.

The mother of the arts, architecture, in such circumstances could have little or no issue. Neither impregnation nor conception upon any social scale is possible. And a restless movement begins the world over. Action is inevitable. It has now begun because, long ago, it was time.

In this human restlessness the new order of culture, structure to emerge as "organic," lies concealed as the child in the womb. Meanwhile, cultural decay of the individual proceeds by way of the commercialized mass-education we have learned to call academic.

Has this modern restlessness anything to turn to? Has it recourse? Yes. Organic architecture with its sense of structure, the sense of the whole, is one great recourse. Religion might be another. These two, now as always.

We have been describing what has happened to art. What, then, has happened to religion so far as it relates to art?

Religion, in its present form, is become "Christianity," the church. The church was the last great client of architecture. The last great urge of human creative energy, upward thrust of human creative power, flowered into stone as it built the great cathedrals. The church was Christianity. What of Christianity, now, as it passes for religion in this general confusion and debauchery of the creative powers of mankind? Neither the teaching nor character of Christianity was such as to inspire the nature-worship of the creative mind.

Christianity took the church to man as a substitute for that law and order of the universe which should have been worked out by him from within himself, law and order made his own by way of the arts. But, as Christianity had it, the man was to be saved by his beliefs, not saved by his works. So, the church substituted beatitudes for beauty. Spiritually the man was invited to become a parasite upon the Lord. That quality in the man that stood tall inside him up against the roof of his mind, which must ever be his true self, can no longer be much encouraged even by the church.

And the ideals of Jesus, the gentle anarchist, remain generally feared because generally misunderstood or yet unknown.

This failure to see God and man as one has disaffected all art for it has betrayed architecture. There is no longer general realization of matter and spirit as the same thing. This is a fatal division of the house against itself. A great wave of ugliness has followed in the wake of this error. Bogus sanctuaries to God stand propped against the sky by steel, as though it were necessary to prove to some court of last resort that the final period of creative impulse on earth is dying of imitation or already dead by mutilation.

With Christianity for tenant today, architecture is a parasite, content with an imitation of an imitation like the spurious St. John the Divine in New York City. To go along with the imported cathedral are such inversions as the Lincoln Memorial, such aberrations as our capitols, such morgues as our museums, monuments, and such grandomania as our city

61

halls. Abortions of sentiment, like the "Great White Whale" at Princeton, a Rockefeller cathedral on Riverside Drive are proof enough that the spirit of architecture has fled from a social era. Corpses encumber the ground. As for religion or art, a pig may live in a palace: any cat can scratch the face of a king.

Upon this, the American scene, emerges the new ideal-structure as organic architecture becomes interpretation of life itself. From within outward is no longer remote ideal. It is everywhere becoming action. With new integrity action insists upon indigenous culture. The new reality.—F. Ll. W.

III. Expression and the Modern World

NEW YORK is a pump that draws into its chambers streams of human beings and then regurgitates them in a vast spray. This diastole and systole of daily urban life is not complete, of course, but it is rhythmic with a short, hard beat. It becomes greater as the years go by. More are drawn in; more flow out. The range and the velocity are greater. Humanity in this collective sense becomes more liquid. It moves faster and farther with each stroke of the pump. It is thinner, less resistant to the draw and push of it. Chicago is a pump; Detroit, flowing down Woodward Avenue, is a pump; Boston, Cleveland, Philadelphia, St. Louis are pumps drawing in, pushing out.

On the other hand are Kansas and southern Illinois, Georgia, rural Pennsylvania and other regions where the suction of the pumps is not so strong. People are farmers there, very likely, or housewives, or local folks of some kind, living their own way, playing their local tunes. But the farmers, for example, are usually commercial farmers. They produce less for their own uses, more for the market. And during winter days or times when outside work lets down they are making fewer things for the house and family and buying

63

more. The exchange function of society increases. Society itself, in this sense, increases in about the proportion that the wholeness of life and the self-sustaining family declines. Life is more fluid, thinner, but has a greater range.

Wherever it may be, the social and personal structures of the world, in the west at least, are vastly different from those of our fathers. And with these differences are closely coordinated the forms of modern expression. Their changes and variegations have had reciprocal effects upon each other. Their movement, like the front of a flood, is a joint movement that leaves departmentalists in the social sciences talking in the wind and specialists in the arts, who interpret expression chastely in terms only of the art or craft that the expression happens to take, as forgotten as yesterday's newspaper. If expression is projecting form and significance on things that otherwise are indifferent to our interest, it is clear that the ways that people live together in the modern world, and the ways that they give significance to things, are part and parcel of the same situation. Whatever seems significant to him, and the significance that he creates, will determine in great measure how a man lives with his fellows. And the ways that he lives with his fellows will in turn affect what seems significant to him.

The world of art and social conduct is full of examples of this interaction between the forms of expression and the structures of life. Even science is such an example, though the case here is not quite so obvious because science is less clearly a form of expression. But science is a kind of expression, nev-

64

ertheless, for it has the power to give its own unique significance to things. It puts things in a world of meaning that is all its own. Though the content of science is strictly fact, not value—and proudly rigorous it is—science beyond that has created an attitude towards the real that is a world in itself. It has made a pattern of significance and value that gives it status as an art. Its creation was a work of art, an imaginative projection slowly clarified through the years, though its practice must be factual and severely disciplined. Science imputed to things a new and gratuitous significance, namely objectivity, and as such became expressive of a new world of intellectual life. Only in a social world that permitted freedom of inquiry could it flourish, but its effect in turn on social life is incalculably great.

Life and expression—it seems obvious enough—influence each other. This, the third part of this book, will discuss the characteristics of the modern world in their relations to expression.

The Norris dam is a wedge of concrete poured between two mountains. It fills the gap accurately. It is clean concrete and sits across the Clinch river canyon of Tennessee in tremendous repose. A road leads up and over it to the other bank of the river. A sign along the rim says, "Do not disturb the wild flowers."

The Norris dam creates a lake among the mountains of Tennessee that has a coast line longer than the coast of Lake Superior. The water coils back among the old ridges almost to Cumberland Gap. It is blue over old farms of the hill folk.

65

It invades the forest coves that mark these southern mountains. The Appalachians are ancient ranges geologically, old before the High Sierras came to be, old even before the Rockies were shouldered up above western seas and sands. And, like old regions, the lakes were drained. Gaps were cut through. The rivers hurried to the sea without hesitation. The Norris dam rejuvenates these Appalachians, as it were, restores the lakes of youth, or others like them, closes the gap. The gods wonder, no doubt, to see the evolution of their hills halted, turned back. Prometheus has returned from Caucasus. On a log church beside the road to Knoxville is a sign: "Property of the Tennessee Valley Authority. Do not disturb this building."

Mountains were moved to build the Norris dam. Along the road are chasms in the hillsides where rock was quarried for concrete and fill. One million cubic yards of concrete were poured into the wedge between the hills. In the town of Norris, built for the workers on the dam five miles away, the streets wind around the hills under the pine trees. A breeze flows in from the east. The lake near by is blue under the bluff. The houses scatter through the woods. No house there is mean or wretched, none shows overbearing wealth. A brick house in a grove of pines, what is it like? It has four rooms smartly paneled in wood, two porches, a bath and shower, a fireplace, an attic. The rent is $36.00 a month. Heat, light, cooking, hot water, refrigeration, washing, ironing, toasting a slice of cracked wheat bread—all are electrical and the bills in winter run from fifteen to twenty dollars, in summer from

66

seven to ten, for generous use of current. In the house live Mr. and Mrs. Douglas McHenry and their children. He works at the dam. She keeps house, cares for the children, and fills the rooms with paintings from her studio in the attic. The pictures are modern in tone, the hills and hill people in subject. She knows the books, Cheney, Bulliet and others, but has taken no lessons.

Over on the hill is the community house for Norris. Within is a large auditorium, an exhibition room for craft work, a soda fountain and candy counter, a library and reading room. Modern books are on the shelves. Prominent among them, and well worn, are Veblen, John Strachey, Shaw, Beard, Thomas Wolfe, Sherwood Anderson. Norris is a worker's village more pleasant than most summer resorts, and more civilized. While the dam was building, construction workers lived there; now it is a village for administrative and other workers. The labor costs on the great dam, according to Chairman Morgan, were less than for private work. This is a consequence of low turnover in labor, good wages, highly selected personnel. It is clear after several days about the dam and its vicinity that the T.V.A. all in all is building more than a dam. It is building a civilization. The visitor there is looking into the next century.

The dam sweeps from the lower river upward in a timeless curve of concrete 265 feet to the coping and the road across the gap. The power is quiet in the concrete. Power is produced there as part of a system crossing seven states and 40,000 square miles. Power is not always noisy. It thrills

67

and burns in silence over the wires. From Norris dam alone can come 132,000 horse power. It is liquid power, easily divisible, easily used far and near, in large amounts or in small. The new Cumberland road to Knoxville, fresh-laid with concrete over a cut and fill, swerves a bit from its straight path outside of town to go around a huge oak tree. On the tree is a sign, "Preserve this tree. Tennessee Valley Authority."

This is the power age, says a philosophical engineer, Walter Polakov. The Norris dam architecturally is an expression of that age. So is a battleship, for that matter, but with a different prospect. The Norris dam structurally is power. It is profoundly identified—mystically, if you will—with the structure of our society. This is a power age. It also is a fluid age. Power and fluidity mark us and the forms of our expression.

What is this power and this fluidity? Their sources are far back in the development of our society and technics. They are the titan sons of Science which in turn was made possible little by little by the ability of western thinkers to distinguish between interest or value and objective systems of reason and of matter. First with the Greeks, who came to think of reason as a self-sufficient order subject only to its own laws, later with Bacon and the great empiricists, who slowly developed the notion of self-sufficient matter as we now have it, through two thousand years of uncertain change and mental searchings were the conditions brought about that make modern science, power, fluidity possible. We have learned now to

68

question those two great autonomies of reason and of matter that are so profound a part of the liberal tradition of the western world. Science itself has reached a point of skepticism where it must turn back to criticize its own origins. But the power and the fluidity of the modern world remain, increase indeed at a terrifying rate, regardless of question and decay among their origins. They are wild children of parents no longer able to control them. Perhaps their parents are dead or have gone away.

The power of the western world refers to our unprecedented rate of doing work. The fluidity of the western world—or should we say plasticity?—refers to the change, the constant, insistent change, and the facility for change, that are associated with modern power. Once power, or the myth of it, meant the fixation of things, as, let us say, in ancient Egypt; it was the ability to resist the roving natural forces, to establish permanence, to hold back the vagrant changes of whim, fancy and decay; but power now is a dynamic notion. Power is the ability not to congeal reality in everlasting molds, but to speed it up in the wild rhythms of moving things.

The facts of this power can have only brief mention here. Through a long line of key inventions and discoveries, such as words and the use of symbols, fire, the lever and wheel, writing as an extension of symbols, metals, the gun and its extension the steam engine, the electrical transmission of power, and many more, have modern power, tools, and machines been developed. When machines, driven by other power-producing machines and supervised by skilled men, tended to replace hand labor with tools, the machine age succeeded the age of craftsmanship. When machines tended to be wholly automatic and used not only less labor but less specialized labor, the power age, says Polakov, succeeded the machine age.

The data of this power are impressive. With power plants already installed America can produce from 700,000,000 to one billion horse power, much more than any other people, and can increase this almost indefinitely as may be desired. Of major machines, such as turbines, locomotives, tractors, motor cars, looms, there are 127,000,000 in America. One billion acres of useful land are here, coal for three to five thousand years, according to estimate, iron in vast reserves; the list need not be continued. The power available per capita in America today is some forty times more than in America a hundred years ago. Perhaps it is a hundred times, for no one knows the upper limits of our power. From a nation of farmers and craftsmen a hundred years ago with an average capacity of perhaps one or two man power, we have grown in energy to a nation with an average capacity of some fifty or a hundred man power with four or five times the population. Our power, in a word, is between two and three hundred times the power of America a century ago.

It is obvious enough : one second-rate battleship of the modern American fleet could destroy the combined fleets of Napoleon, Nelson, and any other fleets of a few score years ago. One shoe factory in Lynn could provide footwear for most of the shoe wearing world of a century ago. One iron mine

70

NTER AT TALIESIN

Iome of Frank Lloyd Wright

in Minnesota could supply iron for the entire world of our great grandfathers. The dramatic contrasts are almost beyond number.

Power, in brief, fluid power is the mark of the modern world. Power and fluidity, in our social structures, in personal life, in the patterns of action and their expression in the arts, is necessarily the focus of almost any interpretation of the architecture of this impressive age. The characteristics of this modern life, so far as they influence expression, are determined in great measure by these factors.

These characteristics may be summarized roughly but tentatively somewhat as follows: the structure of society is horizontal in contrast to the older vertical society; personal life is pluralisic rather than monistic, explicit and external rather than implicit; human action is specialized with sharp cleavage between productive activities and consuming activities in contrast to the integrity of life of our fathers. In these patterns of human life are worked out the power and fluidity of the modern world. They are interwoven, of course, almost inextricably. They are different aspects of the same thing that cannot be sharply separated from each other in discussion. They are profound influences on expression, including, of course, architecture. This billion horse-power America is not the old America intensified by added power. It is a new society. The nature of this society, this personal life and human action engulfing us is not easy to define.

Because modern society is organized more in terms of activities than in terms of persons I shall call it horizontal. The

continuity of certain patterns of activity, such as the manufacture of buttons, that serve an extensive function clear across
the length and breadth of the land, is central in modern
social organization. They are horizontal structures of activity, and their development has been accompanied by a corresponding decline and discontinuity of that other sort of pattern called personal life. Though modern society may seem
dark, violent, complex, and the expression more of power than
of humane values, these are incidental. What matters is the
continuity and smooth organization of these extensive patterns of action, such as modern manufacturing, advertising,
construction, war, education, public transportation. These become always more organized in terms of far-reaching social
activities, and less organized as personal activities. These are
the operating units, so to speak, of the modern world. The
rhythmic pattern of a human being's life, on the other hand,
its functions and development vertically through various and
diverse fields of activity, is not considered an operation unit.
It is contributory only in fragments to the horizontal system.

Modern society is an organization mainly of these activities. They are specialized and impersonal, thinly stratified but
far-reaching. In them all, action is the defining characteristic
and since action is the result of power undergoing change—
or, as I have called it, power and fluidity—it is natural that
social structures should be mainly patterns of action in a world
of great fluidity and power. These activities, such as running
a street-car system, may be partly the actions of people and
partly the actions of machines, all co-ordinated to produce

special result; but only the activity itself counts. If the efficiency of the system requires more machine activity and less human activity, there will be more machine activity. In such a society the citizens, so to speak, are the producers of activity whether they be men or machines.

Public transportation, campaigns to abate mosquitoes, the latest song and dance of a Rogers and Astaire shown simultaneously in five thousand movie theaters, are horizontal patterns of activity. Specialization and division of labor, standardization of output and mass production are their technique. They are the natural working out of a situation in which power is available in huge concentrations. They are, as it were, social configurations of power.

The *Queen Mary*, among the latest of the largest ships, slowly makes her way to sea. The day is calm, and a light mist thickens on the horizon beyond Sandy Hook. Down the harbor, past Liberty, the heights of Brooklyn, Staten Island, through Ambrose Channel, the *Queen Mary* picks up speed. A bone now is in her teeth. She swings towards her left and heads down the great circle course for England. Eighty thousand tons is the *Queen Mary*. The entire Spanish Armada was not more than sixty thousand tons. Two hundred thousand horse power is her capacity for action. Her sides tower incongruously above the sidling, sweet sea, like a hard fact on the blue page of a poem. Across that eternity of blue her wake boils softly, spreads white.

This latest of the large ships rides on the sea, but is not of it. Still she is beautiful, as all ships, it seems, must be; she tells her story with a great voice. Being English and a Queen Mary, she is not wholly modern in her style. Her engines beat quietly in their dance. Their tune is modern. Her controls delicately move the mountain this way and that to within a fraction of a point towards her destination. In most of these operative functions she is modern, with the cleanness and economy of great architecture and engineering. In her furnishings and looks, her superstructure and fancy fittings, however, she is less sincere. She belongs less to the materials, the sea, the power, the disciplines that made her. She carries, for example, fake smokestacks to please a sentimental public. In one, let us say, is an elevator; another can be used for storage space. And inside the ship, she deserts the sea, most beautiful of all things, and piles land luxuries on luxuries in fulsome magnificence to compete with other lines. Still the *Queen Mary* is beautiful and expressive. There is plasticity as in all ships, and discipline in respect to the laws of motion and of the sea. There is greatness and power. The character of the modern age is in her.

Other great works express this modern age of power. The Panama Canal, the locks, massive and smooth running, the great bridges of San Francisco are examples. Great bridges everywhere, like ships, must be beautiful. The necessities of their existence, their response to strain and load, their lift over the water, impose most of the laws of good architecture upon them. The highways, the harbors, the millions of beautiful machines, the dredges and steam shovels, the locomotives on the move; the power of this world breaks through, expresses itself nakedly in beauty and awfulness. These are but a few of the expressions of modern power and fluidity as they find formulation in the horizontal structures of society. They are social not personal expressions.

On the dynamic continuity of certain operations is such a society based, rather than on personal continuity. The operations, such as steel making, are far larger in scope than personal operations could be, and are related to each other in a different way than are the operations within personal life. The objective of these larger operations, aside of course from making profits, is a kind of social efficiency of operation which can be relatively indifferent to personal interests and integrity. They are, in a word, impersonal.

Man, in short, is not the center of the modern social world. Because many do not see this, the modern situation seems to them baffling and contradictory. We are tired of man, it would seem—though many of us do not know it; our sense of his significance is changing. We seek a more stable and trustworthy standard of value. Not man, but an ill-defined idea having to do with the utility of social organization is the modern focus. The accomplishments of social organization, the production that it makes possible, are thought of first. Not man but his power is the point. The power, in short, that may be derived from social organization is nearer the center of modern interest. Society is a machine. The power of that machine is its justification. From this comes the clean surge, the cold grandeur, of some modern works.

The Greeks, we may suppose, lived in a society in which

75

man and man's values and limitations were of primary interest. That, at least, is the myth of humanism, and such philosophers as Protagoras with his "Man is the measure of all things" would seem to bear it out. Since that pagan time there has been much talk but little social emphasis on human values. There has never been quite time for them. They were always to flower after the next push. If God-driven medieval Europe was focused on ideals transcending human values, the naturalistic modern world is also, in its own way, beyond human scale. If angels were out of scale in respect to a lowly, clod-bound peasant, so is a steam shovel out of scale in respect to a man with a pick and spade. If heaven was out of scale for the corrupt fleshlings of this world, so are New York and Chicago out of scale in respect to the person living in them. They defeat his personality. The virtue of Greece, whatever its faults, was its ability to create a world in scale with the people in it. No other Western people has done that thing, and probably does not want to. It may be better so. Our society, our great cities, created by exploiting the power implicit in social organization, run far beyond the scale of the human persons in them.

And this scale, or lack of scale, increases. The small pattern of a life loses significance among giant activities. In contrast to the vertical pattern of an older day in which social relationships were organized more around personal continuities of life and less around extensive and impersonal activities, the horizontal society of this modern age has range and drive and a general functional organization very different from of

76

old. This socially horizontal structure of the modern world should not be confused, of course, with architectural horizontalism, or earth sense, the long fusion of building with the land. Spiritually the two are, indeed, quite opposite in nature. Social horizontalism, to return, makes for profoundly different ways of living from those of older times. People not only act in different patterns, they are different human beings. Would Great-uncle Elisha Foote recognize these moderns? He would have no chance. There are no great-uncles any more —or at least almost none.

Uncle Elisha was born near Middlebury, Vermont, some time before the war of 1812, and as a young man came overland by ox team to northern Illinois. It was in the early thirties that the members of the slow caravan, led by his prospective father-in-law, secured land in the Fox river valley and began the work of building homes and a living. Water, woods and, doubtfully, some of the untried prairie, were sought out for the homesteads. Log houses were erected. Crops were put in.

Uncle Elisha married his prospective father-in-law's daughter and settled himself and family in the black soil of the region. God and hard work helped him—at least that was his philosophy—and the farm prospered. His sons were strong enough to help out with the work. His daughters bloomed like the apple trees in spring. His fine team and carriage were the best in Kane county. For sixty years he lived there on the generous earth.

Uncle Elisha, if analysis be permitted, lived in what may be called a vertical society. His range was small. Once he got there northern Illinois encompassed all his life. The farm, the church, the school, the haul down to St. Charles to ship his hogs or grind his grain, a Sunday afternoon at Cousin Ed's, the weekly singing school, the fall hunt, an occasional day in Chicago forty miles away, this was the area of his living. The context of his experience was coherent with itself in one homogeneous fabric. Of thrill and contrast in the modern sense there was little, though death and danger sometimes were not far away. Of diversity of experience and the mad, magic jumps of life from shoes to ships to sealing wax Uncle Elisha knew little.

It was a meager life, if judged from a modern point of view, for the number of contacts during his eighty-odd years was small. Few people, few books, few foods, few songs, few memberships and recreations. But memories were long, and the people that he knew were deeply known. Their childhood was known; their families were known; their course through life was concurrent with his own. Their lives, in short, were in a complete context. For these lives, these families, or others not so different from them, and the activities surrounding them were the main focus of social organization. They were in the social context. Uncle Elisha's own life was in a context. So too were other things in his experience. Rarely were they casual or incidental. He saw the beginning and the end, the rise and the fall, and himself belonged in them. What moderns must say—or do say—in endless explanatory conversation about themselves was known reticently and deeply with-

78

out conversation by Uncle Elisha and his friends. Memories stood in the stead of talk.

In his family Uncle Elisha found his most impressive and enduring environmental influence. He was imbedded in it. That a life might be foot-loose, casual, with only touch-and-go relationships with other persons hardly could occur to him. Whether he liked it or not, the responsibility for other persons was imposed on him, and he in turn learned to accept their responsibility for him. His was a close-knit personal world. It was personal in scope and size, and personal to a great extent in the range of its activities. The family, always the family, was the symbol—and reality as well—of this.

The families lived in their old houses through long decades, grew into them, around them, over them, like a strong tree filling its enclosure. A wing was added here, a ceiling raised, the garret plastered for another bedroom. Old houses bulged and grew, weathered and wore down around their lives. The notched and worn window sill, scarred by the new saw when Henry was a boy; the old latch on the back door, never exchanged for a modern lock; the house had memories too. In a middle-western house like this Uncle Elisha lived.

"He's a great reader," said Uncle Elisha's wife proudly. But the books he read were few. The Bible and Clark's Commentaries were his main resources. And as for those yellow backed novels: lies, lies of the devil, no good Methodist would touch them. His foods were few, produced mostly at home. His amusements rarely were deliberate, or aware of themselves as such.

Uncle Elisha grew old, with great eyebrows and a gold-headed cane and deep memories of the prairie years that were a different world from this. The vertical pattern of the society of those years is now in great part gone. In sharp contrast is the horizontal structure of the present. It is marked in personal life by great range of contact but not much context. Denotation but not much connotation is another way of saying it. A wide area of fast rippling experience but a shallow volume of life: this marks the horizontal present over against Uncle Elisha.

The effect of this horizontal structure of society on human life is a fragmentation of experience and a dispersion of personal life. They are aspects of a kind of personal pluralism, or pluralistic personality, that is characteristic of the modern world. They are centrifugal and are consequences, of course, not only of the horizontal structures and activities of society but of other influences as well.

On personal life, whatever that may mean, modern society is a disruptive influence. It affects the character and values of people; it affects their expressions in the arts, play, work. A pluralism of personal life appears. It has many aspects, many faces and intricate confusions. Moral pluralism, cosmic pluralism, aesthetic pluralism are all characteristic of the mod-

80

ern age. Even more significant in the temper of the times is a kind of psychological pluralism. This is, so to speak, the pluralistic assumption; the person no longer takes for granted that he is an integral unit of reality. And quite possibly—the thought assails us—this is true.

What is this pluralism that has settled on modern folk with the beating of many wings? Though large-scale organization may be characteristic of the modern world from other than a human point of view, the world to the human person is many-centered, with many fields of reference, pluralistic. Few men escape this multiplicity of reference points, or wish to.

This pluralism of ours has many levels and varied cross sections. There is intellectual pluralism, for example : science, which is one world order, and value or purpose, which is another, claim diverse authority over the same things, and get it. There is the unintentional pluralism of modern physics, temporary perhaps, that uses both the wave and the corpuscular theories of light, or deals with electrons or the neat corpuscular integer called quantum h as if they had both body and not body. Educational pluralism, emotional pluralism, even domestic pluralism are common enough. The monism and the desire for monism of an earlier culture are dying out. We have learned to accept the many and like it.

"I assert myself," says Whitman, and we need go no further. Through all his past, man has intermittently asserted himself, and the assertion, it would seem, is the chief claim to his reality. But a new world is here, and just as his interests and his experiences are scattered widely over many fields so also is he himself scattered. He asserts himself less often. The old, inviolable unity of the human soul, whether it be of slave or serf or freeman, is slowly dissolving in great waters. "Why struggle for futilities?" he might well say. "After all, why retain the fiction of personal unity against such odds? What difference does it make?" And to most people, perhaps, it makes no difference. In the face of pluralism in practice a man tends to abandon a metaphysical form that has less and less content. He is absorbed more deeply in the variegated circumstances of the modern world. Even the physical continuity of the body, its tiredness, its freshness, its cycles and demands, is identified less than it once was with the rhythm and pattern of other things. It is less impressive and less central in the activities of things. It has less effect on them, and they less effect on it.

This psychological pluralism is more tacit than deliberate, and is more evident in the activities of people than in what they say. A modern person acts more often without much reference to the other activities of his life than did, for example, Uncle Elisha. The scope and figure that he follows are, as I have said, rather beyond his vision. Like the primitive man who took things irrelevantly as they came, according to the pattern of nature too large for him to comprehend, the modern man takes things haphazardly as they come in the pattern of a society that lies beyond his vision. What is highly organized from a larger structural point of view may be haphazard from the point of view of the person.

With eleven thousand banks failing in America in the dozen years before 1933 what depositor's security was more than haphazard? With fifteen million men out of work in 1933 what employee's job was relevant to his intelligent planning and effort? The peripheries of modern social structures are beyond men's horizons. A man's work in the wholesale grocery, for example, has little or no reference, so far as he knows, to his excursion to the movies in the evening. His lodge meeting has no bearing on the Sunday afternoon drive to Freeport. He listens to the Minnesota game over the radio without reference to the fate of the League of Nations. And war goes on, burning the life of the world, piling terror on terror, but whether he enters or does not, whether he comes back or does not, are rather casual and accidental incidents as far as the other features of his life are concerned. He lives a plural life. Events do not grow out of each other. Especially is this so in the city. They are not integrated. It is only a natural step to think of oneself in those terms too.

If this be madness, the man at least is calm, comfortable, and successful in it. More and more the modern person accepts himself as an aggregation of somewhat irrelevant interests and attitudes. It follows, of course, that his influence on his environment is also pluralistic. He is many effects. He is scattered, or, better, redistributed in a figure irrelevant to human life. The human as well as metaphysical consequences of the gradual abdication of personal unity are great beyond statement. If western thought has been built around a confidence in personal reality, this tendency towards psychological pluralism may be the mark of another epoch. "I think, therefore I am," might well be transformed into, "This and that thinks this and that."

The photographers several years ago were making composite pictures, say, of Lloyd George, Mary Pickford and Lord Tennyson with somewhat astonishing results. There would be the white-maned, massive head of Lloyd George, the lustrous and innocent Pickford eyes and the laureate beard of Tennyson, and Mary's curls perhaps were added to the picture. The modern multiplicity of life makes a somewhat similar composite. Often, indeed, it is not even a composite, but just curls abstractly located in clear air, eyes somewhere else also in ghostly dissolution, the beard completely autonomous like Ireland, the massive head rocketing briskly into another tense. It is fit subject for a surrealist, a dada or a Dali, but is really the subject of all persons of the modern age. A census, for example, of the rooms and buildings used in an average day by Cousin Nathaniel Foote would show the extreme dissection, scattering and incongruous reassembling of personal life in these times. Nathaniel is the grandson of Great-uncle Elisha and is a very different fellow from the old pioneer.

He awakes, let us say, in a bedroom (1) done in butternut and maple in the best colonial style—colonial for bedrooms. Thence he trots to the adjoining bathroom (2) done in tile, chromium and black enamel—the best room in the house. Having showered, shaved with an electric razor, done his hair with military brushes, he returns to the colonial bedroom, hangs his dressing robe in a cedar-lined closet (3) and dresses for breakfast. He steps into the upper hall (4) of no particular period, descends the stairs to the living room (5), Jacobean oak. Breakfast is ready. He crosses the dining room (6), which inherited Aunt Sarah's mahogany, to the breakfast nook (7) and sits down nookily on a painted bench at a painted table. The grapefruit, bacon, and coffee come and go in their courses; then Nathaniel steps to the coatroom (8), dons his overcoat and derby hat, goes through the kitchen (9), modern—another good room—to the garage (10), no style in particular, and enters his Ford car (11), Tudor. He drives out, goes to the porch (12) and calls, "Hurry up, Lorraine," to his wife, who will take him to the train. They arrive just in time. He hurries through the waiting room (13), railroad style, and gets aboard the last car (14) of the train. In 29 minutes he arrives in Chicago, hurries through the train shed (15) up to the arcade (16) that leads him through the *Daily News* building (17) to the Madison Street bridge.

Thereafter his day dashes through a multitude of rooms, buildings, vehicles and the like that we can only list, and then only in part. Comes the cigar store (18), the drug store (19), cluttered and colorful, the cab (20) in yellow, the grand lobby (21) of the office building, in mellow, cheese-like travertine or imitation, the elevator (22) Otis style, the twenty-third floor (23), the waiting room (24), furnished in 1929 *Saturday Evening Posts* and an office boy, the secretary's office (25), Nathaniel's office (26) with smart Venetian blinds, the chief's office (27) with many anterooms again, the lunch room (28), the wash room (29), the firm's library for executives (30), furnished for the most part with leather chairs and cuspidors, the filing room (31), the business manager's office (32), most luxurious with a secret panel to a private wash room, the shipping room (33), the elevated railroad train (34), style of 1896, the barroom (35), Titian giving way to Ziegfeld, the club (36), the gymnasium room (37), the squash court (38), the shower room (39), the steam room (40), the massage room (41), the artificial sun ray room (42), the locker room (43), the haberdashery (44) for English wool half hose, "Send them out, please," the telephone booth (45), the flower store (46), "Send them out for tomorrow evening, please," the liquor store (47), "Send it out, please," the candy store (48), "Send it out, please," the book and magazine shop (50), "Has next month's 'Gadget' come yet?" the lounge of the Palmer House (51) to meet Lorraine, the Overseas dining room (52), the theater ticket agency room (53), the Priceless Theater (54), the Watchme night club (55), on the train home—29 minutes—they meet Joe and Lennie. "Sure, but can't stay long"; the basement bar at Joe's (56). And so home again to the bedroom done in butternut and maple in the best colonial style—colonial for bedrooms. Cousin Nathaniel is a very different fellow from old Great-uncle Elisha.

The scattering of life, the Rotary Club, the office, the church, the golf club, the summer resort, the town club, the Elks, the Odd Fellows, the Legion, the baseball game, fishing,

E. J. KAUFMAN HOUSE

DURING CONSTRUCTION

Pittsburgh, Pa.

Frank Lloyd Wright,
Architect

Photo by University of Minnesota photogr

THE WILLEY HOUSE

BRICK WALLS ON CONCRETE MAT PAVED WITH BRICK

Minneapolis, Minnesota

Frank Lloyd Wright, Architect
(*Below: plan of the Willey House*)

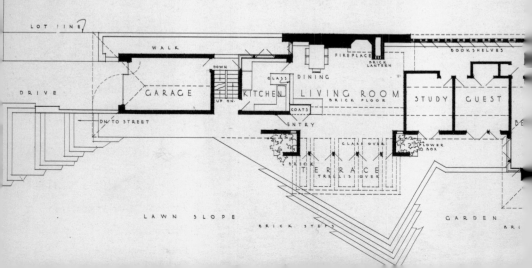

the automobile trip, bridge, the store, the factory, the saloon, the pool room, the garden, the garage, and, yes, the home; the list is endless. In each of them there is little reference to the others. In each and all of them the significance of the whole personality declines. In its place is an aggregation of separate abilities, segregated interests, activities, associations parceled out in various foci of social organization. It is doubtful indeed if there is a whole personality in such cases.

Nathaniel Foote, grandson of old Great-uncle Elisha, is really a multitude of Nathaniel Footes that cannot have much organic relation to each other. They cannot and do not; they are merely aggregative. Life is aggregative. It is a rich, variegated, often beautiful chaos. Its melody, if Conrad Aiken and Houston Peterson are right, is death or disintegration. Dissolution—the modern world is all this and more to one who finds in that quondam focus of life and activity, called the person, whatever it may mean, a sacred entity. From an impersonal point of view, however, this dispersion of the person into activities and functions more or less remote from each other is really a reorientation, not in terms of the person, but of a larger social pattern beyond the person's scope. Highly organized society, in a word, is a disintegrative influence on persons. It moves towards impersonal ends. It gains in power and fluidity at the person's expense.

In fascist Italy, in Germany, in communist Russia this of course has happened. Only less vocally has it happened also in capitalistic countries. In all of them social organization has increased; economic and business organization has increased; political organization has increased; but the person in all of this either is suppressed or scattered into chaos. This defeat of personality, and with it much of liberal and democratic culture, is not inevitable. It is not the march of fate. It is, however, the mark of our changing sense of significance in things.

This dispersion of personality is an aspect of the psychological pluralism in our modern power society. Chaos it may be, but its chaos is limited to man's personal point of view. If it is defeat, it is defeat only of individual man. So far as he wants homemade integrity and self-reliance, as Emerson would define them, it may be defeat, but socially it is a triumph. Nor is this statement entirely ironical. The modern world moves towards the dissolution of what Whitman would call "the single, separate person." There is much to defend that dissolution.

The rivers of Chicago are little more than seepings of the prairie and town. They filter slowly through the sand of the lake shore, humbly around the dunes and bars to find their way at last into Lake Michigan. They enter hesitantly, sometimes not at all.

Once the Chicago river was a great stream, as large as the St. Lawrence, draining the Lake Michigan lobe of the continental glacier into the Mississippi. The Grand Calumet and Little Calumet also had their greater days. As for the Des Plaines, which still flows southward towards the Mississippi, it was a continuation of the Chicago.

But the glaciers retreated. A low continental divide was

formed undramatically among the weeds and rushes and muddy pools between the new Chicago and the old Des Plaines. The lake that had been the great source of their waters became their partial destination. Though Indians knew a way by water from the Chicago through Mud Lake to the Des Plaines, only a sudden freshet now and then turned the river's flow into the old course. When white men came the tide reversed again. In the early days these meddlers with nature dug a short-cut from the Chicago river east to the lake from the bend at Fort Dearborn. Later came the Illinois-Michigan canal to which the city owes its start. Later the Chicago and Calumet were canalized, their bends were smoothed out, turning-basins were built, finally the drainage canal, parallel to the old canal, reversed the flow, carried it back again down the old glacial valley, and made Lake Michigan a tributary to the Mississippi.

The 92nd Street bridge over the Little Calumet carries the holiday traffic south and east to the lakeside resorts. The wheeled legions move massively day after day towards the dune country on the south shore of the lake and St. Joseph, Michigan City, South Haven, Grand Haven, Saugatuck, Muskegon and north along the beautiful Michigan shore where the lake tempers the west winds, and summer is cooler and winter warmer than in Chicago.

The 92nd Street bridge is a transition point, or so it seems to the motorist, between the receding city and the approaching open places, and though his way still has long industrial miles of steel and coke, oil, cement, soap, the glare and stench of furnaces, refineries and processing plants, the motorist knows that he is gradually leaving the city behind. The 92nd Street bridge is a span over the chaos that lies between the sterile noise and order of the central city and the gentler symmetries of the sand hills, water and the sky. It is a lift bridge, dark, surly, powerful in appearance; the new red street cars rumbling across cause hardly a tremor in its frame.

Modern cities are set within peripheries of chaos. Disorder circumscribes them like a kind of doom—rust eating towards the center. The 92nd Street bridge crosses this doom on the way to the country. It is a doom of fires and iron, coal and dead water, rotting ships and the rasp and cough of power shovels in the sand. Work and decay goes on. They seem irrelevant in the vast, timeless murk of the air.

The Little Calumet at 92nd Street bends somewhat and opens north and east into Lake Michigan. Towards the lake a few hundred yards is a turnbridge over the dead stream. A train is crossing. The cars are loaded with crushed stone and coal. They move across as if in a picture; the sounds of them are lost. "Illinois Central," "C. B. & Q.," "B. & O.," "New York Central," "C. B. & Q.," "Rock Island," "C. B. & Q." The vague haze and whiteness of the lake shows beyond the cars. A lighthouse stands there dimly.

"Exide Batteries," "Harbor Tavern," "Set Onions, 6 lbs. 20c," "South Chicago Centennial Committee." Along the shore of the dead river old boats, cabin cruisers, skiffs, even a rotting ore boat, are grounded until some spring or new

90

orders call them into life. "Ropke's Perch, 12c," "Smoke Fish." The stacks of the Illinois Steel Company are smoking. Flames blaze yellow against the black sides.

A railroad track runs close to the river on old ties that in some places are askew. The roadbed is slovenly, lost here and there amid piles of sand, white-gray, clean sand, gravel, crushed stone in loose pyramids and cones, careless geometries of varied color. "Material Service Corp." The wires strung along the track sag. The poles have been there a long time. "Material Service Corp." "Will. Penn Power Gas." Sand piles stand along the track. "C. B. & Q." "Material Service Corp."

Beside one of the tracks is a white picket fence. It encloses a gravestone in a little square not more than five feet by seven. On the stone is cut, "In Memoriam, Andreas Von Zirngibl. Born March 30, 1797, A Veteran of 1815, Battle of Waterloo, Died August 21, 1855." It takes six lines cut on the stone.

Ropke's Perch, 12c, C. B. & Q., J. F. Gallagher Co. Asphalt Paving Contractors. Producing asphalt for W.P.A. projects Nos. 60-64-67-73. The tank cars stand in a long row, strange tubes on wheels back of J. F. Gallagher Co. Asphalt Paving Contractors, and two fire boats in the dead river are tied along the bank.

The Pottawatomies have hunted here among the rusting piles of pipe. Young Gurdon Hubbard jumped ashore and climbed a tree to look westward at the prairie reaching forever across the stacks and furnaces of the mills. Flames are the prairie flowers. The Iroquois Iron Works has a large tract on the east bank of the river and Lake Michigan.

Derricks point their empty fingers to the sky, a hundred smoke stacks; steel cranes are unloading a freighter at the wharf. The river curves, dead water, a dull red fence runs east from the 92nd Street bridge. "Great Lakes Dredge and Dock Co.," "Calumet Brass Foundry." Two clam-shell shovels are working in the piles of sand. A barge rots by the junk yard, piles of pipe, a rusted bell buoy lies on its side, piles of pipe, six-inch pipe in about six-foot lengths. The derricks point empty fingers overhead.

Now look away. The flat rim of earth. A gas tank bulges over the horizon. Smoke is the horizon, also the earth. "Chicago-New York River and Harbor Improvements." A low building of tan brick, no inside, only outside. "Lake Sand," "Industrial Supplies," "Fish Caught Daily." A low building of tan brick is shoveling sand. Steel, angular sand screens stand along the old Indian Boundary Line. They gave the Pottawatomies their village at St. Joe and took this instead. By-Products Coke Corporation and dead water, a plume of steam against black sides, a plume of steam over flat water. And Ropke's Perch are shoveling sand geometries; red gravel on Thanksgiving Day. The 92nd Street bridge over the dead Little Calumet pauses, is shoveling sand. C. B. & Q., J. F. Gallagher Co. Asphalt Paving Contractors.

The modern world that everyone talks about has a different meaning for almost every person. What it does to people and their experience in terms of behavior may be as good a way as any to get at it. What happens to human experience in the modern world? The tale of multiplicity, fragmentation, pluralism goes on.

Our experiences have relatively greater range. There is more distance between them, not only in space, but in quality and tone. They have, as it were, more coverage. The young man in his sixty-dollar second-hand Ford is acquainted with Kansas and California, Boston and St. Augustine. He also knows, very likely, jazz and Beethoven, or at least the former; maple sirup and avocado pears; blondes, brunettes, and red heads; strawberries in January, ice cream in July. His experience has range, if not organization. Though his contacts and activities may be agglomerative they have wide reach. His life includes diverse and mutually remote things.

Modern experience also sustains a large number of contacts. Jackie Coogan is acquainted with many more persons than George Washington ever met, or at least Lawrence Washington. Adelaide Howard no doubt knows fifty persons to her grandmother's five. Walter Merrill, who entered law school this year, is in touch with more things, knows more kinds of tea biscuit, cigarettes, automobiles, dictators, cheeses, comic strips, brands, trademarks, popular songs, football scores and a multitude of other things than his grandfather ever heard of. The multitude becomes greater, it would seem, with each generation.

In a world where more and more attention is given to social connective tissue and the vast horizontal network of social relationships, human experiences become more fragmentary, and the patterns and values of personality change. Ten per cent of the working population in 1870 was engaged in distribution and transportation, for example; but in 1920 there was twenty-five per cent so engaged. Today there are far more people whose life-work is to sell other people's goods, move other people's productions, and to make merchandise of everything that human beings want. The very structure of experience, as well as content, changes. We move from agrarian and craft life and their moralities to a new life and morality of the city.

Because more things come to their attention people are keener, quicker in perception, more discriminating. More things interest them in a modern horizontal society and there is more diversity among those things. Alertness is necessary, brings success and becomes a general attitude. The segregation of interests and loyalties in a modern society also has its effect. Business loyalties are separated from church loyalties. Sport loyalties are separated from class-room loyalties. Home and marriage loyalties are separated from loyalties to persons known elsewhere. Labor loyalties, national loyalties, neighborhood loyalties, sex loyalties, race loyalties, age loyalties, job loyalties—there are a multitude. They cross and contradict. They compete with each other without coherence. Consequently, loyalty as a principle declines. Loyalty to principles also declines. What remain are certain loyalties to people, to organizations and to local situations which shift and veer according to the circumstances. Expediency tends to re-

94

place loyalty. In a horizontal society, again, a person's duties are dispersed over various unrelated fields. There are duties in the factory or office, duties in the home, duties as a citizen, a church member, a lodge member, and the like, each related to a different personnel. The boss in the factory knows nothing of a man's duties at home, nor cares. The wife at home knows nothing of a man's duties as corporal in the field artillery unit of the national guard. A modern man's responsibilities are usually subdivided. They have no integrating principle. No person knows him all through. No life is concurrent with his. Because of these things the sense of responsibility declines. Pride in the continuity of one's personal life weakens because there is no continuity of personal life— at least no significant continuity. Why be consistent? Why hold to these fictions of honor? In any case there is less rigorous pride in personal honor. Persons trust more in organization—fools though they may be—and less in persons. And they themselves are less trustworthy.

So it goes: the fragmentation of experience, the dispersion of personal life, the pluralism of personality that stands over against the horizontal structure of modern society; moral pluralism, cosmic pluralism, aesthetic pluralism, the entire ideology of the modern person's life; to say the least, it is thoroughgoing.

Such is the city and its organizations. In contrast to this is the country. The architect for John Frederick's silo near Elkhorn, Wisconsin, was not Frederick himself nor even the cement firm which gave him free plans, specifications, and full instructions for building. The architect was the price of corn in winter and the pressure of ensilage at the bottom of a forty-foot column. The architect was the ratio of the silo's capacity to the size of farmer Frederick's herd and the strength of round walls of monolithic concrete. These were the voices that said what the silo should be, and no other architect was there to carve wild roses around the coping, or to add a gargoyle or superfluous flying buttress. John Frederick's silo was built to serve a definite function and every pound of cement in it works toward that end. In some ways his silo had the greatest of all architects: necessity. Its form was necessary, so to speak; nothing could be different, given the conditions.

Its form, really, is a function of the raising of live stock and the life of the farmer who raises it. It is architecturally honest because it expresses this pattern of the farmer's job without fake or pretense. It is architecturally good because the life behind it is good. John Frederick's life has a certain integrity of pattern. It has simplicity and a reticent but profound reliance on the rhythms of the native season and the soil that we have learned through age-long experience to call good. This is not all of the story: the salt sweat of the summer's day, the bitter milking in winter, the loneliness and crudity, the harsh stupidity of nature and of men, all have their part, but pattern there is, at any rate; the simple, concrete silo by the barn belongs to it. It stands gray-white, tall with a fresh curve of surface that is in lively contrast to the long angularity of the red barn. It is a sturdy column, to

96

which, thank God, no eclectic stockman yet has tried to give flutings or a Doric capital.

Why do most of us like silos? Were it possible to explain their simple assertion of beauty, why their volumes and proportions and the suède textures of concrete are "right," the long mystery of value would be cleared away. But that is not probable. The mystery no doubt lies in the very structure of human experience. To solve it might destroy the structure of all that is most real.

Silos, in any case, are built some thirty to forty-five feet high, and run from ten to twenty feet in diameter; one will provide winter feed for six months or more for a herd of dairy cows that may number a dozen up to sixty. These are the basic facts of silos, in case they are required, but farmer Frederick can give many more. There are wood silos, for example, brick, steel, concrete stone and concrete monolithic silos; the farmer builds the kind that cost, materials at hand, and the degree of skilled labor permit. For the silo must be water tight, air tight, strong against wind storms and possible lightning and fire. It will be built course by course above the shallow silage pit. Finally, a Norman roof will cover it.

The silo has agrarian repose. The stocky tower, though vertical in silhouette, is self-contained. It stands on the earth, and from the earth has assured stability. It is, so to speak, a tower of good harvest and a reserve when crops are poor. How many silos there are may be known deep in the archive rooms of the U. S. Department of Agriculture, but it makes little difference. Over the great live stock belt of this country they stand on their domain on every forty acres or so up to one hundred sixty acres.

From this agrarian architecture and the contained lives that underlie it we return to the strain and scatter of the city. There is John Frederick's silo, near the little town of Elkhorn, Wisconsin, and there is the moral, cosmic and aesthetic pluralism of metropolitan society. There are no silos in the city.

Morals in the city are many. The plural personality of a contemporary human being will naturally have plural codes and standards of action. We have been bred to think that our conduct has one moral law, one standard of right and wrong, but conduct in the modern world has many authorities. Though this always has been true to some extent, the present era gives new emphasis to our moral pluralism. Not since monotheism was imposed on the Western world have the authorities of conduct been so diversified and at times so contradictory. Our gods, it is true, are few, at least our recognized divinities, but the sanctions of our conduct are no fewer than if we found gods in every sunrise and every ocean wave.

Our gods, or half gods, are a strangely assorted company, and their Olympus, which lies no doubt above the ghostly smoke and violence of the railroad yards at Clearing, Illinois —greatest of railroad yards—has neither peace nor purity but seethes with power. There is, of course, the god of business, a shrewd fellow with four hands and no legs, whose principle of action is, "Exchange everything for something else," and whose method is, "You get yours and I'll get mine, and the devil take the hindmost, so long as I am not hindmost. In that case I should have government assistance." His apotheosis of the principle of exchange is one of the reasons for the extreme fluidity that marks the modern world. And there is, for example, the god of sport, who invents new and gratuitous ways to compete. His is the principle of antagonism limited. Be a friend and gentleman towards your opponent in all but one particular, and beat hell out of him in that particular. Never boast of victories nor remember them, never complain of loss. Take it, if you must, as the saying is, on the chin, but remember it is better to give than to receive. And there is the inevitable god of love still hanging around, a burly fellow now, with great shoulders able to carry any load. He strides here and there, his voice roaring above all others. He beats his chest, "In my name, anything, anything, I say, goes." Other gods too numerous to mention, many gods, including, of course, Jehovah, many codes, standards, authorities; each one becomes more a pattern of its own as it matures; each one lays out a world without much reference to the others. Such is the pluralism of modern authority for conduct. Conduct and its sanctions are centrifugal in tendency.

These divisions of authority are, roughly, the source of conflict in modern moral life: there is sacred over against secular authority. Although secular authority, as found in the law of the land, the family, in the school, in the football team, in the factory, has grown in power and complication at the expense of sacred authority, there remains a significant

99

influence of the sacred or divine even in modern life. There is also rational and irrational authority. By no means is all irrational authority confined to what may be called sacred. The social authority of German Nazism is irrational in basis, proudly so, as contrasted with Russia's communistic rationalism, yet both are definitely secular. There is, again, what may be called humanistic as contrasted with organizational authority. This division of the modern moral complex cuts still another way. Whereas the democratic or protestant thesis, theoretically, bases authority on the human being as an experimental and rather free agent, communism, fascism, catholicism alike find authority not in the human being but in the organization. With this again is involved the naturalistic authority of science based on free experiment and observation. From six or seven primary sources come the sanctions and authorities of modern conduct. Often they are not co-ordinated; sometimes they are in profound conflict. Our moral world is pluralistic.

The modern man stands in a great room amid the clatter of insistent machines. Through the room move many conveyors or belts that carry in endless procession a large number of different things in process of manufacture. The man, unlike Charlie Chaplin, has not merely one belt but several belts to attend to. He makes an adjustment on one article on one belt, then turns to another belt, then to another, and so on from belt to belt. The ends of each belt are lost in the distances of the room. The man busily adjusts himself to each belt in turn, belongs, indeed, to each system consecutively,

100

the limits of which he does not see, then turns to enter another system. The belts move on their rollers out of the darkness into a spot of light and on into the darkness again. The man lives in that spot of light. Perhaps he is that spot of light. He lives locally in relation to a brief section of each belt, turns to a brief section of another belt, but can see no significant unity between one belt and another. Like this is the plural authority for conduct. The modern man participates briefly in one system of sanctions after another; he cannot, or does not, belong wholly to any one system. Neither can he find unity in the cross section of the several systems.

In such a world no building can house a life, nor can one god sanctify it. Structural continuity is not there. Living is not coherent. As a result some aspects of the modern situation find expression, or refuge, in the arts and some do not. Many cannot escape the overburden of tradition. In architecture the organizational sanction of conduct, in contrast to the human standard, is given form in many works in the great cities. The tall buildings, the railroads, the steamship lines have the beauty of great power and organization. They are clean-lined now and usually express the abstract energy that made them. But the old craft arts decline. They remain only as a sentiment and must be deliberately promulgated to remain at all.

This pluralism of the modern world may seem to be in contradiction to the well-known uniformities of the age. We use the same slang, read the same best sellers, wear the same cut of clothes, don our straw hats together, eat the same food, and by standardizing the denotative aspects of our experience impoverish the connotative or imaginative context of it. Wherein then is the pluralism? But the regimentation, so often pointed to as the disastrous goal of modern tendencies, is a broad social regimentation that far overreaches the horizons of the people in it. It is beyond their scope, beyond their organizational capacity, and in its effect is pluralistic morally, intellectually, culturally, yes, personally. Observe the experiences of modern people; regimentation there is, but is there moral or intellectual integration in those uniformities? Quite the contrary: the great organization destroys those integrities of life and incorporates the fragments. The classic rubble from the temple, a splintered bit of cornice, a broken capital, is built into the Turkish fort.

If the moral order of the modern world becomes under these pressures many moral orders, so too the intellectual order, the very cosmos of the modern man, breaks into glittering sections that cannot be co-ordinated. Whatever the philosopher may have, or may think he has, in the way of a universe, the average man—whether he be salesman or scientist, lawyer or laborer—has several universes. For not only is his authority for value and goodness in the moral world a plural and sometimes conflicting committee of gods and scattered interests; his authority for truth also is several different things. The structure of his intellectual world, in other words, is not coherent with itself. He is the owner and operator, as it were, of several cosmoi.

The main issue between these diverse worlds is still no doubt the naturalistic in contrast to the revealed truth.

102

Modern sophisticates and others retain them both, often from discretion. They closet them each in its place, with insulating indifference between. Thus they find peace, but peace only by psychological escape and bizarre substitution. They forget at a price. They ignore the cosmic incongruity of gods and science, of values as forces, at a heavy cost. I need not go into this ancient problem except to point out that the universe for modern man as a practical reality is not one universe but several. He has several sources of authority for truth, several different standards of the real. He accepts the consequences of naturalism, from modern plumbing to the planetesimal hypothesis of the earth's origin, and he accepts also the power of a god's hand and the "force" of values and purposes. This lack of intellectual homogeneity in the modern mind is a characteristic of the age. It is a kind of pluralism that relates, in this case, not to the code of values involved in action but to the system of facts of the world's structure.

The consequences in expression of this pluralism are of great and still unrealized scope. The modern arts have their continuity, it is true. They burn with the same flame. They move in their respective fields towards somewhat the same culmination. But that culmination is in some respects the culmination of human disintegration in the face of increasing social organization. The arts flame variously. Buildings tower into the sky on the one hand, or lie along the low prairie slope on the other. Literature burns from fever to fever. A Dreiser and a Robinson Jeffers, an Ogden Nash and a Eugene O'Neill, endless contrasts crowd the modern age. They emerge each from his own cosmos, each from his moral code and traditional authority to build the strange clash and pluralism, endless contrasts, diversity, bewilderments of the modern situation.

The modern pluralism of taste is inevitable in such a world. The standards of expression are many and diverse. And taste, what is taste? What conscience is in morals taste is no doubt in the realm of aesthetics. It is a mysterious authority, neither learned nor reasoned but there regardless. So we like to think. "I am no expert, but I know what I like," is heard from London to San Francisco. But taste has its vicissitudes and conditions like other human things. In simplest terms taste is indeed what we like. For reasons that we need not go into we take to things, like them, often want them. In the modern world, however, taste is not homogeneous. And culture, so far as it is based on taste, is variable and violent in its contrasts. It is learned or somehow acquired from many sources. It is pluralistic.

Many of these variations in taste are honest enough and derive from essential differences in background and environment. The Jew, for example, ordinarily likes the city. He lives there, thrives there, and his taste usually runs to the urban manner. He accepts with pleasure the extreme professionalism and virtuosity of the arts. He enjoys the division between audience and expert that marks so much of city life. He turns towards brilliance and facility of intellect, but like the urban Greeks cares little for the slow growth and feel of material construction and for craft carried on for the activity of craftsmanship. All this is urban in culture, and the Western

104

Jew comes by it naturally enough. Other diversities of modern taste are less honest. The promiscuous imitation of styles in residence buildings along Chicago's Sheridan Road is meretricious and vulgar, but a mark no less of modern culture.

This pluralism of taste is called eclecticism. It is a process usually of taking rather than creating, of capture or purchase rather than production. With the wide reach of the money economy in our horizontal social system this pluralism of taste becomes predominant. Academic training, for example, is almost always eclectic and usually debases any artist that it touches. It is founded more on the phrase "learning about" than the phrase "producing with." Modern travel, "picturesque travel," the trips and tours that slide sentimentally over the surface of the earth, seeing the world from a paying visitor's point of view, have the same eclectic influence. Shopping, for that matter, often with unearned money, flitting here and there from thrill to thrill, or the dull grind of factory work or routine of the office to earn the cash to buy what is worth while, all tend to break down the integrity of taste. The eclectic attitude replaces it. Gothic for churches, classic for government buildings, pig-baroque for movie palaces, renaissance for clubs, anything for residences—this is eclecticism. Historical styles, by some strange subdivision of sentiment, are used as different functions in the modern situation. This may apply to different buildings or to different parts of the same building. A Gothic church stands beside a classic library, but here is a woman's club building with a Gothic entrance, a renaissance lounge, a modern dining room,

a classic washroom, a romanesque ballroom, a Moorish library
and so on, arrangements unlimited. The total result is techni-
cally a disorganization that in mental life is called insanity.

We live, as a fact, eclectic lives. This no doubt justifies in a
sorry way the eclecticism of much modern art and architecture. The horizontal structure of our society, the pluralistic
character of our personal lives, are influences towards eclecticism.

Drive out on Sheridan Road along the "north shore" of
Chicago. The road winds over the bluffs and ravines along
Lake Michigan. Elms overarch the way in long, living vistas.
The apple trees, lilacs, cherries bloom in Spring in sheets and
billows of soft flame. The jonquils are sunshine on the earth.
In the fall the maples, oaks and sudden poplars flare into
exaltation. They burn through the weeks, October, Novem-
ber, against the smoke-blue sky, on towards December. It is
a gracious scene.

But man's works along the drive rarely suit that scene. The
blue lake is there beating upon the sand. The trees and the
ravines lie under the sun and rain. But the buildings along
the way rarely incorporate them in their structures. The road
sweeps on beautifully over the ravines in lithe conformity,
but of man's work along the shore that curves north unbroken
three hundred miles, it is too often only the road that is beautiful. Here is a French peasant house with rippled roof and
imitation thatch, the dear old thatch in our school books. It is
set quaintly near the corner of Ridge Avenue and Sheridan
Road. Here is a Swedish house with its blueprint logs and

106

rough-cut lumber, with sentimental wooden storks beside the chimney. From the dark hills and timbered valleys of the north it comes to nestle here on the N.E. corner lot. It nests here cozily at the corner, let us say, of Perkins Avenue and the drive. Here is old Spanish next, with plaster courts and curves, delicately pink according to some architect's specification. A French château, Italian, German, Moorish, Tudor, Colonial, Georgian, the whole museum is there, all, no doubt, with excellent plumbing. Italian, French, Elizabethan, Spanish, Dutch, Classic, German, Colonial, French, Italian, Renaissance, Swiss, Venetian: they march down the great drive, pretentiously cozy, borrowed, but the plumbing is the thing. There is the honest work hidden behind it all. Thank God for modern plumbing!

The great road swings up the shore under the dusky blue of northern Illinois. It sweeps over the ravines; it curves across the contours of the dark earth. Through a swarm of billboards that settle like flesh flies on a fine horse, between the rows of costly houses—Italian, Tudor, Classic, Byzantine; Italian, Classic, Tudor, Swedish—the purchased sentiments of Chicago's elite, the road sweeps on, brushing them off, as it were, and gets free at last magnificently into the country. A red barn and a farmer's silo are worth more architecturally than most of the costly imitations that line the early reaches of the drive. Most, but not all; there are some good buildings there.

Such wares show alertness to see and imitate detail, and to sell it. They have no responsibility, however, to the real na-

107

ture of the situation. They are explicit without context. They are acquired bodily without creation. The result is architectural heterogeneity. It is a *mélange* but not an architecture.

That personal life is explicit and external today rather than implicit might well be inferred from modern architecture. We refer of course not to the natural architecture of those magnificent expressions of social power and fluidity, such as the steamship or Golden Gate bridge, or to the simple honesty of the silo or gasoline engine but to the architecture that takes pains to be correct, tasteful, pretentious or pretending as the case may be. In this may be seen the pluralism and heterogeneity of taste and personality and the fragmentation of experience. There can be seen also the emphasis on the explicit and the external in personal life.

A man today lives in a great organization. And because he has no visible history, no memory, no context in that organization he must talk more. He must explain, always explain. A modern society is a talking society. A man will depend on talk, must depend on talk. His world will be more verbal, more conceptual, less imaginative and kinaesthetic. Meanings and values will be less implicit, more explicit, and the created thing will be of more interest than the act of creating. This is one reason for the clutter of Italian, Swedish, Moorish, Classic, German, Tudor, Colonial houses on the drive. This is one reason, at least, for the modern tendency to acquire things of value rather than to create them. They are more explicit.

The man who passes a little mountain cabin as he drives

108

south on U.S. 41 or some other continental road has only the most brief and denotative experience of what the cabin is and means. He drives past many cabins, hundreds of cabins across Kentucky, Tennessee, Georgia, Alabama, more cabins than Walt Warrick, the gray-eyed reticent hill-man living in Pine Cove, ever saw. He drives past thousands of cabins; all his life he is driving past cabins or things like them, and his experience of each one is like the last. It is fragmentary; it is explicit; that is all. There are few connotations. There is no context of any depth.

This explicitness of experience and personal life, whether it be in modern travel, shopping, university work, or wherever, is related to the derivative art and culture that characterize so large a part of the modern situation. Where experiences of things are limited to narrow fragments of those things they cannot include in themselves intimations of their genesis and history, the remote tones and colors that enrich their being, the structures, skills, many-sided realities implicit in the things in question. The context, the growth, the potentialities of things are simply not there.

Thus the modern person is likely to turn to the past— which is always explicit—for the things which he values. He acquires the sharp, sure things already created. He takes what he finds, raiding other cultures past and present, and sometimes understanding them. He derives his appreciative life from other sources than his own world. He accepts derivative culture on the principle that a bird in the hand is worth two in the bush. The acquisition of a thing already made is better than the uncertain potentialities of a thing not yet created. He raids the certain past to avoid the unsure future. He captures the thing done. Because his experience is aggregative rather than whole and organic the native growth of original art is for him impossible.

This derivative culture of modern times is due in great part to the fact that no person—that is, no one person—is associated with the complete production of a thing. In a horizontal society this division of production becomes more and more usual. Power and mobility have replaced personality in our productive methods. In consequence the whole activity of production is not experienced by the modern person. Things come to us made, or partly made, and we do not know or see or feel the making. They are derivative in the sense that the finished result is not identified with the whole creative activity of making them. Their production is out of human scale. They are derived, in effect, from elsewhere than our own lives.

I have discussed thus far in this part of the book the horizontal structure of modern society, the pluralism of personal life in its various aspects and the explicitness and externality of personal life, and I have tried to show their consequences and correlations in architectural expression. There remains the modern cleavage between production and consumption in the activities of people. This of course is closely related to the material already discussed, and has a perhaps even more significant influence on expression. In any case changes in systems, values and activities have taken place.

110

Production is different; so is consumption. The implicit and contextual values of persons and things virtually disappear. The things taken for granted in Uncle Elisha's life are now neither known nor taken for granted. The explicit and the verbal take their places. In this modern emphasis on the explicit is a primary reason for the derivative architecture of these times.

Were these the only influences, all modern architecture would be what much of it is, feeble eclecticism and imitation. But the modern age is complex. There are other influences. The fluidity and raw power of the modern world has also its truth. It breaks through these aesthetic crusts in vast floods and eruptions, creating impersonally, as it were, its own forms and unconsidered beauty. In architecture and poetry, at least, and probably in dancing and music, if not in the art of living, this era has made a major contribution to world art.

It is a complex age. The power and mobility of it expressed in one configuration results in mean and meretricious work, in another soars to an honest, if cold, glory.

The cleavage between productive activity and consuming activity is the third and last feature of my interpretation of the modern world in its influence on expression. This division of human activity into two sharply separated phases is in

111

some ways the most drastic of the human changes of the modern industrial age, and in some ways is also the most tragic. In terms of industrial and social organization, on the other hand, it has huge efficacy in the production of goods and in the smooth operation of the great horizontal structure of activities that is the mark of modern society.

By breaking down the activity of a person into parts called production and consumption, and reassembling those parts, like with like, with the activities, similarly divided, of other people—mass production was achieved. This involves, it should be remembered, not only great quantity of production but the inner coordination of production by this method. Only by this segregation of the functions within personal activity—a kind of inner division of labor—could the modern horizontal structure of society be built. In such a system people are associated with each other not as whole persons, but as productive units in a factory or work place, or as consuming units, or as some other special units. The result, of course, is the great efficiency of our industrial organization and a society in which power and mobility have reached unprecedented amounts. The result is also, as I have said before, the surrender of personal unity and integrity. In the western world, with its Christian and romantic tradition of personal value, this may seem to be the ultimate disaster. This should not be taken for granted, however; it is not necessarily disastrous. The extreme emphasis on personal value and the value of persons in the western tradition is unusual, if not freakish, in the history of man. Humanism, indeed, is something of a novelty.

112

Though the cleavage between productive and consumptive activities is not, of course, a discovery of the modern world, it is put into effect in the modern horizontal society to an extent that makes it virtually a new principle of relationship between the activities in a life. In Great-uncle Elisha's life, production was often distinct from consumption, to be sure; he too sowed and reaped that he might eat; he too sacrificed the enjoyment of the moment, postponed values, in order to perform tasks whose interest was less in themselves than in what fruits they produced. But the cycle was short in Great-uncle Elisha's life. More than likely he himself and his immediate family consumed, or enjoyed, the things that his work and his hands produced. If they did not, the pattern was not beyond his scope: he saw the things that he produced, used, and enjoyed, or at any rate he saw the things that he produced. He followed through the rhythm of their making from beginning to the end. In the modern age this is different. The workman can neither enjoy his product nor see it enjoyed, nor does he see even the activities of production in their entirety.

The activities of modern people are highly skilled. Skill, more and more specialized, is a primary industrial and social advantage gained by the separation of production from consumption. It is an age of skill. Millions of men and women attain a proficient speed and accuracy of movement, a sure technique and confidence in the mastery of certain operations and materials. Never in all probability have there been so many skilled persons or so high a proportion of them in a society. The attitude and temperament of our society and public opinion are largely determined by it. That these skills have not the scope or wholeness of the earlier crafts is true, but they are skills no less. They are attached, without legs of their own, to the massive industrial and social machine and are carried by it, but they are highly developed within their limits. Though Polakov points out that machines themselves take over many of these skills as industry emerges from the machine age into the power age, skill remains still the dominating character of modern activity.

It is five o'clock, and we face the homeward rush on Madison Street at Wells. Who are these hurrying people? Here is a skilled typist. Her smart skirt swirls about her silken legs as she dashes up the stairs to catch the Shopper's Special to Jarvis. A skilled filing clerk is with her. A skilled riveter strides by from the construction job on Clark Street. A skilled reporter, a skilled copy reader, and a skilled telegraph editor walk past together. They are talking about the whims and failures of a skilled night editor, a skilled editorial writer, a skilled drama critic, a skilled copy boy. A skilled motorman brings a street car to a stop. A skilled shoe salesman, a skilled window washer, a skilled saxophone player, a skilled hairdresser for women, a skilled gold-leaf letter-layer get on. In the crowd in the vestibule they jostle a skilled garage mechanic. On the long seat inside sits the champion hog castrater of America arrogantly confident of his skill. Beside him is a teacher of English equally arrogant in his nice knowledge of "would" and "should." A skilled boxer, cauliflower-

114

eared, gets off at Randolph street. A skilled sign painter gets his seat. A skilled waitress, tired on her feet, dangles on a strap. A skilled policeman, newspaper under his arm, is on his way home from duty. Not all of these belong to the so-called skilled trades, but skilled they are nevertheless. They and thousands more will devote most of their lives to the limited set of operations in which they have become proficient.

As producers they are skilled; as consumers they accept the skilled ministrations of others. Skilled, classified, specialized, reassembled as it were, they produce what others will enjoy, they enjoy what others produce. They rarely produce and enjoy in natural cadence. Today Dizzy Dean pitched for St. Louis and thirty thousand fans sat in the stands and watched their baseball game. Home after the game for a moment, then off to Wentworth avenue and 22nd for a Chinese supper; a radio plays—Chinese or no—singing tonight will be furnished by Kate Smith. And a concert down town for the evening, for we are cultivated—a concert, let us say, by Albert Spalding; the brilliant violinist will give us our hour or so of music. We enjoy what others more skilled than we produce for us. A great system of exchange develops. Money becomes both a mystery and a god, for it measures this exchangeability of things.

This is the city. It is created in the character of its labor and living, its culture, recreation, art, its great buildings, its facilities and services, by productive and consumptive activity segregated from each other in this way. The sharp limitation of a person's work-time activity—as well as his experience—

115

marks it. A modern woman may know the wearing of a gown but nothing of its making. A seamstress may know the making, or part of it, but have no decent dress to wear. A girl may know the taste of beaten biscuit but nothing of their baking. A man knows his office companions in business but nowhere else. The space zones of the city, the time zones, the occupational zones segregate his friendships. A boy moves from group to group, from school friends to college friends, from college friends to early business friends or professional friends, from business friends to friends in later leisure and success, with few or no persons carrying across these zones of time. He may have even his successive wives zoned in each group. His activities are compartmentalized. In modern urban life production is not usually enjoyed; it is exchanged for enjoyment. Thus the principle of exchange goes deeply into the fiber and activity of life. Instead of participation in the complete cycle of an operation there is division and subdivision. Instead of identification in the integral cadences of action there is exchange, specialization, and the mobile transfer of parts.

And today the great cities burden the earth. They are the prime creation of these modern methods of action. Their success or failure is the success or failure of modern civilization. They are both orderly and disorderly, beautiful and hideous, constructive and destructive. These paradoxes are focused in general around the differences between the personal and human aspects, and the organizational and social aspects of the situation.

116

The modern city is orderly in a way and to a degree that medieval cities—in spite of the encomia of some antiquarians —never approached. The older cities were industrially and socially aggregative. They were collections of people—tradesmen, craftsmen and others—whose lives were organized with a good deal of completeness about their own personal or local centers. Their lives were organically whole. They were integrated. But the city was merely an aggregation of these lives. Its structure as a city was subordinate or absent entirely. It was less orderly in this sense, far less orderly, than the overpowering cities of today. The city of today is more orderly as a social system but the lives in it are less orderly.

So, too, the modern city is beautiful as a vehicle of social power and mobility. It is beautiful in its verve and speed and wild color. It is hideous in its effect on the lives of millions of people. It has the beauty of marching men, the massive beauty of great structures, the exact beauty of machines. It drives, overwhelms like a storm, and it leaves its wreckage.

In like manner the city is constructive. Its organization is continually more powerful, more miraculous. Its grasp extends over more of the country. Its bridges and buildings, its music and dancing, dining, dressing, its plumbing and its drama, its vast thrust of life, all of these are constructive. They are constructive and these are the results. But men disintegrate under the destructive pressure of it all. The city is that primary paradox of human civilization, namely, society at war with man—with man, at least, as we traditionally know him. Though man's society it may be, it destroys him.

117

The ends and objectives of modern society, in a word, are not in many cases human ends and objectives; they often are anti-human.

Thus it can be said, in terms of this conflict between society and human life, that the modern city is both orderly and disorderly, beautiful and hideous, constructive and destructive. It depends, of course, on which of our ambivalent standards we happen to be using.

Most of the expressive architecture of these times is the architecture of society triumphant over human life. The factories and towers, the machines and boulevards, bridges and battleships have grandeur and cold power. They are authoritarian. A world great in its power and fluidity raises its authorities and its symbols of authority. A battleship is authoritarian, obviously. A Field Merchandise Mart is authoritarian. A Clearing freight yard is authoritarian, coordinating, classifying, imposing patterns, regimenting. All these things lay authority from without upon their materials. Their architectural forms are external. They are compulsive over the material. They exist in construction for much the same reason that both fascism and communism as social authorities exist in political life. The efficiency of great organization is in them triumphant. For this reason they exist.——B. B.

IV. Some Aspects of the Future of Architecture

THE chapter on the past and present of architecture ended with the ideal of an organic architecture—the New Reality.

If architecture has any future more than revival or passive reform, we must speak of future architecture as organic. It is apparent that the pagan ideal of architecture—we call it classical—has broken down. In practice, then, speaking out from experience in the field, what does this term, organic architecture, mean? Already it has been said—*lieber meister**—declared it—and biology knows and shows us that "form follows function." But the physicist cannot interpret the word "organic" as it applies to architecture. Not until we raise the dictum, now a dogma, to the realm of thought, and say : *Form and function are one*, have we stated the case for architecture.

That abstract saying "Form and function are one" is the center line of architecture, organic. It places us in line with nature and enables us sensibly to go to work. Now accepting that fundamental concept of architecture as interior discipline, how can we work it out in actual practice?

Let us rebuild a building with phrases as I have built one with bricks and mortar and men. I have built one, as I believe, naturally.

* Louis H. Sullivan.

"Form and function are one" is the thought in the back of the mind that will now shape an attitude towards everything in our sight, including Mr. and Mrs. Domestic Client and progeny or, it may be, towards the capitalist-captain, the unfeeling corporation, or the baron.

Before we begin to build, however, what is the "nature" of this act we call architecture? That quest will discover certain elemental truths with which building, as organic, is concerned. Form and function being one, it follows that the purpose and pattern of the building become one. They are integral. This, in a sentence, is the ages-old thesis, which, made new, we call the norm of organic architecture. This new integrity, "from within outward," is now evident as the modern architect's guide and opportunity. "Out of the ground into the light" is opportunity. The nature of materials is also his opportunity and no less limitation. All three opportunities are limitations but they are a condition of success. Human nature, too, is one of these materials, served by the building and serving it.

With the purpose or motive of the building we are to build well in mind, as of course it must be, and proceeding from generals to particulars, as "from-within-outward" must do, what consideration comes first?

The ground, doesn't it? The nature of the site, of the soil and of climate comes first. Next, what materials are available in the circumstances—money being one of them—with which to build? Wood, stone, brick, or synthetics? Next, what labor, or means of power, is available and advisable in the circum-

120

stances? Manual, machine, or both? The labor union or the factory, or both? Always with this "from the nature within" in mind, working in imagination towards a significant outward form, we proceed always within the circumstances.

Here we come well in towards the processes of thought that properly employ science in the erection of an organic building. But, still, the most desirable and valuable element in creation is lacking. It, too, is primary. We call it "inspiration." It seems to us a mysterious element. But it is of the "from within outward" and it is a qualification that gives finality to the whole structure as creative. To give life to the whole is "creative" and only that. We imply the structure of that life when we say form and function are one, or organic.

What, then, is life?

To answer that question the organic structure must now appear not only as "entity"; entity must appear as individuality. We are concerned with organism. We may say the organism is a living one, only when all is part to the whole as whole is to the part. This correlation, such as is found in any plant or animal, is fundamental to the life of organic architecture, as it is to any life whatever. But more important, and what finally makes any building live as true architecture, this building we are building must finally come to terms with the living human spirit. It must come alive where that spirit is concerned. Now what is this "*living*" human spirit?

First, it is a quality of the mind really informed with a sense of man's universe. It is a mind wholly in life as life is in it. It is the spirit in life for what life may be. It desires living

121

to the utmost. Such spirit is seldom lost in any part of the whole. Such a mind never for long loses the direction of the center line of "sentient entity." The "living spirit" would, at least, be the spirit capable of that. Let us call the living spirit, then, the new-old integrity that in architecture, as in all else, is the bridge by which man's past reached the present and by which his present will reach the future, if his present is to have any future at all. If our present in architecture contains any future worthy of the living human spirit, it will cross over this bridge. I am trying to present that architecture here in words as architecture "organic": the living expression of living human spirit. Architecture alive.

As already said, such architecture is and, as a matter of course, must be actual interpretation of social human life. Such living architecture is a new integrity in these modern times. It enters a distorted world where capital has got ahead of labor; where individual qualities of the personality are rendered invalid by new dimensions for money and where education is no longer on speaking terms with culture.

We shall go on in thought now with this building we started to build.

We start with the *ground*.

This is rock and *humus*. A building is planted there to survive the elements. The building is, meanwhile, shelter and human dignity, though inevitably destined to succumb to time in due course.

Why should the building try to belong to the ground instead of being content with some box-like fixture perched upon the rock or stuck into the soil, where it stands out as mere artifice, regardless where it stands up and "off," as "colonial" houses do, and just as all houses not indigenous must do?

The answer is found in the ideal stated in the abstract dictum, "Form and function are one." We must begin upon our structure with that.

The ground already has form. Why not begin to give at once by accepting that? Why not give by accepting the gifts of nature? But I have never seen a "colonial" house that did or could do this. Inevitably that house looks as though it hated the ground, with vast vanity trying to rise superior to it regardless of nature, depending upon a detachment called "classical" for such human values as habit and association of ideas could give to it.

Well, then, rejecting the "classical"; what of the ground?

Is the ground a parcel of prairie, square and flat?

Is the ground sunny or the shaded slope of some hill, high or low, bare or wooded, triangular or square?

Has the site features, trees, rocks, stream, or a visible trend of some kind? Has it some fault or a special virtue, or several?

In any and every case the character of the site is the beginning of the building that aspires to architecture. And this is true whatever the site or the building may be. It is true whether it be a dwelling among Wisconsin hills or a house on the bare prairie, the Imperial Hotel at Tokyo, or a skyscraper in New York City. All must begin there where they stand.

123

For our "case in point" we shall take the Imperial Hotel at Tokyo and try to put into words something of the thought process that tended to make that structure organic.

A social clearing house, call it a hotel, became necessary to official Japan as a consequence of new foreign interest in the Japanese. A new hotel becomes necessary, because no foreigner, no matter how cultivated, could live on the floor, as the Japanese do, with any grace or comfort. It was also necessary for another reason: a Japanese gentleman does not entertain strangers, no matter how gentle, within his family circle. So the building will be more a place for entertainment with private supper rooms, banquet hall, theater and cabaret than it will be a hotel.

No foreign architect yet invited to work in Japan ever took off his hat to the Japanese and respected either Japanese conditions or traditions. And yet those aesthetic traditions are at the top among the noblest in the world. When I accepted the commission to design and build their building it was my instinct and definite intention not to insult them. Were they not a feature of my first condition, the ground? They were. The Japanese were more their own ground than any people I knew.

So while making their building "modern" in the best sense, I meant to leave it a sympathetic consort to Japanese build-

124

ings. I wanted to show the Japanese how their own conservation of space and the soul of their own religious shinto, which is "be clean," might, in the use of all materials, take place as effectively for them indoors in sound masonry construction when on their feet as it had taken place for them when they were down upon their knees in their own inspired carpentry.

I meant to show them how to use our new civilizing-agents —call them plumbing, electrification, and heating—without such outrage to the art of building as we ourselves were practicing and they were then copying. I intended to make all these appurtenance systems a practical and aesthetic part of the building itself. It was to be given a new simplicity by making it a complete whole within itself.

Mechanical systems should be an asset to life and so an asset to architecture. They should be no detriment to either. Why shouldn't the Japanese nation make the same coordination of furnishing and building when they came to be at home on their feet that they had so wonderfully made for themselves at home on their knees?

And I believed I could show them how to build an earthquake-proof masonry building.

In short, I desired to help Japan make the transition from wood to masonry, and from her knees to her feet, without too great loss of her own great accomplishments in culture. And I wished to enable her to overcome some of the inherent weaknesses of her building system where the temblor was a constant threat to their happiness and to their very lives.

There was this natural enemy to all building whatsoever:

the temblor. And, as I well knew, the seismograph in Japan is never still. The presence of the temblor, an affair of the ground, never left me while I planned and for four years or more worked upon the plans and structure of the new hotel. Earthquakes I found to be due to wave movement of the ground. Because of wave movement, foundations like long piles oscillate and rock the structure. Heavy masses of masonry inevitably would be wrecked. The heavier the masonry the greater the wreck.

The feature of the ground that was the site itself was a flat 500 by 300-foot plot of ground composed of sixty feet of liquid mud overlaid by eight feet of filled soil. The filling was about the consistency of hard cheese. The perpetual water level stood within fifteen inches of the level of the ground. In short, the building was to stand up on an ancient marsh, an arm of the bay that had been filled in when Tokyo became the capital of the empire.

But the mud beneath the filling seemed to me a good cushion to relieve earthquake shocks. A building might float upon the mud somewhat as a battleship floats on salt water. Float the building upon the mud? Why not? And since it must float, why not extreme lightness combined with the tenuity and flexibility that are a property of steel instead of the great weight necessary to the usually excessive rigidity which, no matter how rigid, could never be rigid enough? Probably the answer was a building made flexible as the two hands thrust together, fingers interlocked, yielding to movement yet resilient to return to position when force exerted upon its mem-

126

bers and membranes ceased. Why fight the force of the quake on its own terms? Why not go with it and come back unharmed? Outwit the quake?

That was how the nature of the site, the ground, entered into the conception of the building. Now, to carry out in detail these initial perceptions.

I took a preliminary year in which to acquire necessary data, making tests for the new type of foundation. Finally flexible foundations, economical too, were provided by driving tapered wooden piles, only eight feet long, into the strata of filled soil, pulling them out and throwing in concrete immediately, to form the thousands of small piers or concrete pins two feet apart on centers upon which the jointed footing courses were laid. Nine pile drivers dotted the ground, each with its band of singing women pulling on the ropes lifting and dropping the drive-head—twelve ropes, one for each pair of hands.

The good sense of careful calculation so far: now what about the superstructure?

The building was going native, so intensive hand methods would have to be used and native materials too. The nature of the design therefore should be something hand methods could do better than machinery. It was impossible to say how far we could go in any direction with machines, probably not very far.

Evidently the straight line and flat plane to which I had already been committed by machines in America should be modified in point of style if I would respect the traditions of

127

the people to whom the building would belong. The Japanese, centuries ago, had come nearer the ideal of an organic architecture in their dwellings than any civilized race on earth. The ideals we have been calling organic are even now best exemplified in their wood and paper dwellings where they lived on their knees. As I have already said, I wanted to help the Japanese get to their feet indoors and learn to live in fireproof masonry buildings, without loss of their native aesthetic prestige where the art of architecture was a factor. Trained by the disasters of centuries to build lightly on the ground, the wood and paper homes natural to them are kindled by any spark. When fire starts it seldom stops short of several hundred homes, sometimes destroys thousands, and ends in complete destruction of a city. After the irresistible wave movements have gone shuddering and jolting through the earth, changing all overnight in immense areas, islands disappearing, new ones appearing, mountains laid low and valleys lifted up taking awful toll of human life, then come the flames! Conflagration always at the end.

The cost of metal frames and sash at that time were prohibitive, but the plans were made for an otherwise completely fireproof building and the designs were so made that all architectural features were practical necessities.

The flexible light foundations had saved one hundred thousand dollars over the customary massive foundations. Now how could the building be made as light and flexible? I divided the building into sections about sixty feet long. This is the safe limit for temperature cracks in reinforced concrete in that

128

climate. Wherever part met part I provided through joints.

To insure stability I carried the floor and roof loads as a waiter carries his tray on his upraised arm and fingers. At the center all supports were centered under the loaded floor-slabs; balancing the load instead of gripping the load at the edges with the walls, as in the accepted manner. In any movement a load so carried would be safe. The waiter's tray balanced on his hand at the center is the cantilever in principle.

This was done. This meant that the working principle of the cantilevers would help determine the style of the structure. So the cantilever became the principal feature of the structure and a great factor in shaping its forms throughout as the floor-slabs came through the walls and extended into various balconies and overhangs.

Tokyo buildings were top heavy. The exaggerated native roofs were covered deep with clay, and the heavy roof tiles laid on over the clay would come loose and slide down with deadly effect into the narrow streets crowded with terrified humanity.

So the outer walls, spread thick and heavy at the base and tapering towards the top, were crowned there by a light roof covered with hand-worked sheet copper tiles. The light roof framing rested upon a concrete ceiling slab extended outward over the walls into an overhang, perforated to let sunlight into the windows of the rooms beneath.

Now as to materials. What would be desirable and available? Again we go to the ground.

A stone I had seen under foot and in common use in Tokyo

building was a light, workable lava, called oya, weighing about as much as green oak and resembling travertine. It was quarried at Nikko and was floated down on rafts by sea to Tokyo and then by canal to the site. I liked this material for its character but soon found that the building committee, made up of the financial autocracy of the empire, considered it sacrilege to use a material so cheap and common for so dignified a purpose. But finally the building committee gave in and we bought our own quarries at Nikko. We used oya (the lava) throughout the work, combining it with concrete walls cast in layers within thin wall shells of slender bricks.

Large or small, the pieces of lava could be easily hollowed out at the back and set up with the hollow side inside, as one side of the slab-forms for casting the concrete. In this way the three materials were cast solidly together as a structural unit when the concrete was poured into them.

Copper, too, was a prominent feature in our list of available hand-worked materials.

Thus the "Teikoku" (Imperial Hotel) after these measures were taken became a jointed steel-reinforced monolith with a thin integral facing of lava and thin brick, the whole sheltered overhead by light copper tiles. The mass of the structure rests upon a kind of pincushion. The pins were set close enough together to support, by friction, the weight calculated to be placed upon them. To the lengthwise and crosswise work in this particular structure all piping and wiring were made to conform. Both were designed to be laid in shafts and trenches free of construction. The pipes were of lead, sweeping with

130

easy bend from trenches to shafts and curving again from shafts to fixtures. Thus any earthquake might rattle and flex the pipes as they hung but could break no connections. Last, but by no means least, an immense pool of water as an architectural feature of the extensive entrance court to the hotel was connected to its own private water system. This was to play its part in conflagration following in the wake of earthquake.

During the execution of these ideas I found the language a barrier. Men and methods were strange. But the "foreign" architect with twenty Japanese students from Tokyo and Kyoto University courses in Architecture, some of whom were taken to Taliesin during preliminary plan making, and one excellent American builder, Paul Mueller, made up the band that built the Imperial Hotel. Hayashi San, the general manager of the Imperial Hotel, was in direct charge of everything. The principal owner, the Imperial Household, was represented by Baron Okura. And there was a board of directors composed of five captains of Japanese big business—ships, tobacco, cement, and banking.

The original plans which I had worked out at Taliesin for the construction I threw aside as educational experience for the architect only and worked out the details on the ground as we went along. Plans served only as a preliminary study for final construction.

These Japanese workmen! How clever they were. What skill and industry they displayed! So instead of trying to execute preconceived methods of execution, thereby wasting this precious human asset in vainly trying to make the workmen come our way, we learned from them and willingly went with them, their way. I modified many original intentions to make the most of what I now saw to be naturally theirs. But, of course, curious mistakes were common. I had occasion to learn that the characteristic Japanese approach to any subject is, by instinct, spiral. The Oriental instinct for attack in any direction is oblique or volute and becomes wearisome to a direct occidental, whose instinct is frontal and whose approach is rectilinear.

But, then, they made up for this seeming indirection by gentleness, loyalty, and skill. Soon we began to educate the "foreigners" as they did us, and all went along together pretty well.

As the countenance of their building began to emerge from seeming confusion the workmen grew more and more interested in it. It was a common sight to see groups of them intelligently admiring and criticizing some finished feature as it would emerge to view. There was warmth of interest and depth of appreciation, unknown to me in the building circles of our country in our own day, to prove the sincerity of their pleasure and interest in their work.

Finally, out of this exercise of free will and common sense, with this unusual Western feeling of respect for the East and for Japanese life and traditions in view as discipline and inspiration, what would emerge?

A great building is to be born; one not looking out of place where it is to stand across the park from the Imperial Palace.

132

The noble surrounding walls of the Palace rose above the ancient moat. The gateways to the Palace grounds, guarded by blue-tiled, white-walled buildings nesting on the massive stone walls, were visible above the moat across the way. It was architecture perfect of its kind and as Japanese as the countenance of the race. I conceived the form of this new associate— the Imperial—as something squat and strong, as harmonious with this precedent as the pines in the park. It should be a form seen to be bracing itself against storm and expected temblor. Appeal has already been made to imagination in a realm scientific; but pure reason and science must now wait there at the doorstep.

Wait there while something came to Japanese ground— something not Japanese, certainly, but sympathetic, embodying modern scientific building ideas by old methods not strange to Japan. No single form was really Japanese but the whole was informed by unity. The growing proportions were suitable to the best Japanese tradition. We have here in the individuality of the architect a sincere lover of old Japan, his hat in hand, seeking to contribute his share in the transition of a great old culture to a new and inevitably foreign one. Probably the new one was unsuitable. Certainly it was as yet but imperfectly understood by those who were blindly, even fatuously, accepting it as superior to their own. A great tragedy, it may be.

Looking on then as now, it seemed to me as though tragedy it must be. The Far East had so little to learn from our great West, so much to lose where culture is concerned.

133

I might ameliorate their loss by helping to make much that was spiritually sound and beautiful in their own life, as they had known it so well, over into a pattern of the unknown new life they were so rashly entering. To realize this ambition in concrete form, apparent in a structure that acknowledged and consciously embodied this appropriate pattern, was what I intended to do in this masonry building 500 feet long by 300 feet wide. It was a world complete within itself. It now may be seen. It is known far and wide as it stands on the beaten path around the world. Said Baron Takahashi to a conscientious objector from America, "You may not like our Imperial Hotel but we Japanese like it. We understand it."

Two years later—1923—in Los Angeles: news was shouted in the streets of awful disaster. Tokyo and near-by Yokohama were wiped out by the most terrific temblor in history. Appalling details came in day after day after the first silence when no details could be had. As the news began to add up it seemed that nothing human could have withstood the cataclysm.

Too anxious to get any sleep I kept trying to get news of the fate of the New Imperial and of my friends, Shugio, Hayashi, Endo San, my boys and the Baron, hosts of friends I had left over there. Finally the third or fourth day after the first outcry, about two o'clock in the morning, the telephone bell. Mr. Hearst's "Examiner" wished to inform me that the Imperial Hotel was completely destroyed. My heart sank as I laughed at them. "Read your dispatch," I said. The Ex-

134

aminer read a long list of "Imperial" this and "Imperial" that.

"You see how easy it is to get the Imperial Hotel mixed with other Imperials. If you print the destruction of the new Imperial Hotel as news you will have to retract. If anything is above ground in Tokyo it is that building," I said, and hoped.

Their turn to laugh while they spread the news of destruction with a photograph across the head of the front page in the morning. Then followed a week or more of anxiety. Conflicting reports came continually because during that time direct communication was cut off.

Then—a cablegram.

"FRANK LLOYD WRIGHT, OLIVE HILL RESIDENCE, HOLLYWOOD, CALIFORNIA.
FOLLOWING WIRELESS RECEIVED TODAY FROM TOKYO, HOTEL STANDS UNDAMAGED AS MONUMENT TO YOUR GENIUS HUNDREDS OF HOMELESS PROVIDED BY PERFECTLY MAINTAINED SERVICE. CONGRATULATIONS.
                                            OKURA."

For once in a lifetime good news was newspaper news and the Baron's cablegram flashed around the world to herald what? To herald the triumph of good sense in the head of an architect tough enough to stick to it through thick and thin. Yes, that. But it was really a new approach to building, the ideal of an organic architecture at work, that really saved the Imperial Hotel.

135

Both Tokyo houses of the Baron were gone. The splendid museum he gave to Tokyo was gone. The building by an American architect, whose hand he took to see him through, was what he had left in Tokyo standing intact, nor could love or money buy a share in it, now.

When letters finally came through, friends were found to be safe. And it appeared that not one pane of glass was broken in the building—no one harmed. Neither was the plumbing or the heating system damaged at all. But something else was especially gratifying to me. After the first great quake was over, the dead lying in heaps, the Japanese came in droves, dragging their children into the courses and up onto the terraces of the building, praying for protection by the God that had protected the Teikoku. Then, as the wall of fire that follows every great quake came sweeping across the city toward the long front of the Imperial, driving a continuous wail of human misery before it, the Hotel boys formed a bucket line to the big pool of the central entrance court (the city mains were disrupted by the quake) and found there a reserve of water to keep the wood window frames and sash wet to meet the flames. The last thought for the safety of the Imperial had taken effect.

Early in the twentieth century, a world in itself, true enough to its purpose and created spontaneously as any ever fashioned by the will of any creator of antiquity, had been completed within a sector of the lifetime of its one architect. Such work in ancient times generally proceeded from generation to generation and from architect to architect. Strange! Here expert

136

handicraft had come at the beck and call of one who had, up to that time, devoted most of his effort to getting buildings true to modern machine processes built by machine.

Here in the Far East a significant transition building was born. Are really good buildings all transition buildings? But for the quality of thought that built it, the ideal of an organic architecture, it would surely have been just "another one of those things" and have been swept away.

While the New Imperial only partially realized the ideal of an organic architecture, the pursuit of that ideal made the building what it really was, and enabled it to do what it did do. The fact that were I to build it again it would be entirely different, although employing the same methods and means, does not vitiate my thesis here. It greatly strengthens it.

Now let us glance at what followed this natural approach to the nature of a problem as a natural consequence. Opposition, of course, followed until finally Baron Okura took full responsibility and saw the building through. There was the unfriendly attitude of Americans and Englishmen. Though none too friendly to each other, they opposed this approach. They had owned Tokyo up to now because, where foreign culture was being so freely and thoughtlessly bought, they were best sellers. The Germans were there, strong too, but they were almost out of the running by now. My sympathetic attitude, Japan for the Japanese, was regarded as treason to American interests. I encouraged and sometimes taught the Japanese how to do the work on their building themselves. The American construction companies were building ten-story steel buildings with such architecture as they had hung to the steel, setting the steel frames on long piles which they floated across the Pacific from Oregon and drove down to hard pan. I suppose they were built in this fashion so the steel might rattle the architecture off into the streets in any severe quake? These companies were especially virulent where I was concerned.

The Western Society of American Engineers gratuitously warned me that my "scheme for foundations was unsound." The A.I.A.—American Institute of Architects—passing through Tokyo when the building was nearly finished, took notice and published articles in Tokyo papers declaring the work an insult to American architecture, notifying my clients, and the world generally, that the whole thing would be down in the first quake with horrible loss of life.

Finally, when the building was about two-thirds completed, it came directly to the directors from such sources that their American architect was mad. Now every director except one (my sponsor, the Baron), so worked upon continually for several years, became a spy. The walls had ears. Propaganda increased. General Manager Hayashi was "on the spot." My freedom was going fast and I worked on under difficulties greater than ever. Hayashi San, the powerful Okura, and my little band of Japanese student apprentices were loyal and we got ahead until the final storm broke in a dark scene in a directors' meeting. Then the Baron took over the reins himself to see me through with my work, and the building of the New Imperial went forward more smoothly to conclusion.

138

I have learned that wherever reason shows its countenance and change is to take place, the reaction in any established order, itself not organic, is similar. Therefore organic architecture has this barrier to throw down or cross over or go around.

As for government, I should say here that no permit to build the Imperial Hotel was ever issued by the government. I explained to the proper Imperial Department our intention, registered the drawings. The result was visitation by Japanese authorities, more explanations, head shakings. But the attitude was entirely friendly and sympathetic in contrast to the attitude that might be expected in our own country. Finally we were told no permit was needed, to go ahead, they would watch proceedings and hoped to learn something from the experiment. They could not say that most of the ideas did not seem right but, having no precedent, they could not officially act. They could wink, however, and "wink" the government did.

This "wink" is the utmost official sanction organic architecture or any thought-built action of the sort in any medium may expect from a social order itself inorganic and in such danger of disturbance if radical examination is permitted that even an approach in that direction is cause for hysteria. Institutions such as ours are safe, in fact remain "institutions" only upon some status quo, some supreme court, which inevitably becomes invalid as life goes on.

Now—so far as the Architecture of the Future is concerned, what is to be deduced from this particular and by no means typical instance?

Let us take an example with a broader application. The problem of the moderate cost home for that unfortunate—the "average American."

Suppose, then, we consider briefly a much broader application of the principles of an organic architecture: the moderate house for the citizen in moderate circumstances. For some reason—probably not a good one—five or six thousand dollars seems to be as much as the better part of the average citizenship of the United States can afford to pay for a house and the lot he builds one on. This lot is usually a fifty-foot lot for some other reason, certainly not a good reason. He may secure sixty or seventy feet, and has been known in rare instances to acquire title to as much as one hundred feet on some street front where sewer, water and gas, or electricity are available. The "lot"—the word is short for "allotment"— varies in depth from 125 to 200 feet, with a sixteen-foot "alley" at the end opposite the street end. Each lot on each side must range lengthwise along neighboring lots, so privacy is unlikely or impossible to any great extent. Corner lots are exposed to the street on two sides, with more taxes to pay accordingly and even less privacy than the inside neighbor has.

The result is a row of houses toeing an imaginary mark

called a building line—a line predetermining how near the street the houses may come; and sometimes they must stay away several feet from the neighboring depthwise lot line. Oftentimes not: the feeling being pretty general that when a man buys a piece of ground it is his for better or for worse, not only from side to side but from the center of the earth to the top of the sky, although the "top of the sky" has been the subject of recent regulation.

Fortunately the owner's imagination, though ambitious, is limited. And he can go about as far as his neighbor goes and no farther. That is about all the actual discipline there is. Within that limitation each proceeds to be as original—"different" they call it—as each can be, with the net result, of course, that all look monotonously alike in their attempts to be "different" because the thought involved never changes. To be perfectly sincere—no thought at all ever enters into the affair from beginning to end. There is only habit, fashion— a certain association of ideas and the idiosyncrasy called "taste." The citizens talk of comfort and convenience without knowing very well what either really means. They spend two-fifths of the cost of the whole house to do as well as their neighbors in appearances, or to outdo them. Emulation or competition are in it all, but constructive thought does not enter. A certain shrewd common sense has to serve as it may, and such taste as may be.

Then the department store delivery wagon appears out front and the furnishings begin to come in from the chief source of furnishment. Countless items in the prevailing mode,

141

all bought in some big establishment with the help sometimes of the interior decorator, whom even the undiscriminating are learning to call "the inferior desecrator."

So the interior is Marshall Field, Wanamaker or Kaufmann's at this level, instead of the Montgomery Ward and Sears Roebuck of the next level down—say the three thousand dollar bracket—house and lot. Now it is well to realize at this point that these houses so furnished are usually investments. They are homes, that's true, but they are homes afterward. Nothing must be done that detracts from the likelihood of profitable resale—on occasion. And American life is continually making that occasion for some reason, probably a good one this time.

A privy used to grace the backyard; perhaps there was a small stable for a horse and buggy, which necessitated a driveway along the north side of the house. And there was (still is) a north side which the sun never sees because the streets are all laid out square with the points of the compass—they had a reason for this but I could never find out what it was except that it was a surveyor's convenience. This scheme (or lack of one) gave every house a hot front or a cold front. The south belonged to one front alone. The morning sun shone in the east windows—the afternoon sun in those to the west. No one questioned the inevitability of all this, and only rarely is it ever questioned now. The net result of all the placing and fixing (and fussing, too, because they were awfully fussy about this) were the long rows of houses, all facing the street

142

to the north or south or east or west, and set back to give thirty percent of the ground to that street for general effect. This dedication to the street is a marked characteristic of all American towns.

The "backyard" thus left was divided from the neighbor by a fence or hedge, or none. Modern plumbing came to take the privy into the house. The motor car came to add the so-called garage to every house in place of such stables as there were, and privacy was something none understood though some few did desire it. It would take too long to say how all this came to be. Of what use to say it now?

Into these inorganic circumstances so curiously, unthinkingly compounded to confound simple living comes this organic $5500.00 house with the automobile as much a feature of life as the bathroom and the kitchen. When error has confused an issue hopelessly it is time to begin again. What can this house do to have a better beginning? Go to the country or go out in regional fields where ground is not yet exploited by the realtor. That is all. And it must go because to this house a garden is no backyard affair—an acre is necessary. The street cannot be desirable so far as this ground consideration is concerned except as a way to get to the place as unobtrusively as possible.

What, then, is desirable to this new house?

Well . . . *first*, free association with considerably more ground than the old house was allowed to have.

Second, sunlight and vista, a spaciousness conforming to

the newly developed sense of space demanded by modern facilities. No north front because the house will not be set square with the compass.

Third, privacy, actual, not imaginary or merely makeshift.

Fourth, in the arrangement of rooms a free-pattern for the occupation of the family that is to live in the house. As the families vary, so must the house. The rooms should be as much as possible on a single level for several reasons, all good.

It would be ideal to have all these requirements meet in some integral harmony of proportion to the human figure; to have all details so designed as to make the human relationship to building not only convenient but charming. For this building which we are considering is intended not to make shift with life but to give life more easy conditions that will cherish and protect the individual——not so much in fostering his idiosyncrasies and sentimentalities as in protecting his vital necessities and fine sentiment. Above all, we must see this new house as the cradle of continuously arising generations. So, while appeal to reason is intrinsic, it is insufficient. There must also be beauty——beauty of which man himself is capable, the utmost beauty of which he is capable without getting himself into trouble with the installment system and the tax collector. We are hinting at a new simplicity of appearances where this new home is concerned. It can only appear in a drawing or model.

We must achieve that new simplicity too, as well as establish a finer logic of use and want, but the new house won't pay two-fifths for it. It will pay nothing at all. Now, here we

144

are with the acre essential to an individual human life on earth. The acre is level, with a few trees in one corner or more, but an acre fit for a garden. The house sees that garden to begin with, arranging itself about and within it so as to enjoy the sun and view and yet keep privacy.

The living room is where the familiar life is lived, so it must take first place. It is a room common to all, with a big fireplace in it.

Because of modern industrial developments the kitchen no longer has a curse upon it; it may become a part of the living room by being related to another part of that same room set apart for dining. An extra space, which may be used also for studying or reading, might become convenient between meals. In such a house the association between dining and the preparation of meals is immediate and convenient. It is private enough, too.

Next in importance to this decentralized central unit is the toilet unit, the bathroom. Only it should now be a triplicate bathroom, one section for man, one for wife, one for offspring. The fixtures are placed to have the economy of close connection but the three bath compartments themselves are large enough for dressing rooms, closets for linen, etc.; even wardrobes, with perhaps a couch in each. The bedrooms adjoining this unit are small but airy. Both bedrooms and the triplicate bathroom would be alongside the garden, easy of access from the living room.

The indispensable car? It is still designed like a buggy. And it is treated like one when it is not in use. The car no longer needs such consideration. If it is weatherproof enough to run out in all weather it ought to be weatherproof enough to stand still under a canopy with a wind screen on two sides. Inasmuch as this car is a feature of the comings and goings of the family, some space at the entrance is the proper space for it. Thus the open car-port comes to take the part of the dangerous closed "garage."

While the car is yet far from being well designed, it has more in common with our sanitary appliances and modern kitchens than the older cars could have with the older houses. The proportions and lines of this organic house are those the industrialists are trying so hard to get into their products, succeeding only superficially in doing so. But they are doing so sufficiently to make congruous the house, car, kitchen and bathroom. Furniture too is coming to reflect this new sense of unity and congruity. They are calling it modernistic, or streamlined, or just modern.

Except for the more advanced triplicate bathroom unit, not yet executed, I have been describing here a particular house, the house of Herbert Jacobs being built at Madison, Wisconsin, and illustrated herewith. It was let by contract for $5500 to Harold Grove.

The drawings will tell more than any verbal description. What I want to say in words the house itself alone can say. But perhaps enough has been said to suggest the ideals and processes of thought at work that are giving us an indigenous and, probably, a greater architecture in every respect than has existed before.

146

I could go on with many instances in the widely varying fields of our American activity and show how a new development in building design is bringing order out of chaos. I could show pretty clearly how a new technique of building is growing up into the American scene—a new technique as well as an integrity of design that does bring to the house builder and home owner the benefits of industrialism and the efficiencies of the factory. Instead of the criss-cross of the open field we are developing building schemes that utilize the economies of standardization without its curse, using the simple unit system applied to building, meaning buildings put together upon a horizontal and vertical unit system much as a rug is woven on its warp.

The implications are as aesthetic as they are scientific and economic. They go far beyond any space limits available in this book. But I hope enough has been said to indicate that organic architecture has already gone far enough, that standardization is no real obstacle to freedom of individuality. Standardization is not a real obstacle in spite of the international style, the "permanent wave," the realtor, and "housing."

A future for architecture depends upon a new sense of reality, a different success ideal, a deeper social consciousness, a finer integrity of the individual—that there may be promoted the integration of a whole people with their own soil or ground. This will in turn bring about freedom from a false economy. It will bring about the end of labor, money, ground and buildings as speculative commodities. It will bring about the rise of cultured sentiment to take the place of educated sentimentality. It will abolish commercial standards that are only profit-taking. It will close institutes, museums and universities until new ones may be created to bring culture to youth by way of action in an atmosphere of truth and beauty. It will train youth to want and utilize its own ground. There is also necessary a new type of architect and a new structure of government that governs only where individuality may not exist. Such a government will function as a business of the whole people in matters common to the whole people, and only so, instead of as a policeman and a politician. A further essential is a popular realization of organic structure as the basis of all culture in the development of the whole life of a whole people. Such a future as this must grow slowly. Finally the abandonment of ultra-urban life is necessary. A new type of city must be realized. There will be organic structure in government, organic structure in society, organic structure in the economics of both.—F. Ll. W.

V. Society and the Future of Expression

HIGHWAY U. S. 41 is a ribbon of concrete that runs north and south across the United States from the cold, fresh waters of Lake Superior to the warm, salt waters off the southwest coast of Florida. It crosses the pine and iron lands and the cutover country of the northern peninsula of Michigan, enters Wisconsin along Green Bay, drops down across the latitudes through Appleton, Oshkosh, Fond du Lac, Milwaukee. It crosses Chicago, down Sheridan Road and Michigan Avenue and along the south shore. It bends around the brick encrusted southern end of Lake Michigan, then southwest on a causeway over the marshland and reedy lakes that make a flat interval between Lake Michigan and the prairies of Northern Indiana. It goes southward over treeless, townless corn-land to the Wabash—southward through old Vincennes and Evansville to the Ohio river; it crosses magnificently over a bridge to Henderson, Kentucky, moves on through tobacco lands and horse country to Nashville, Tennessee, crosses the Cumberland plateau to Chattanooga, the mountain cabins, the great gap, the battlefields. Now it swings down out of the mountains to Atlanta, Georgia, to Macon; crosses the cotton coun-

149

try, the black belt, Valdosta, peach and pecan groves; passes through Lake City, Florida, the tung oil plantations, Satsuma and tangérine groves and on to the great springs of Ocala. Southward to Tampa it moves into the phosphate lands and the orange regions. It swings along the fisherman's coast, mangrove, coconut palms, through Sarasota, Punta Gorda, the truck district of Fort Myers with their acres of eggplants and peppers, mangoes, grapefruit, December tomatoes, potatoes, papayas. And it ends at last, more than two thousand miles south of Lake Superior, in the Everglades near Naples.

U. S. 41 is a prophecy; it is a symbol of America today and of the Western world tomorrow. It is extensive and flowing. Though it lies geometrically across the country, it is nevertheless the plasticity of a people. Wheeled multitudes flow in millions along its course. Trucks and trailers, Fords, Cadillacs, Chryslers, Studebakers move across zones of sovereignty and climate, of soil, altitude, vegetation, in smooth freedom and continuity. Rigidities and absolute break down. U. S. 41 is the plasticity of a new world.

"Everything flows," said Heraclitus, or so it is reported. Everything flows: there is a way upward and a way downward according to the law of flow. Change has its route, fire and water their destination. The Greek misanthrope, hating man in the sunlit world, preceded by several thousand years the modern doctrine of plasticity. The Heraclitan principle of flow in the modern world has many forms and media of expression. In the arts it is called plasticity. In social life and economics it is sometimes called mobility. In the physical sci-

150

ences, the theories of relativity and of the electrical structures of matter have at least some structural similarity to it. In morals on the one hand and religion on the other the immutable absolutes are breaking down and provisionalistic beliefs and standards take their places. All of these have their Heraclitan aspect. The great roads, U. S. 41, U. S. 12, U. S. 6, U. S. 99, U. S. 87, U. S. 30, and many more, are the ways up and the ways down. They are routes of flow.

If flow is one feature of the modern world, power, I may say, is the other. Together they describe the disposition and the tendencies of things today that are greatly influential on tomorrow. Though only words, to be sure, except as they are embedded in activities and the concrete stuff of machines, people and the physical and social structures of our environment, they are words that are significant in the long precipitation of the future onto this present earth. Flow and power, I surmise, are the words best suited to interpret what is to come.

Since this fifth section of this book will be concerned with the future of man and his social life in relation to expression, the words "flow" and "power" will be key words in the discussion. They are prophetic, and though presumptuous it may be to prophesy—the future is itself a presumption—it is worth while.

But prophecies are of various types and have various motivations. They vary up and down the scale, and I should make clear, no doubt, the kind of prophecy I expect to utter and what realms of the future I hope to explore. First of all I should say that prophecies rarely have much value in fore-

151

seeing the temporal future or in preparing for it. They do help oftentimes in penetrating the present and in living more integrally in it. My prophecies, such as they are, will have this intention. The world is too irrational, too streaked with chaos, and its expressions in the arts are too broken and complex to permit prediction to any great extent. But discussion of the present in terms of what that present may become, were it to continue unbroken in development, or broken by forces now on the scene, gives a reverberatory insight into what this present is. In all this the words "flow" and "power" will come again and again, for the flow and power of the modern world are its future. They are, as it were, the change principle and the will principle in nature. They bear the future on their shoulders.

Prophecy usually takes one of two forms. It foretells what may be the state of things in the future, and in this sense is usually involved in what the prophets desire; or it foretells what probably will be the state of things in the future. In the first case prophecy is a province of literature. It is involved in values and throws over itself the mantle of the prophet chiefly as an artistic device to give concreteness to values that have no body now. The realm of utopias is here. The cities of vengeance and hope are built by these prophets. Compensatory devices and romance, pastures where thwarted ideals may graze and where the uneasy selves of men find expansive freedom and prestige, are provided by these means. The Christian heaven and the Marxian ideal state after the revolution are such prophecies.

152

The other form of prophecy is scientific in temper, or at least hopes to be, and tries to eliminate desire as a prophetic instrument. It observes the natural processes in material things, in human lives and societies and assumes that they are orderly and successive. On these bases it predicts what will happen. Sometimes it is right. It fails in the long run, however, must fail, because all the data in this complex world never are at hand, nor can the prophet know accurately the balances and complications of tendencies that create the future. He builds on the fiction, furthermore, that our world is completely ordered. Though the fiction is necessary, no doubt, in a completely intelligible present situation, it breaks down under the load of the future. The future, indeed, is a fracture in the orderliness of the world that no rational fiction can completely seal.

In this field of prophecy, or a modification of it, is the executive or the engineer who constructs forms for the future, such as buildings, institutions, organizations, patterns of various sorts that will determine the outlines of the future. In this kind of prophecy all of us spend much, perhaps too much, of our present lives. It involves will and desire, to be sure, but it uses the dynamic facilities of the present world to attain its ends. It resorts to observation, test, and rational prediction on the basis of objective data here. It is scientific, or at least mainly so.

A third form of prophecy, rarely recognized as such, is the ability, as it were, to draw down the future into the present and to make it live now. Instead of projecting the present into things to come, it incorporates the future, or strains and elements of it, in the present situation. Strange guests enter the scene. Magic irrelevances shine in the fabric of the present. The glisten of unknown fish is seen in the net of existence. Prophetic art and philosophic mysticism sometimes bring these things about. From the future come migrations into the present. They enrich the present and stimulate it. They add new and beautiful dimensions. The present becomes more integral and more universal.

The future, from this point of view, may be an enrichment within the present rather than a draining from the present. Though the main moral characteristic of this western world is no doubt its tragic postponement of values, its continual sacrifice of the realities and riches of this moment for an abstraction called the future, or success, or progress, or heaven, or utopia, or some other image, it is still possible, in a measure, to repudiate the barren regress of values and to fix and incorporate the future, or the principle of the future, as an enrichment and a new reality within the present. This art can do, to some extent, by means of the magic that only art can use. Expression in art differs from mere statement in carrying an overburden that cannot be found among the data of the explicit present. It enriches the present. The future is implicit there. It is flame burning in the present, burning in this luminous hour.

Thus expression, which after all is the theme of this or any other book on art and modern life, is deeply involved in this

154

mystical unity of the tenses. It emerges from a realm, the dimensions of which are different from those of our traditional time, space, particulars, pluralities. It emerges from that realm bearing the flames of a deeper more inclusive mode of being. Expression in the arts, and particularly in architecture, involves this generalization of reality embodied in particular concrete things. It discovers the eternal, as the poet would say, makes it articulate, imbues this moment, this building of stone or steel, this sound of pipes or strings with its great continuity. It fuses the past, the future, the timeless and the timed in the immediacy of this moment.

Lao Tze, who defied in his way the separation of matter and spirit and refused to tolerate a distinction between the abstract future and the concrete present, is an appropriate philosopher for this point of view towards expression. He permits no universal to escape from the concrete. He allows no abstractions, or images called the future or the past, to wander about, irresponsible and loose, detached from this living present; or at least I so interpret him. He embeds time and the eternal, value and spirit in some tangible, concrete thing of this world. Their significance is there. Their reality is recognized only in their fusion with particular, even material, things. For Lao Tze the Platonic "idea" would be an abomination. It would mean for him a fatal schism between spirit and matter and between time and the eternal. Such an easy isolation of value, beauty, goodness from the material stuff of things, the one yearned for as the true being, the other repudiated as the unfortunate failure and necessity of our crass flesh, is not the truth or discipline of the real world as Lao Tze sees it.

These easy absolutes of Plato and the classic and Christian schools that followed him have led to the great cleavages that mark the western world and that disintegrate western life. Spirit, or the "idea," is contrasted with base matter; heaven is contrasted with this wretched earth; the future, and a life sacrificed to it, is contrasted with this present; "success" and savings is contrasted with joy in work; consumption is segregated from production; art, particularly fine art, is segregated from living and practice. These are some of the Platonic cleavages that have given the western world much of its character and power and most of its disasters. With such cults of the absolute and their accompanying specialism and facility Lao Tze, I think, would have little to do. For him the eternal is within the concrete sound or scene, within action, within the dance or the palpable object in the present, and the absolute, if such it may be called, lies in the furrow of the relative. "These two things, the spiritual and the material," says Lao Tze, "though we call them by different names, in their origin are one and the same."

Expression in the arts, from this point of view, is not the purification of matter. Nor is it the elimination of matter so that the abstract "idea" may shine forth. Neither is it the use of matter as a humble vehicle for the chance burden of eternity. Expression is the revelation of the character of matter, the wood of wood, the glass of glass, and the synthesis of their

156

native realities. The structural elements of the situation are by plastic expression given form and unity. Time and the timeless are joined in it; the material and the spiritual, the person and the social figure and outline in which he moves, become one living thing.

If the Heraclitan principle of flux describes the movement and power of the modern world, the naturalistic mysticism of Lao Tze—or of Walt Whitman—interprets that world's expression. If the flow and power of the modern world, on the one hand, has destroyed the old absolutes such as the atom and time and space and the fixed orders of creation and social institutions, plastic expression, on the other hand, has broken down old orders and absolutes in the arts and values. The two philosophies are complementary in a sense, and both prophetic.

We face, then, a new and relativistic world. It is a world where absolute and irrevocable patterns of material reality have been revoked, and revoked not in favor of some other absolute system, but in favor of flexible, tentative, even indeterminate forms, the validity of which depends on their organic place in the entire situation. It is a world where fixed and final standards of social life have become no longer fixed and are replaced by experimental attitudes wherein the criteria of action are relative to the changing, variegated streams of life. It is a world where the perfections and authorities of expression have become imperfect and unauthoritative. Art is no longer preciously complete in itself. It is no longer abstracted like some costly essence, and distilled out of the dross and heaviness of concrete things. It is in them and of them. It gives them voice.

There are, to be sure, resurgences of absolutes and external authorities in the modern world that may control the future. Social and intellectual authoritarianism and their concomitants in the fields of expression have risen to impressive heights in modern Russia, Germany, Italy, Spain, Turkey, Japan, Brazil, Roumania, Poland and elsewhere, and the old authorities of the Catholic Church meanwhile hold on. These various and variegated absolutes may become dominant. They reject the experimental attitude that marks the scientific approach to reality. They reject tentative ideas, in which the future is a part of the form of the present, and hold to dogmas that resort above all to power for their enforcement. They require power, and much of their present success lies in the fact that new concentrations of power and new mobilities in the modern world have been their able instruments. The power of the modern world, on the other hand, is the offspring and constant protégé of science. It would seem that an authoritarianism that makes impossible the scientific attitude would in the long run lose the power required to enforce its dogmas. This probably is true, for it is not likely that scientific method can for long be promoted in activities relating to mechanical invention and technology and at the same time prohibited in social, economic and other fields. There will be a permanent and probably fatal contradiction at the core of dogmatic systems that make the attempt. Science, in a word, rests on an ideology that probably cannot be segregated in compartments devoted exclusively to technological skill and invention. It must be a general attitude towards all reality or it must gradually disappear. In the meanwhile, however, the new authorities and despotisms may destroy science and its tradition by the use of concentrated and mobile power derived parasitically from that science and from the liberal institutions coordinated with it.

And just as theoretical communism in Russia and theoretical totalitarianism in Germany and Italy may destroy science, so practical capitalism in England and America may make the experimental attitude on which science is based increasingly impossible. There can be little doubt that capitalistic ideology, as such, is also adverse to the scientific point of view. It is a power policy, as communism and fascism are power policies, and depends on dogmas, drives, and superimposed restrictions that are not native to the materials and people in the situation. Its debt to science is great, but endless instances during recent decades indicate that the power of capital is exerted less to maintain the flexibilities, the freedoms and the experimental changes that made science' as well as capitalism possible than to fix material acquisitions and privileges and at the cost of human welfare to secure property. Only the fact that capitalism as such is less highly organized, less aware of itself and less inclusive as an ideology than are the totalitarian dogmas of Europe and Asia, permits science and free institutions to develop.

Against the great streams of modernism which I have called experimental and provisionalistic have arisen, indeed, new certitudes and new resistances. New absolutes, as it were, are thrust up against the new relativities of science and of human values. If the tendency towards organic flexibility and relativity seems to be in keeping with some irresistible movement forward of events, we should remember that the irresistible logic of events in this somewhat unreasonable world may be less irresistible than we think. The traditional future, in a word, is still open.

But resurgent absolutes and despotic abstractions, dangerous though they be, are rooted in weakness. The power that they must feed on comes only from a host whom they seek to destroy. They are desperate authorities, it is true, but they are not self-sustaining. The orderly development of experimental and creative activity and of freedom, of relativistic and organic conceptions of reality, probably will continue.

In the outline of the future of society and expression I have noted one great conflict that enters into the future and thence reverberates into the present, as it were, and makes these days of ours different. That conflict is the modern relativism in contrast to absolutism. Though orderly development lies, I think, in the increasing relativism and plasticity in life and art in contrast to the obstruction by the resurgent absolutes and external powers, what I think or hope, or what orderly evolution may be, is not necessarily what the future will be.

In addition to this primary conflict of tendencies, three other great conflicts or contrasts will be discussed. They are: (1) the conflict of urbanism with agrarianism or some mod-

160

ern form of agrarianism; (2) the conflict of security with opportunity; (3) the conflict of specialization with integrity. Together the four give, in terms of conflict and doubtful outcome, something of the topography of the future. The conflict between relativism and absolutism is primarily intellectual. The conflict between urbanism and agrarianism is primarily in the social field. The conflict between security and opportunity and between specialization and integrity are primarily problems of the individual human being.

Southeast of Chicago the highway called U. S. 41 turns suddenly from the heaps and ruck of slums, "saloons," signs, billboards and minor business houses, and on a low causeway crosses the marshlands towards the sand ridge that once was the shore of Lake Michigan. To the right is marsh-water, fog, a remote scatter of chimneys, trees, a lonely house or so. To the left, across the flat and beaten peacefulness of the marsh, rises a dome of industry. It is huge in the distance, like a walled town, smoke burdened. Above the low layer of water, it rises compactly, a gray mound of buildings each with its slender stack or battery of stacks pointed in thin lines towards the sun.

Once the dunes and the sand beaches around the south end of Lake Michigan were occupied by sparse groves of oak and a few birches. Juniper grew there, and now and then a cactus

161

dared the northern winter. Marsh grass and sedge lined the slow ponds and backwaters behind the dunes. The streams were blocked by shifting sand, were backed up. They seeped through long twisting detours into the lake. Then grass would capture a dune, or part of it, trees would follow, and the hill's wanderings were over.

But strange seeds were planted there in the years after white men came. Crops grew that killed the sun and the sandy soil. Harvests of steel, cement, smoke, the stench of oil are now the products of the region. Chimneys, hundreds of chimneys, in marching columns, pour their smoke into the sky. The gray mound of buildings across the marsh-water rises abruptly with the harsh certitude of a volcano. Smoke smears the feeble sun. The city of industry dominates all nature.

What is urbanism? What causes it? This city of smoke, the piled structures of the mills across the marshes from highway U. S. 41, is urbanism. And in one sense it also is its cause. In the contrast between modern urbanism and older agrarianism this is the dominating influence. Modern urbanism rises from the industrial methods and organizations that this dark, magic city of the marshes represents.

The cause of urbanism, so far as single causes can be assigned to so complex a state of things, is in the convergence of two influences, one physical, the other organizational. The one is the power of the modern world derived from new resources in coal, iron, soil, labor and the like. The other is the organization of this power and productive capacity into what I have called an economically horizontal type of order. Power

162

the modern world has, a hundred times more, perhaps, than the world of our grandfathers. Its organization, and the organization of industry and of society in general, involves areas of huge scope, along with specialization, standardization, mass production. These are characteristic of the modern world. They lead directly to urbanism.

Modern urbanism, or great city life, involves the extreme concentration of industrial and mechanical power, the concentration of production and of the instruments of production, the concentration of property, or its management, so far as property relates to the means of producing goods, and the concentration of population. It involves extreme development of exchange, and methods of exchange, and of money as an agency of power and a standard of value.

In the arts urbanism promotes professionalism and virtuosity on the one hand, and on the other an increasing vicariousness in which people tend to accept others' production of art in place of their own. In education urbanism fosters the compartmental subdivision of subject matter. It promotes specialism both in professional and "liberal" education. Because large numbers of students must be handled, grades, credits, degrees and other standardizing instruments have great emphasis. Education as well as the arts becomes impersonal. It becomes intellectually corrupt, decadent, snobbish.

People live anonymously in cities. Family influence declines. Personal life is distributed over the industrial and social structure without much unity of its own. Because of the complex impersonality of events, gambling becomes a major occupa-

163

tion. And for the same reason standards of personal honor and morality change and often decline. The responsibility for the order and welfare of society is in great measure relinquished by the individual. The tempo of life increases. More things are experienced. Fewer things are contemplated. This, or something like it, is, briefly, urbanism.

Urbanism depends on a number of complicated artifices of which various forms of rent, or analogies to rent, are in many ways central. Rent of land with huge land values, rent of money with wild and whirling activities around it, rent on the added increment from machines leading to greater and greater concentrations, as my colleague, Mr. Wright, likes to point out—all these pile up in mazes and mountains of abstractions. Paper, exchange mechanisms, sellers, credit; all move towards salesmanship.

History indicates that urban ways of life are not self-sustaining. They move through their cycle towards the breakdown. Though modern cities are very different from those of old, it is not clear that they are more stable. Their destiny seems to be about the same, printed boldly then lost in the pages of history. Over-centralization takes its course. The costs of "overhead," of crowded land, congested streets, overburdened "utilities" and services mount up, so that even to be housed in the modern great city costs more, as Borsodi shows, than the average family of moderate means can possibly afford. The slums engulf them, or semi-public housing projects paid for by great subsidies are carried out in their behalf. The city, so far as it furnishes decent living quarters for its in-

164

habitants, is parasitic. It is parasitic, privately or publicly, on the home owners, the rural regions, and other tax payers and consumers of the nation. It is parasitic in other ways. Over-centralization lays its curse not only on the family, on labor, on industry, but on morals, art, ways of living.

The city arises from this tendency towards concentration in social, economic and political organization. (It is a more or less cyclical tendency, a rhythm of growth and decay that some philosophers of history like to point to as the inevitable course of social evolution.) Though fixed, rhythmic destinies of this sort are probably not so fixed nor so rhythmic in the complex human world as an orderly philosopher's mind might desire, there is little doubt that these concentrative tendencies in a measure are repeated in different cultures and civilizations and lead repeatedly to decay and downfall. Breasted, for example, in his book *The Conquest of Civilization* shows how the small, land-holding farmers, first of the Hellenistic world, later of the Roman world, were gradually deprived of their land. War and empire took the men away. Cheap labor deprived them of markets. Wealthy nobles and capitalists acquired their lands and organized great plantations. Other lands were destroyed by erosion, returned to weeds. The small farmers drifted to the cities, got jobs, went on relief. The cities filled up. The land became empty. Civilization declined and fell.

Though the city is an example of human coordination that is amazing in its complexity and power, it is predatory in character. Its tense and brittle inner structure is founded on predatory competition and control. Its relations to the world outside its gates are based on exploitative principles. In materials and men and money it takes more than it gives, and though it performs a function, the "rake-off" is excessive. The city lives at the expense of others both within and without its gates.

These doctrines are inherent, usually unconscious, in the arts and expression of urban life. The handsomest skyscraper, glittering and proud, captures the air and sun at the expense of lesser buildings around it. Its feet stand in the darkness and clamor and the inhuman pressures of life that its presence helps to create. The fashionable art dealer, to use another example, selects five young painters for pushing and promotion. Fifty or one hundred and fifty other young painters may be as worthy, but the laws of competition and profitable trade require that only a few be built up, their prices doubled, tripled, quadrupled, a small turnover and a big profit, while the other painters starve.

For the profits of the city lie in the mass standardization of taste. When the shifting millions rush for one book, one artist's paintings, one composer's music, one crooner's songs, one actor's Hamlet, profits are compounded. Native art, folk art for the many and variegated little neighborhoods of expression, declines. Advertising is a professional technique for standardizing taste and demand around one product issued in quantity. Though standardization of this sort has its obvious benefits, it has also its cultural disasters.

The evils of urbanism are obvious to many persons. The

166

Photo by University of Minnesota photographer

E WILLEY HOUSE

Minneapolis, Minnesota

Frank Lloyd Wright, Architect

Interior, showing open kitchen partition, dining table arrangement nearby

BROADACRE CITY DETAILS

Tourist Cabins of Canvas and Wood

Cantilever Gas Station, Neon Tube Lighting

Gas Bells Suspended with Flexible Hose Pen

ways to correct those evils, however, fall into two groups that in some respects are opposed to each other. One attitude towards this primary problem of modern civilization is based on the assumption that the evils of the great city are for the most part due to an immaturity of modern cities and industry that will be corrected by further growth. The other attitude is based on the assumption that the concentrations involved in great cities are the source of a trouble that cannot be removed except by the disintegration of the city itself.

Socialist theory, which in general is based on an urban conception of life, proposes that the present evils of the city, the slums, the injustice, the predatory savagery of man towards man, can be removed by the evolution of the industrial urban system—the dialectical evolution, indeed—towards more mature forms of organization. This evolution will take place, they think, through the mechanism of class conflict. This is again the competition motif, applied now to classes, that is characteristic of the modern city and of the capitalistic system that produced it.

Other utopians believe that without class war or revolution the city will evolve more or less automatically into a happy place to live. Still others believe that reform, "clean-up," publicity, and democratic methods can bring the city to a tolerable state of living. To this group belong the quondam muck-rakers, the reformers such as Lincoln Steffens, the civic virtue groups, most of the so-called liberals. Although this group is no longer so confident as it once was, it represents still the most powerful of conscious influences towards the improvement of the city, and it probably has made some progress. It believes that democratic forms of life and culture are still possible in the city, though it admits, of course, that radical readjustment of those forms to urban conditions will be necessary. Nor can we be sure that this group will not be successful. Changes in governmental pattern, such as the city manager system, civil service regulations, changes in economic set-up such as cooperative producing and purchasing groups, collective labor bargaining, bonus systems, employee participation in profits and management, industrial labor unions, changes in cultural habits, adult education groups, parent-teacher groups, social service agencies, city planning, parks and recreational planning, and many other efforts to get the problem under control have had considerable success. Certainly this liberal or progressive group, whatever its failings and hesitancies, is the only group that has actively accomplished any part of its purpose. It has at least seen action. The others thus far have only talked, at least in America.

The public housing projects have been a part of this liberal program. These housing projects since 1933 have become a most important feature in the government and public business of great cities. Though they do indeed require subsidies that must be paid by other taxpayers, they are carried out in the belief that they will pay for themselves in reduced crime rates, better health, greater productivity and consumption and other benefits, the lack of which now add greatly to the city's cost to itself and to the country as a whole. They are, it is true, another movement towards

168

socialized production, but they are primarily ameliorative and as such would no doubt be rejected by the socialists themselves.

If city housing projects cost more than they return directly towards the upkeep of urban organization, it is also true that the slum areas, which they are designed to displace, also cost more than they return. In Cleveland in 1932, for example, slum areas inhabited by ten percent of the people of the city, according to the "Survey" magazine, were taking twenty-six percent of the costs of the police, fire, health and sanitary services and thirty-six percent of the city hospital service. In an area containing 1.73 percent of the land within the city's limits and occupied by 2.47 percent of the population taxes were paid amounting to $1,972,437 whereas the costs of municipal services in the district were $3,719,839. This is a sample that will find parallels in all the greater cities of America. The liberal is therefore likely to say that it is better to have good housing in cities even though it lays a heavy burden on many tax payers not directly concerned, than to have *laissez faire* slums which also are a burden on tax payers not directly concerned. He usually accepts the fact of the city and asks what can be done within the limits of those facts.

And some of the facts of this situation are the following: Fifty-nine percent of all families in America had incomes of less than $2000 a year during the "prosperity" of 1929. Forty-two percent had less than $1500 a year. Twenty-one percent had less than $1000 a year. This means that about one-fifth of all the families of America had less than $17.00 a month to spend on housing. About two-fifths had less than

169

$25.00 a month for the same purpose. Since housing construction in the cities, due to antiquated organization method, costs far more than $17.00 or $25.00 for decent family requirements, the result is that a great proportion of families in the cities must be subsidized in respect to housing or live indecently, and be subsidized anyhow.

As a fact, they do live indecently. In sixty-four typical American cities 25 per cent of the dwellings have no bathing facilities; 17.1 per cent have no private indoor toilets; 33 per cent have stove heat; 8 per cent have no interior water supply, according to an inventory taken by the U. S. Department of Commerce. One-third of the people of the United States have never been decently housed. Two-thirds are inadequately housed.

With facts such as these in mind a beginning has been made towards subsidized housing for people of low income in the cities. The movement has varied foci of attack and numerous agencies. No less than the Home Owners Loan Corporation, Federal Home Loan Bank System, Federal Housing Administration, Reconstruction Finance Corporation Mortgage Company, Resettlement Administration, and the Housing Division of the Public Works Administration have been organized by the federal government to advance housing construction. Only the Resettlement Administration and the Public Works Administration, however, have aimed at collective housing projects for persons of small income. In the large cities these projects have been handled by the Public Works Administration.

170

At the end of 1936 fifty-one such projects in forty cities were completed or underway on allotments totaling $133,-445,761. Though this indeed is only a drop in the bucket compared with what is needed to house decently our urban population it points the way towards a solution, or a hoped-for solution, based on acceptance of the city. It is amelioration on a grand scale that must be grander still to be largely effective. The projects are carried out on a 45 percent federal grant with a loan on 55 percent at $3\frac{1}{2}$ percent interest. And even this, according to the "Survey," quoting Evans Clark, cannot produce housing at costs low enough for the low income group of people.

For the two-fifths of American families who cannot pay more than $25.00 a month for housing, the rents that must be more than $8.00 per month per room to keep public housing projects out of a deficit are too high. Costly as they are they must be more costly to the public, if they succeed at all, or production costs must be lowered or savings made elsewhere. It is a dilemma, it would seem; still the housing projects go on, with a considerable measure of human success if not financial profit.

In the Techwood project in Atlanta, for example, more than 45 percent of the tenants have incomes less than $1050.00 while 41 percent have incomes less than $1300.00 a year. In decent, modern, even attractive apartments these families are housed. Their children have grass to play on, sunshine to cleanse the air that they breathe. Verminous old shanties, broken houses on a filthy street, had been their homes before.

171

On the basis of so low an income no other housing in the city could possibly be available until the government took a hand. Ameliorative such projects are. It is true perhaps that they help to make a permanently bad situation tolerable. But in terms of human values they probably are justified. They are part, only a part, of an attack on conditions that must be fought on a broad and varied front.

Another type of housing project is the Greenbelt towns built by the Resettlement Administration. Three of these are built or underway, one on the outskirts of Washington, one on the outskirts of Cincinnati, one on the outskirts of Milwaukee. In this project the focus of interest is not the slum areas in the central areas of the city, nor the farm areas outside, but the urban periphery or so-called suburban region. In this respect the plan accepts the modern tendency towards growth in the peripheral regions accompanied by decline both in the rural regions and the central regions of the city, according to Rexford Tugwell; it tries not to check but to go along with that tendency. The project is, secondly, based on the construction not only of houses but of all the facilities, utilities, and instruments of city life. That construction is, furthermore, limited. The number of houses cannot exceed three thousand. Sewer systems, electric services, fire stations, schools, streets and the like are built only to that maximum; and, because the size of the towns is fixed by plan, great economies are possible. The homes in these towns cost from $9000 to $10,000. When the fact is recognized that these costs include all the services and municipal equipment for the entire town these costs for the houses are low. They are built, furthermore, for a period of sixty years or more of use. In such a planned town the houses themselves cost less than 45 percent of the total, but carry the entire burden.

The Greenbelt towns differ from the slum clearance projects in being somewhat less ameliorative and more revolutionary as a project. They are planned towns and limited by plan in size. In these respects they stand counter to the natural tendency of modern city growth. On the other hand they accept the desire of the average family to have a house of its own and to live in the suburbs, or at least we may assume that it is the average. The Greenbelt towns build with the old and for the old, but they introduce controls, planning, maximum size that may recall early New England but really are progressive methods that can be maintained, no doubt, only by government authority. As experiments, small though they be, they are justified by their human results in better housing for some three thousand families, if for nothing else.

But the great city and its satellite suburbs are not necessarily a certain feature of the future. There are signs that the great city is disappearing. As congestion increases even its business efficiency declines. It was estimated a number of years ago that New York City alone and the people in it pay $500,000,000 a year as the cost of extreme and ever-increasing crowdedness. Traffic delays alone take a large part of that sum. In terms of human health, human efficiency and happiness, in terms of stable civilization, native culture and individual integrity, the cost is far greater. The cost indeed may be the nation itself and its people. There is reason to think that the apparent disintegration of western Europe and the modern economic and social disasters in America are, as it were, natural functions of the overgrown urbanism and cosmopolitanism of these times.

The abstractionism of the urban system increases. Money, credit, property rights, on the one hand, education, intellectual life, books, radio, movies, tourism, professional sport, professional art, professional amusement facilities, on the other hand, are examples of easily concentrated, easily manipulatable functions. By means of conceptual abstraction and the vicarious use of life great chains and clusters of power are made. They become more manipulatable, more concentrated, more standardized. The stubborn concrete stuff of immediate experience gives way to exchangeable concepts. Poetry gives way to rationalism. The city moves on towards doom.

Though no one would wish to abolish these instruments and economies of organization, they are, in the city, out of scale. They are predatory, or instruments of predatory men, and because they are out of balance with life they destroy life. But the doom of the city may have several forms. The city conceivably may continue to exist, become permanent, and thus be its own doom. It may, on the other hand, ride on to destruction of a cataclysmic sort. Or it may break down into other forms, as a pile of manure rots away and becomes in time the sweet fabric of flowers.

Some of the agencies that may lead to the gradual disappearance of the city are already available. Electrification, both

174

in communication and in the use of power, is a way of using energy that has many advantages and opens many avenues towards decentralization. Electric power is easily divisible. It can be used cheaply at remote distances from where it is produced. It is flexible, fast. It brings distant homes and villages into contact with each other. It helps to make production and manufacture in the home and the small town feasible. Through electricity space is brought under control. The advantages of close contiguity of people with people and of productive machines with other machines are not so great.

A second agency is the internal combustion motor. This again makes power divisible and cheap. Motor cars, hard roads, airplanes, motor ships, farm pumping plants, are a few of its associated phenomena. The gasoline motor tends to decentralize the systems where it operates.

A third agency, associated with electrical and gasoline power, is the development of mechanical refrigerators, heating plants, lighting plants, small power looms, small power tools, drills, lathes, washing machines, ironers, toasters, cleaners, wheat and coffee grinders, milk separators, incubators, cultivators, tractors. Power tools and services of this sort, and automatic tool techniques, now make the home establishment once more comparatively independent of centralized service systems in the city.

A fourth agency is the use of new materials such as concrete, glass, steel-in-tension, sheet material and insulations of new fabrics and compositions. As my colleague, Mr. Wright, says elsewhere, they are more adaptable to small uses than corresponding materials once were. They can further decentralization in many ways.

A fifth agency is the mass production of machines. Though this may seem contradictory to the decentralization principle, it is true that mass production in some fields makes decentralization in other fields more possible. The future of whatever decentralization there may be will not be, in all probability, a return to the simple agrarian system of our grandfathers. It will involve a differential movement. In some respects greater concentration of production may take place in order that decentralization by means of those machines may follow. In fields such as the heavy industries, in the manufacture of automobiles and of other power tools, in fields such as electrical power production, railroads, the navy, road building, the mails, the radio, greater concentration may well take place. Perhaps a third of our production and services will be centralized, very likely under government control or ownership, in order that the other two-thirds may be decentralized and made free.

The machine, in short, is not only the creator of the great city and its centralizations; it will also be the agency of decentralization and the disintegration of the city. Mass production of these machines and low cost distribution, whether they be automobiles or electric hair curlers, can make it possible for the family unit and the small town to meet the competitions and pressures of the city. A new machine regionalism already is developing.

If the urban apartment projects designed to clear the slums
176

are efforts to ameliorate the necessary communal life of the great cities, while the Greenbelt towns are projects in individualistic home architecture on a communal basis, projects such as Borsodi's Suffern foundation are rejections entirely of the city and its communal pressures. This project abandons the city and by the use of modern technological devices builds up a self-sustaining family unit of land and labor which is free of urban compulsions and necessities.

In 1920 the Borsodis were a family of four living in a rented home in New York City and dependent, as Mr. Borsodi says, on a somewhat precarious white-collar job. The housing shortage of that year was rising to a crisis. Buyers' strikes, renters' strikes, protest meetings were boiling in ineffectual fevers and heat. Prices rose. Rents doubled, tripled. Then the house in which the Borsodis lived was sold over their heads. Their reply was not the usual discouraging search for other quarters of the city. They bought a small place, less than eight acres in all, and moved into a small frame house about two hours from New York. No modern improvement was available. They moved in; but such things as plumbing, running water, gas, electricity, steam heat, all were procured by gradual purchase later. Mr. Borsodi kept his city job at the beginning. Mrs. Borsodi was not unacquainted with country life. Soon both knew their way about on the simple, sustaining soil of their farm.

From this small and rather uncomfortable start the Borsodis, without capital, have built up at Suffern, New York, an extensive project which is almost wholly self-sufficing and independent of outside income. A number of other families have become associated with them. Productive acres, good buildings, home-built for the most part, home recreational and artistic facilities, comforts and conveniences greater than those of city life, and above all stability of life, are now accepted facts of their existence. Home food production and processing, home weaving and sewing, home wood and metal working, home management and education occupy less of their time than working hours would require in the city. Life is integrated, though not easy. It is complete, stable, significant, though not luxurious. It is beautiful, according to their report, though not without work and service.

Mr. Borsodi kept his white-collar job in the city for some years after he undertook the project. By this means he provided a cash income to buy land, shelter, equipment, power tools and other practical necessities of a modern attack on the problem of self-sufficiency. He was able, as time went on, to effect such savings in living costs that cash income became less and less important. He cut down his time in the city, first by one day a week, later by two. Finally he gave up his city job. Since then he has made a go of it on his farm, without a city job.

Chickens and goats, fruit trees, gardens and hay fields, bees, and domestic machinery of various kinds are his allies. Nature furnishes the raw material for the family needs. Domestic machinery makes unnecessary the traditional drudgery that has hitherto accompanied the transformation of that raw material into goods ready to enjoy. The Borsodis have appropriated the

178

industrial technique and machine skills of the factory, decentralized them, and reoriented them in respect to their family uses. They have in a word reformulated the structure of society so far as it applies to them. They have made the Borsodi family the center of their industrial structure. They have refused to be captured by and made incidental to the organization of production. Production is for man, not man for production.

In a world where human life is made secondary to productive effort by machines and men, the Borsodis have made productive effort secondary to human life. They have, indeed, created a structure, which is architectural in a larger sense. Work and production is deeply integrated with the use and enjoyment of the product. In such a structure, and we think only in such a structure, can industry and life find mutual coordination and fulfillment.

A three and one-half acre self-sustaining project can be undertaken, suggests Dr. Borsodi, with a capital of about $900.00. To this should be added, no doubt, considerable intelligence and work. He apportions this money—for the Dayton Homestead Units—as follows: Land, $250.00; building materials for the first section of the home, $300.00; materials and equipment for other buildings, $50.00; well and pump, $75.00; tools and implements, $25.00; livestock, $75.00; seeds, plants, trees, $25.00; sewing and loom room, $75.00; preserving and kitchen equipment, $25.00. Native ingenuity, persistence, and the pioneer's overwhelming yearning for freedom and self-dependence are also necessary. We would add, in

179

view of these, another ninety cents to the table of equipment costs. This will buy a copy of Emerson's "Self-Reliance."

The Borsodi project and others like it, and to some extent the Resettlement projects of the federal government, have in view not a pattern of life dependent on a cash crop or a cash earning job which is exchanged for shelter, food and other necessities of life in more or less abundance. They have in view a world in which a great part of production and consumption, the basic polarities of life, shall be in a short cycle. It is a life relatively independent of any great social organization. It is socially distributive, decentralized.

Such a life, and such a structure of society, if it be modern, will involve, to be sure, concentrations in some fields and mass production of some kinds of goods. It will require them to an extent and with an efficiency that no doubt will surpass the machine-power production of today. So, too, government in some respects will necessarily be more concentrated, more in control of some functions of society in order that self-sustaining life may be protected from predatory interests. In the modern world, at least in the West, there can be no return to the primitive agrarianism that Gandhi urges on India. But such concentrations, where necessary, can be, and perhaps will be, only in the interest of more independent, more self-sufficing life.

The popular assumption that centralization in one function or in one product must involve centralization in all is a fallacy that becomes more obvious as it receives further study. Because centralized production of automobiles or of machine

180

tools is more efficient does not mean that centralized production of food stuffs, music, drama, textiles, dancing, furniture, education, amusement, pottery, sport, conversation, horticultural products, literature, housing and life itself is also inevitable and desirable.

Life is practice; art is practice. The centralization of life, of industry, of art in vast horizontal structures of mass productions, exchange systems and vicarious enjoyments is neither necessary nor humanly efficient. It is a despotic and unwieldy kind of social organization that can have only one human consequence, disaster. The modern revolt against urbanism will in time succeed, or man as we know him will fail.

If the great factory building with its smoke, its chimneys, and its dreary rows of workmen's cottages is the characteristic architectural expression of the modern age, as Bertrand Russell suggests, the expression of the future, we may hope, will integrate living with production. Around the home and in it, and in the small community, in the neighborhood and region, productive activity will have its numerous foci. It will be merged in the living process rather than abstracted rationally into factories. And the home and village, or their analogies in the future, will become richer architecturally, more significant, more functional, honest. They will be the scene of balanced life and varied cycles of behavior that will have their counterparts in building. For work itself can be a slow dance of beauty when it collaborates with life. It has its lyric aspects and significance when the schism between production and enjoyment is reduced, forgotten, and the two are one vital unity

181

of living. Production and use may be one integrated action.

But the arts and architecture of today express the fatal cleavage. They are frivolous or they are brutal, as the case may be; weakly decorative, derived from dead traditions, or insensitive and harsh. Not all is thus, for in modern art are intimations of the future. But the art today that expresses our day, suffers from this dichotomy. The factories smoke or stand cold and silent. The workmen's houses are hunched in drab, dirty clusters around them. Their windows are dead eyes. Their doors gape open, sag on broken hinges. The smoke of the factories swirls through them into dark interiors. Smoke is the life of these houses. Rain streaks the old boards and drips to the mud and cinders below.

I may assert—though with some foolhardiness, no doubt—that the urban expression in modern architecture and the other arts has reached its apogee. It has climbed its limit from the earth. Toppling, terrible, it rises in rash defiance of the slow power of earth, snatching man from the soil that loves him and endows him with what reality he has. These piles of logic, these tall buildings, these concepts, sterile abstractions, story above story, higher and higher above the native silence of the soil, these cities of substitutes, vicarious rationalisms, piled up into clattering remoteness from the direct simplicity of life—in them human integrity cannot survive. They will fall.

They are dazzling to the casual visitor and to him who need not leave the boulevards and the luxuries along the city's glistening façade. Their boulevards and bridges, their great parks

182

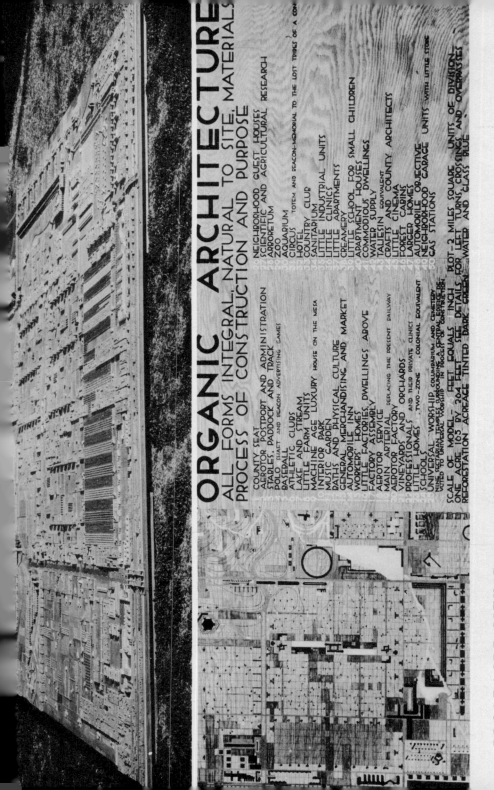

BROADACRE CITY Perspective of Model and Key

Frank Lloyd Wright, Architect

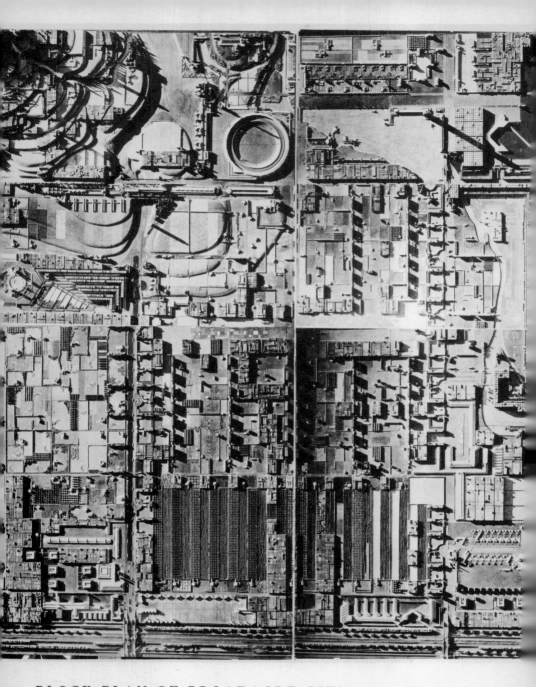

BLOCK PLAN OF BROADACRE CITY

LOOKING DOWN ON MODEL TWELVE FEET SQUARE

Frank Lloyd Wright, Architect

and bathing beaches, their sewer systems, engines, elevators, and their dynamic organization of powers and pressures into a beating, burning whole are, indeed, architectural expressions of a high order. But life in them becomes ever more disintegrated. Man breaks down in them, especially the majorities of millions in the slums, and where man breaks down they will break down too.

The new architecture will be focused on the human being, at least we may so hope. Less grandiose but more lived in, less pretentious but more honest, the architecture of the future will turn from glorifying gods and big business and express more intimately the life and the needs of men as they are. If the architecture of the medieval world was characterized by the serf's miserable hut and the soaring cathedral or the castle tower, if the architecture of today is characterized by the drab rows of workmen's cottages beside the smoking factory, the architecture of the future may well be the sunlit expression of a life whose values will remain on earth, in the earth, and of the earth that gives it being.

Clustered buildings in small groups will appear upon the land. That strange and unnatural separation between what we call "living rooms" and "working rooms" will disappear. For "work" may be "living" too, if we will see it so and will make use of the skills and technological facilities now available. Clustered buildings in small groups built to the scale of a man, a woman and their children, or to small groups and villages of people, will appear once more and will have, we may suppose, the prestige that now attaches to the city. In them will live stable folk who have learned that the values of life are primarily in this active moment, in this immediate experience of living.

Is this "utopian," after the pattern of a dream? Does it transmute people into creatures whose complex drives and earthy desires are miraculously coordinated and brought to perfection? I think not. Such a future requires education, to be sure, in so far as the people in it may realize the possibilities, technological and social, of the world that lies about them. It does not require, however, a transformed human nature. It is founded on the deep desire for stability, for integrity of life, for a world in which work is significant and enjoyment is fused with productive effort. These things are not "utopian." The lack of them in the modern social structure and in its architecture is bringing the urban system towards downfall. This, it seems to me, is the contrast between urbanism and the new agrarianism.

The road swings southward from the marshes and mills of Gary and Hammond, leaves the dunelands of the dead end of southern Lake Michigan, slopes over an ancient rim of sand and points, like a bird migrating in the fall, straight for the Ohio River. The road comes out of the great pot of smoke south of Gary. It moves across the surface of the earth like a concrete meridian, a time line, as it were, clean, bare, Euclidean, where Monday might stay on one side and Tuesday on the other. St. John, Schneider, Enos, Morocco, Kentland, Earl Park, Carbondale, Attica, then the road crosses the Wabash, Sterling, Turkey Run, Clinton, Terre Haute, Sullivan, Carlisle, Vincennes, Princeton, Evansville, and now it crosses the Ohio.

Highway U. S. 41 is new-laid in its course through Indiana. It drops down straight along the western border of the state avoiding the towns, crossing, in this three-hundred-mile stretch, only four cities of size. They are Attica, Terre Haute, Vincennes, all on the Wabash, and Evansville on the Ohio. The other towns are little more than cross-roads, railroad stations, or prairie markets for the farmers around.

At Schneider a dark towering elevator stands crowded between the highway and the railroad tracks. At Kentland, U. S. 41 crosses the main highway from Detroit and Toledo to Peoria, Quincy and Kansas City. A shining front of glass stands at the intersection. Behind it girls are making waffles, drawing ice cream sodas, serving steaks to travelers who pause there. Busses from the North, East, South, West draw up at the service stations. Cars from Florida are parked beside cars from Oklahoma and New York. Trucks rumble through or stop just off the road while their drivers get a cup of coffee.

At Earl Park an elevator of gray concrete stands on a little hill. It seems astride the road, looming larger and larger, a massive cylinder, sharp cut like a formula written against the sky. It rises above the trees on the knoll, above the scattered box cars along the railroad tracks. Geometrical, sharp, it stands

185

above the slow curve of the prairie like the naked concept of construction itself. Clearly it is something made. So abstract a thing never grows.

Carbondale, where coal wagons haul the black bones of the banksides, Clinton, Carlisle, Princeton, the little towns are much alike, small cross-hatchings on the plain. The cars roll through the little towns and out on to the prairie again. It is the great prairie. The slow, rolling slopes were left by the glaciers, as deep, black soil. A man could plow a furrow in it straight from eastern Ohio a thousand miles to western Nebraska without serious obstruction by hill or wood or stone. The cars roll through the vague little towns and across the gentle prairie slopes. They roll in thousands across the empty, abstract space of the great land.

Who are these people? Where are they going? Some of them are near-by farmers on their way to town to buy meat, butter, and seed for the early garden. Some of them are "traveling" men with a line of goods to sell at the next village. Many of them are neither farmers nor "traveling" men nor any other of the sort. They are citizens of the road, at least so far as they now use it, just traveling. The Fords go by, the Plymouths, Chevrolets, Buicks, Pontiacs, Studebakers, Packards, La Salles, in a loose procession.

These people of the road have homes, no doubt, but homes do not hold them. They have jobs—sometimes—but jobs are activities to get away from. On the road they find freedom, or at least the freedom that their world affords. It is more a freedom from things, to be sure, than freedom in things. And it is less a free quest than a free get-away. But freedom it is, nevertheless, though few persons would call it significant freedom. They roll across the world, up and down, back and forth, in strange, restless migrations, from St. Paul to Miami, from New York to California, through Kentland and Earl Park, Carlisle, Clinton, minor cross-roads, lunch-room intersections, cross-hatchings on the map, water-tank towns one after another, where they pause only for fuel and food to go on again. The sun-bare road is their empyrean escape. They are empty angels, with no message, free in the blank bliss of space.

In the modern contrast between security and freedom these people are the cavalry of freedom. For them freedom is in cutting loose, but security on the other hand is not in fixation. They find what security they have in infinite mobility. Of this freedom and of this kind of security the great road is the modern architectural expression. As Heraclitus might say: in all this world only the path of motion is firm.

Freedom in the modern, western world has been generally synonymous with opportunity. It is an independence of conditions and controls that holds people, in a tighter society, within the confines of one social and economic status. It is freedom to change according to the individual's own capacity and desire. It also involves not only freedom to change but an abundance of land, jobs, business openings, things to do and to acquire that a free man with initiative and ability can seize upon and therein make his fortune. The western doctrine of opportunity is based on the assumption that the world has unlimited room for active men. Give them freedom in that world and they will

187

provide their own security. And in that kind of world they probably will, as a fact, provide their own security.

But in recent decades men have found themselves less and less secure. The early assumptions of democratic America obviously are not in perfect working order. Freedom men have, to be sure. They may come and go as they wish without much legal hindrance. But their freedom is without opportunity. They have independence, at least politically. They can quit work, change, loaf, hunt, or walk the rails to the next town. But their independence is without security. On the job or off they are subject to vicissitudes and disasters over which they have little control. Twenty-three million persons have recently been on government relief rolls in the United States. Millions more have met defeat, broken hopes, disastrous fear in their struggle for existence. Four-fifths of the population of the United States in all probability have neither security nor the confidence that hard work and honest effort can give them security.

In such a state of affairs it is clear that the doctrine of freedom, good as it is, does not now involve opportunity nor security as automatic concomitants. The modern world faces a dilemma: no longer may we expect freedom *and* security but freedom *or* security. The ideas are now in conflict. This conflict is of critical importance in determining the future of society and its artistic expressions. In our highly organized urban world the fields for initiative and fresh exploitation become smaller and smaller. The economic opportunities for free development become less in about the proportion that economic

188

organization becomes more complete. In a system of economically and socially horizontal relationships that have little or no responsibility to persons involved in them, human security declines as productive power increases.

We are in a paradoxical world where personal freedom in many ways is greater than in any period in our history, and where personal power in some respects is unequaled by the past. The few have greater personal freedom and power, no doubt, than the autocrats of earlier generations, and the many still have more freedom and power in some fields than their ancestors ever had. Still, they all are without security. For personal life, in spite of its power and freedom, is disorganized. It is scattered, irresponsible. It cannot under these conditions be secure. Military insecurity, economic insecurity, personal disorganization are all parts of the same picture.

The doctrine of freedom and opportunity has two aspects. In both cases security tends to be destroyed. In a rich and relatively unorganized state individual free opportunity can rove, as it were, at will without immediate encroachment on the security of others. It may enhance that security, indeed, through the formation of loose protective communities and associations, and become in its way successful. But such a state of free individual opportunity is not permanent, for the opportunity to create great organizations and powers in industry and social life in time exhausts or crowds the field, as the case may be; great populations arise; urban, closely correlated relationships develop; opportunity for most people disappears, while in the hands of a few the power and freedom acquired under the old

189

conditions remains to control events under the new. As a result of this kind of management, and in spite of the complex organization of their world, most people are hopelessly insecure.

In response to this situation the collectivists reply: "Since security is more important than freedom, give up freedom and the pretense of opportunity that goes with it and insure security by complete collective control of industry and social life. For most people opportunity is a lost hope, anyhow; it is better to restrict the free opportunity of all in the interests of security." The collectivists accept the fact of great cosmopolitan organization and urge only that it be more so.

Another type of response is a re-definition of freedom. Freedom from this point of view is control from within of the means of life rather than the extension of control over others. It is freedom to be relatively self-sustaining rather than predatory. Opportunity is the chance to develop one's capacities, but not by a process of private acquisition that destroys the security as well as the opportunities of others. For persons who answer the problem in this way, the modern city is a curse that leads not only to the destruction of freedom, as they define it, but to the loss of security and of personal integration as well. For these persons the modern city is not inevitable. By attacking its causes, or some of them, they hope to disintegrate the city, without losing all of its advantages, and to reintegrate human life. These responses have mainly to do with the individual aspect of freedom and security.

A second aspect of the doctrine of freedom and security is the national phase of the problem. Bertrand Russell in his book

"Freedom versus Organization" develops this aspect of the doctrine and shows how the principle of freedom and self-determination carried onward to nationalism has resulted in highly organized states intensely competitive with each other, free as states, but restrictive of individual freedom within their borders. Military insecurity in these states, the constant fear of war and war taxation, of death by land or sea or air or slow strangulation by blockade, is a tragic compensation for the measure of industrial security that their defensive collectivism brings about.

The doctrine of opportunity, indeed, is at best an aristocratic concept that may be socially dangerous unless hedged about with protections for the "other fellow." Industrially it has broken down the equalitarian principle of democracy and made of freedom either a predatory hunt for booty or a restless wish to flee. To those individuals able to get power and wealth by work, brains, graft, gambling, inheritance or other means it sometimes gives power and wealth, but the selection nowadays is at best haphazard. Unless the doctrine of opportunity can be made less dangerous to the security of the people in western society it will move on towards a disastrous culmination, industrially and nationally, such as recent war and depression have only hinted. If social intelligence advances, however, which we trust is not too much to hope, the principles of opportunity and security need not be incompatible.

The future of society, in any case, will be determined in great measure by the outcome of this conflict between freedom —or opportunity—and security. In the light of the disasters of the last two decades, many people have become convinced that social effort must be devoted mainly to making human life more secure. Most of these efforts have been expressed in collectivist systems of various sorts designed to protect the individual—or the state—by means of social organization and power.

These collectivist systems are many. Collective defense in the army and navy programs is one of them, limited in this case to nations or to groups of nations. Collective financial security is sought in systems of guaranteed bank deposits, stock market control, federal reserve systems. Collective industrial security is sought in federal subsidy, tariff, loan systems to industries. Equalization and land saving systems try to give security to farmers. Home loan, pure food, advertising control systems try to give security to consumers. Social security systems, insurance, workman's compensation, child labor laws, minimum wage and hour laws, collective bargaining laws try to give the industrial worker security. The modern world is not unaware of its critical need for security. Most of these efforts, designed to aid the employer, the capitalist, the farmer, the consumer, the industrial worker, take the form of greater collectivism.

I grant that these are necessary—or many of them are—simply because society is a group of living persons who must be kept alive during any operative procedure designed to save them. Such efforts are emergency measures in a sick world. I assert, nevertheless, that greater collectivism as a social ideal is essentially insecure, unstable, destructive of human values

192

of life. Man, I believe, is not naturally, or happily, an urban animal. The price of great cities is human disintegration.

Other efforts have been made, conscious and unconscious, to bring about social and industrial decentralization and in this way to stabilize life and give it security. In the past, free homesteads have been a strong influence in this direction. In some regions today tax exemptions on homes or homesteads are designed to further the same end. Restrictions on chain stores, on chain banks, on monopolies, are efforts—perhaps mistaken —towards this end. Agricultural loans, farm tenant aid, county agents, research and educational services for farmers also have their influence. Income tax exemptions for heads of families, laws to restrict corporate ownership of land, corporation taxes, holding company laws are also efforts to aid regional and rural life. The U. S. Senate itself, as a regionally representative body, was planned with this in mind. Thus far these various efforts have not held their own against increasing centralization in management and financial control. The violence and oscillations and insecurity of urban life increase.

The most effective influence towards greater security is the profound technological change brought about by the electrical distribution of power, the internal combustion motor, the mass production of power tools for use in production and service in the family and small community. Though technological developments such as these depend upon highly organized production methods and standardizations over large areas, they do not bring with them inevitably the blight of the great city. They are influences in general towards a distributive type of

193

property system and of living. Even in their production, as in the case of the Ford works, decentralization has been accomplished to some extent. Machine production and new technological methods have in the past tended to distribute consumers' goods widely and at the same time concentrate producers' goods in fewer hands. It is not impossible, perhaps it is even probable, that these influences will tend to distribute producer's goods in the future.

The future of the conflict between opportunity and security is now emerging within the borders of the present time. It is still uncertain and without definite headway. That the forces focused in the ideology of opportunity are self-destructive seems clear after two decades of war and economic failure. But security is not necessarily the outcome. On the contrary, there is much to indicate that the remnants of security left in the modern system will be destroyed in a world-wide increase of disaster. Technological revolution may restore security to human life and society, as medical science has restored it to physiological processes, but that is by no means certain.

In the fields of expression the same confusion and anomaly exists. The trailer house, for example, to which thousands of people are turning, is a mark of unstable, unrooted home life. The roller coaster is an architectural symbol of a modern man's life and prospect. He turns to it, and to similar devices, in order to find symbolic form and expression therein of a life that is drab, noisy, routine but threatening, fast but going nowhere. He seeks the empty peace of noise, thrill, the unknown people of the crowds, hot-dogs, a thousand Coney Islands. The

194

roller coaster in some ways is the most expressive of all modern architectural creations.

Movable homes, abstract office buildings, factories where no life takes root : life is the drifting of sand across them, through them. Portable houses, portable furniture, portable radios, portable typewriters, portable pianos, tools, instruments—they are characteristic of a world where only motion is peace. They are symbols of people who have no place on the soil or in it. Even death fails to return them to the earth. There is no earth to which they belong, no home place; their ashes from some crematory drift out into the winds that blow here and there irrelevantly.

After it crosses the Ohio river, U. S. 41 loses geometrical simplicity. It is no longer a new road cut for transcontinental directness. It forsakes the abstract and becomes in Dixie a winding route from town to town. Obviously, it is an old-time local road, or succession of local roads, remodeled on a larger scale. It turns amiably around the shoulder of an old farm. It angles off to reach a little town. It moves southward between low boulder walls or the white board fences of the horse farms. The smooth, glaciated contours of the hills have given way to somewhat sharper ridges. The rock bed emerges here and there as the road lifts out of a valley.

The road clearly belongs to the country. It follows the towns and fence lines, the contours of the country and the patterns of life. It was not laid upon the land, superimposed as it were, for reasons remote from the little town and valley, the tobacco drying barns outside Springfield, the grist mill near the bridge. It was not cut through, driven by a distant power, going to a distant place, for purposes of speed and space and continental organization. It is a local road in character. Cars from Minneapolis and Milwaukee, Fond du Lac, Chicago, Detroit, Sioux Falls course around its intimate curves. But the road requires them to pause, and to some slight extent incorporates them in the scene.

The old South has retained its regional character more definitely perhaps than any other part of the country. The road does not alter it greatly. North of Nashville a turn to the left is possible. It detours the city, passes the stately quiet of Andrew Jackson's home, and slowly climbs to the Cumberland Plateau. It coils beautifully from ridge to ridge. There are woodlands and farms, cabins and the rangey houses of the more wealthy. Fox skins are for sale at stands along the road, fox skins, quartz crystals, bed quilts of homely native pattern. The road enters the valley of the Tennessee and approaches Chattanooga.

The South is the least wealthy part of the country. It was broken by war and by looting after the war. Large parts of its population, the poor whites, the tenant farmers, the textile workers, the negroes, live under conditions that offer little or no hope of a good life. Great areas of her soil are ruined.

196

Much of her forest land is slashed and cut-over. Her resources are greedily exploited by northern capitalists and by many of her own more powerful business men and politicians. The South for many years indeed has been rather out of the currents of so-called progress that have set so strongly across other regions of America. It is a sad land under its sudden violences, its sunshine, its sentiments and memories, its brief terrors and hopes. The dynamic gaiety of the North is not there, nor is the northern indifference. If the South suffers these misfortunes and handicaps, however, it also escapes some that are perhaps less obvious. It has not undergone the disintegrative consequences of industrial urbanism in most of its regions. It is still rooted, still in the earth. Its folk can live more integrated lives than is possible in the cosmopolitan North, or in the shifting, ambitious West. The process of industrial and educational division of labor has not gone so far. Specialism—that realm of half-life—has not encroached so completely on life.

The conflict between specialism and integration—or the ideologies that center about them—is an influence of major importance, the third and last that I shall here discuss, in determining the character of the future and its expression. In that conflict the old South has retained something of the old American tradition, or what I like to think is old tradition, that many other parts of the country have lost. For this reason statistics based on what is bought and sold in the South present a picture that is darker than the reality. To a greater degree than elsewhere in America the South, we may suppose, de-

197

pends on immediately self-sustaining activities without resort to trade or cash income. Much of its life does not get into statistics.

Life in the South, in spite of misfortune and the pressure of poverty, has its compensations. It is more contained. It is more integral with its surroundings. It "belongs," as the saying is; its cycle of functions—economic, social, cultural—is more naturally contained within the scope of the individual person, or the family, or the small community than are the great impersonal systems of the North. The South, in a word, is more agrarian in attitude. And by that I mean not an economy based on the cash crop—though that, God knows, has had its overemphasis in the South as well as elsewhere—but a relatively self-sustaining life founded on the soil. It is a life in which the cycle of production and consumption is short. People tend to produce what they consume and to consume what they produce. Such a life is economically integrated. It may also be socially, culturally, artistically integrated.

The conflict between the specialized pattern and the integrated pattern of life is essentially a conflict between the ideal of life as an instrument and the ideal of life as an end. In the one case life is devoted to specialized activity because in large-scale organization a more efficient production can be maintained when people become highly specialized parts of the physical or intellectual fabric. They give up their general interests and competence. In the other case the living process is thought of as the end and value of living. The living process in all its natural balances and diversity is a system in itself. It is developed, enriched, accepted as having formal value of its own. The practice of living is the value of life.

In many fields specialization is characteristic of the modern age. The huge, horizontal organization of our economic system carries with it extreme division of labor. This results in a person's life becoming more and more specialized. It is limited more and more to particular functions as the general organization of society becomes more complex.

This is obviously true in modern industry. Management is separated from ownership and becomes a specialized job. Labor is separated both from management and ownership. It in turn becomes more highly specialized and sometimes is higher paid. It is separated, so far as ownership is concerned, from the tools and machines that it uses. In the same way labor is separated from the homes that it lives in, from the ground that it walks on. On the books it is balanced by a cash wage and a cash wage only. The controls of the tools, the homes, the land, are in other hands. The workman's life is disintegrated, sub-divided, narrowed by the process of specialization. On the other hand his skill is intensified. The same process and the same consequences are largely effective in the white collar man, the executive, the financier, the professional man. They are also effective in the farmer.

Education has followed the same course. The universities today are failures from any liberal intellectual standard. The professional schools in a greater measure are doing what they profess to do, but they too are failing to train their students adequately for the social and professional responsibilities of the modern world. The universities in general have accepted the vogue of specialism. In some ways they have created it. They have entered a difficult world blindly and ignorantly, with no idea where the cult of specialism belongs and where it does not belong. They have come forward with considerable arrogance to supervise the intellectual destinies of the world and, instead of enriching and unifying intellectual life and giving it significance in a world that needs above all a consistent and creative attitude towards reality, they have helped to destroy its cultural integrity.

They have done this by the process of specialization carried to disastrous extremes. The world for them is sub-divided into fields of knowledge: departments, courses, lessons, degrees, credits, grades, all the intricate compartmentalization of an academic system that is moved more by the acquisitive desire for large quantities of their product than by any sincere effort to see the world whole and to adjust human life and values to its changing contours. Their system is similar to their industrial counterparts, such as an automobile manufacturing concern, for example; the process of division of labor and specialization is carried to a point where educational and human integration is destroyed. And they lack what even an automobile concern provides for its product, an assembling plant.

The ballyhoo, the lack of standards and of courage, and the toadying of many university administrators is related to this deep failure in educational integrity. The intellectual snobbery and the failure, on the part of most of the members of the faculties, either to teach or to produce significantly, are

200

almost inevitable in the present structure of the academic system. The indifference, the dull and scattered minds of students are the natural consequence. When we see what the universities do to the natively fine material of which most of the student body and much of the faculty is composed we realize the extent of the modern educational tragedy. The educational system built around the principle of specialism has failed.

In religion in its organized forms may be seen the same sources of disintegration. Religion in the western world, indeed, has been traditionally established on the cleavage between production and consumption, or as the Christian epic has it, earthly life and heaven. This primary separation of the instrumental values from the values that Dewey would call consummatory is no doubt the traditional source of the characteristic ideology of the west. Plato with his antithesis between matter and spirit—or the idea—began it, but the life of the Pagan Greeks, as contrasted with Platonic philosophy, was more integral than ours. We have inherited the Platonic tradition through the church. The great cleavage has remained not only in the church but in our secular activities. The abstraction of the spirit, the segregation of the instrumental and its multiple subdivision into specialized fragments, has reached a disastrous culmination in the modern life. The fragmentation of experience, the disintegration of the person is the result. Specialism as a pattern of life is centrifugal. Life is shattered.

Integrative tendencies in the modern world, on the other

hand, have also power and significance. They may not be noted in the clatter and intensity and the dust storms of specialism. There are sincere efforts in the schools, particularly the lower schools, really to educate the young for a significant life rather than merely to "learn" him. There are sincere efforts on the part of thousands of individuals to make their lives superior to the centrifugal influences of their world. An important group in the Catholic Church, led by Hilaire Belloc, Father Michel, Father Rawe, Father Stewart, and others, as well as groups in the Protestant churches, realize that social and economic centralization lead to the disintegration of personal life and the spirit. An even more important power to bring about the integration of life is the Tennessee Valley Authority under the leadership of Arthur Morgan. By means of this great instrument, with cheap power, soil control measures, education, and in some cases resettlement, village and home production in the Tennessee Valley is made efficient and significant in the integrated pattern of life. The Borsodis and others have made of their lives and work a successful experiment in the practical synthesis of work and reward, of production and enjoyment, in their homesteads. Gandhi has led in India one of the great movements of all time towards an ideal of integrated life. His repudiation of science and modern technology, however, makes it a movement that cannot have a counterpart in this respect in the west. The west, we may assume, is pledged to the use of the machine. It is better so. With the machine the abundant west can move towards the integration of life and at the same time

202

retain abundance. Without the machine it can have integration only by a return to the scarcities and impoverishments of the past.

But a more important influence towards the integration of life than any thus far mentioned is the traditional ideology of the democratic west. Even in the great cities of America many, if not most, of the people are small town or farm folks in temper and desire. They have been detached from the land only for a few years or for a generation. They are at home in the country and can return to it without the helplessness that marks the traditional urban type. They are not urban "bourgeois" in attitude, and in their hearts do not wish to be. Nor are they fixed temperamentally as city "working men." These millions of Americans are not only folk of American rural and pioneer stock; they include many from the peasant stocks of Europe who have migrated to America, taken jobs in the city because they must, but are rural still. There are, to be sure, large numbers of immigrants in America, as well as some who have been in America for several generations, who are city bred and urban by long tradition. They have little sympathy for rural life. They prefer the crowds, the quick facilities, the "conveniences," the wage and salary systems of the city. They are groups of considerable influence and vocal activity, but they are not by any means the real power of America. Nor do they represent its temper.

There is little doubt, for example, that urban life with its enforced specialization, its limitation of activity to narrow fields, and its expansion of vicarious life to widely scattered and unrelated areas of experience, destroys the kind of people that millions of Americans are. They are not the sort of folk that flourish under such conditions. Few, if any, human beings are. Intense psychological strains develop. Insanity and nervous breakdowns increase. Physical and reproductive ability decline. Restrictions forced on the individual by modern conditions, such as delayed economic independence, delayed sexual independence, the postponements of rewards of all kinds, result in profound tensions and maladjustments in social and individual life. And to drain off these anxieties religious, radical, and patriotic fanaticism and other violent phenomena develop. Escape devices in morbid literature and newspaper stories, in wild amusements, drink, narcotics, sadistic sport spectacles, fakery and hullabaloo are characteristic of a society in which life activity is limited to rigorous special operations. Surely one of the main influences towards a more integrated life and culture is the nature of the American people. They are not suited to urban lives and extreme specialization. The agrarian tradition is deeply in them.

In the arts the expression of this conflict between specialism and integration takes various forms. The literature of revolt of the 1920's, as well as the defeatism and cynicism of much other writing, has its bearing on this conflict. When romantic escape was no longer possible and became frivolous, revolt or candid defeatism became appropriate. If Sandburg's poetry is, in part, a revolt against social injustice, and Jeffers' is revolt against life itself, T. S. Eliot's "Wasteland" is defeat, candid and bitter but not profound.

In painting there is a tendency to turn metaphysically into the substance and structure of visual experience and to find there, mystically, a spiritual form that is identified with, not segregated from, concrete things. The more profound post-impressionists—Cézanne, Van Gogh, Gauguin—have done this, less to escape romantically the false compulsions of their age than to go through them to the essential significance of the materials from which they arise.

Another tendency in painting is to seek "pure" abstract form removed from human and social contexts, to enter into sensuous irrelevancies in color, mass, and line, or into specific insanities. They are vehicles—any vehicle will do—in which a removal from the commonplace, the massive reality of things, can be effected. This tendency in painting is more rationalistic and symbolic in ideology, though not in method, than the mystical post-impressionists. The cubists, Kandinsky, the futurists, the surrealists belong here.

Another tendency in this field is the penetration into the regional and unique characteristics of life and the expression of them, creatively, on canvas. Among the regionalists are Grant Wood, Benton, Hopper, and many more. There is in modern painting, moreover, a deep tendency to integrate form with matter. It is a tendency to express the characteristic stuff of things and of events in terms of their own realities. Lao Tze would approve of it; Plato would not.

In music, too, may be found sharp contrasts in tendencies. All of them are characteristic of the situation from which they arise. There is, as in painting, an experimental, rationalistic group of musicians reaching for new forms, new tone scales, new time sequences, new textual and tone-quality effects. They are, as it were, the end of a cycle which began with the gradual personalization of music through Beethoven, Wagner, and the romantics, and moved from personalization to particularization, from emotion to abstraction. Scriabin, Ravel, and to some extent Stravinsky are examples of this group. They have moved from melody to tonal texture in their emphasis, and in some cases to experimental abstraction.

Another tendency in music is the violent surge of folk song. We today call it "popular" music; it is written for the instrument more than for the voice, but folk song it is, nevertheless, in function and form. The savagery and voluptuousness of jazz music, swing music, or whatever its latest variation may be, is apparent to all and unpleasant to some. But this in no way changes the fact that modern American music is one of the most vital and most dynamic expressions of life in art in the entire history of music. Not only is it heard by everyone through one agency or another, it is sung, tooted, strummed, hummed by millions. Millions of folk dance to it. It is music in action. Nor does the average American feel that he must leave the composition of his songs to professional experts. If there is one, there are five thousand persons in every country-side, in every city of size, writing a song or working out, no doubt with one finger, a tune that he likes.

In poetry, too, art in great measure has returned to the folk from which it must always eventually come. Under the leadership of Harriet Monroe and her magazine of verse in Chicago, poetry became an amateur art, as it should be, and ten thousand poets began to sing where a few hacks and professionals had sung before. With new freedoms in form and with new scope and significance in subject matter, poetry became a normal mode of intense expression. It was no longer written exclusively by a few specialists. It became integral in the lives of thousands of people. For poetry above all is the practice of poetry. The creative act cannot be delegated, if one would have sons.

The regional development of prose (and this includes most biography) is also a part of the modern tendency in the arts to express life integrated with the spatial, temporal, and material surroundings. In America almost every region has its literature and every pasture its poet. Authors, often with no specialized training, are appearing over the entire country trying, often with distinguished success, to formulate in words the rich beauty and texture of their part of the world. Zona Gale, Carl Carmer, Ruth Suckow, Faulkner, Caldwell, Sherwood Anderson, not to mention Robert Frost, are examples of this group. Important tendencies in the arts towards regionalism, non-professionalism, and the plastic expression of the realities in which living is embedded indicate that the significance of an integrated life, in contrast to expertism, is well recognized. From the development of folk poetry and agrarian prose to boys' high-school bands there are indications of a desire for the native integrity of life. From the rise of garden clubs to the La Follette movement in Wisconsin there are signs of revolt against urban specialism.

In architecture the conflict between the expertism of the city and agrarian integration is even more intense than in literature. On the one hand the great commercial and industrial buildings, skyscrapers and factories, stand crowded on the city's floor. They are the housing of specialized activities. None of them houses a whole man or a whole life. They are created by specialism. They express it, and in turn create it. The street cars, the elevators, the toilet rooms, the jails, the barber shops, the offices, the machine rooms, hundreds of specialized housings for special activities performed by masses of disciplined people—these are the material realities of the city. The great buildings are shells built around these activities.

In some modern dwellings, on the other hand, a real sense of integration begins to find a place. The old separation of functions symbolized in the "dining room," the "library," the "reception room," the "parlor," the "sitting room," the "sewing room" and various other sub-divisions of formal family activity is now often ignored. The main activities of indoor life are sometimes assigned to three or four rooms. These may be a work room where the preparation of food, dining, and other activities take place and where the children are; a study, where books, music, quiet conversation or just silence may be enjoyed; a bedroom or two; a bathroom. Such a house may not only integrate the lives within the house; it may, by the use of terraces, courts, large windows, unify the

208

indoors and the out-of-doors so that the contrast and separation between nature and a housed life is no longer as drastic as it once was.

House design that is integral with the lives in the house, and with the materials of which it is composed, is all too rare; but such houses do exist. They are plastic, expressive creations that belong to life and to nature, to the building materials and to the environmental society. Such houses also create new integrations of nature, life, materials, society. Their dynamic form re-creates the world about them.

With such design a house rises from the soil, as it were, or rests upon it. The house is an extension of the rock and the earth. Trees are glad to grow beside it. And children of the earth will live in it as naturally as clover plants grow in the soil.

The future of society and the expression in the arts of that future has not the sharp clarity that we might wish. The future is clear, however, only to the extent that the present is clear. It is obscure only as the present is obscure. Great contrasts and greater conflicts mark this present. Great influences and ideologies surge together in a roiled and broken pattern of conflicting life. The modern conflict of relativism with absolutism and the conflicts between urbanism and agrarianism, between security and opportunity, and between specialization and integrity—if I may state them in their ideological terms—these conflicts in the present are no doubt creative principles of the future. The future of society and expression is here, in other words, within this present day. The obscurity of it, the smoke hiding the fire, is obscurity in the present. The future is only as clear—no more, no less—as the present.

This future, which is the only future that we ever actually possess, is a spiritual design in the present. It is in essence the mystery of religion and the arts. It is the gratuitous addition to reality, more real than the real, that the arts give imaginaively to this moment of the present. Expression in the arts is the future in this mystical sense. It is all the future that we really have. It is the magic of another dimension brought by art into the present world. It is expression of the present but withal the creation by that act of more than the present.

But expression also is a function of society and of man. Society lives when it truly expresses itself. Without expression it can be no more than a halting, over-complicated machine.

What is social expression? It is the integration of the variegated influences, interests, materials and other characteristics of a society in one illumined whole. What so-called consciousness is to the individual, social expression is to society. It is the dynamic focus of that congeries of relationships called social life. The many things that society are become one in such expression. It is the creation of social integrity.

The arts or their allies are usually the vehicles of social expression. Through music the wild jazz rhythm of a mad society is expressed. Beauty, brutal dullness are there. Through

210

painting the lithe distortions and entanglements of the modern world of space and color are given form. The search below space and below time for things unknown in the old "pictorial" representation, and unknown also in the old conceptions of the natural universe, find in modern painting at least some expression. Through poetry and other literature the modern structures of society become realized. They are less a description of society than the creation of its form. They assemble it, give it contour. They make of the scattering crowd of human events, relationships, movements, conflicts, intimations, a new synthesis. It is a design of social life seen imaginatively for the first time in the minds of the people. And because it is a design held in the thought of people it is a creative influence in society. In other arts and ways of doing things society finds expression. In the sports and in laughter, in the routines of work, in the smooth craft of machines, the rhythms of movement, the roar and dance of the streets, there is social expression.

The world to the artist is plastic. Whether it be the social world or the physical world that is in his hands, the creative spirit finds it plastic stuff to be molded into forms appropriate to its nature. The grim verities of the social or the natural order, structurally rigid though they may be from the point of view of people in them, are for the artist part of his plastic material. He finds forms, creates them, out of the nature of that material. He does for it what we may fancy it would do for itself if it could think and feel. The artist is its mind.

This is the social function of expression. As we view the

"works of art," conventionally so called, that clutter up so much beautiful blank wall space, or burden the fine emptiness of the land, it is clear how far away from vital expression much so-called art may be. Impoverished imitations of older styles, that once may have been expressive, can hardly be expressive now. Vulgar assemblies of other men's work in the so-called eclectic manner can cover only a shoddy failure. Social expression in the arts has immediate value or it has no value at all; nor is it expression. Social expression never is derived. It is direct, never over-washed with colors from elsewhere. It comes direct from its material, like light from an incandescent rod of steel.

Social expression through architecture is a powerfully creative force. For architecture more than other arts, unless it be dancing, is muscular or kinaesthetic in many of its implications. It requires more than visual response as in painting, more than auditory response as in music, more than tactile response as in sculpture. Architecture requires of those who live in buildings a muscular response. It directs action. It gives design to our comings and goings. Though other arts also are kinaesthetic or muscular to a degree not often recognized, architecture is directly involved in physical activity. So long as a man lives in a building, or works there, he will move about in figure of action that is determined in great measure by the plan that the architect has wrought into the building. The number of his steps, his right turnings and his left turnings, his climbings and descendings, his repose and his exertions will be written into the building by the architect as a composer writes the orchestration of a theme into the musical score. The man will dance, indeed, the long dance of day-by-day life, to a tune that the architect has made in stone and wood, in rooms and passageways, in terraces, and in the light flooding a window.

Architecture, for this reason, is a powerful influence in creating the future in the present. It may formulate the future, create it indeed, and give the present new character and direction. And because architecture redesigns the activities of people who inhabit its works, it is able to carry these creative influences, these futures as it were, into the active life of man. It can bring families together or separate them. It can bring different groups and classes of people together in friendliness, or it can segregate them. It can weary people and make them irascible through constraints and obstructions and the continual frustration of normal rhythmic activity. It can debase their taste and their moral judgment with structural fakes and ostentatious decoration. It can seal them in dull monotonies of expressionless life through indifference to human welfare. Or it can give to life a gracious pattern of action. It can release powers and abilities for significant achievement that otherwise would be absorbed in frittering. It can provide a rhythmic pattern of activity that transforms the present, gives it new dimensions, depth, and significance.

This indeed is the expressive function of all art. Not only does it reveal life; it creates life. In creating new forms and relationships, in making new significance or reviving old, it really is creating life over and beyond the life that nature gives. It gives to "natural" life additional dimensions and significance, forms and futures within the present, that nature without art never could provide. It is nature and more than nature, "super-nature" as it were, and the only supernatural influence that we need consider here.—B. B.

VI. A Balanced Society

WHAT is balance in society? We live today in a social system that becomes more unbalanced as it continues to evolve. Though balance and unbalance are relative terms that depend in great measure on what seems a good balance or a bad unbalance according to the standards that people use, it is still possible to outline roughly what a balanced society according to my standards might be.

I have discussed the character of society in the present world. I have discussed the character of society and of expression as I think it may be in the future. In this part of the book I shall neither hold to the present, though I shall describe some of its features, nor shall I prophesy the future. I shall sketch what society in America would be if it were laid out structurally in proper balance. And I shall sketch not only what it might be but what it can be, in view of the conditions, facilities, resources in this country, if social balance were the guiding principle. It will be a rough and hesitating sketch to be sure. The situation is almost infinitely complex and difficult. But the achievement of such a balance is not beyond the capacities that Americans have shown in other fields. The attainment of America's present situation and status, unbalanced, dynamic, dangerous as it is, was possible only through great capacities on the part of our people. But the results in some ways are disastrous.

I shall discuss eight kinds of balance and in each case suggest what a good balance should be. They are : balance in population, industry, property, politics, art, religion, education, human life. I shall outline, in short, the structure of an integral society in America.

Social balance is a stable correspondence between different parts of society so that there is a completeness and inner reciprocation of functions. This makes for social efficiency. It makes for dynamic cooperation. At the same time it is coordinated with a stability of human life that in a measure is independent of social organization. This conception of balance is based on the assumption that a social system is a necessity arising from man's proximity to man. It is an instrument towards life, not primarily an end. It should be made efficient, serviceable, protective, but not the all-absorbing aim of living. In the population of America there should be a proper balance between rural and urban groups, between old and young groups, between male and female populations, between occupational groups and between regional groups. In respect to racial and national stocks there may be some advantages in balance, although it is doubtful whether this is preferable to homogeneity of stock. In respect to economic and social classes, as well as in religious groups, there are now some factors of balance,

216

but this is of doubtful benefit. Balance, in a word, is desirable in some fields. In other fields its value is doubtful.

This means that balance in social life is different from compromise. A compromise between the government of Chicago and the alki gang is not an example of balance but of weakness. The oft made remark that some graft in government is necessary to motivate our public officials is not balance but corruption. Social balance applies to factors that in themselves are functional but become dangerous without compensating factors in another direction. Balance relates to the organic aspect of social structure.

The balance between rural and urban populations in America should be determined by two considerations: first, the optimum number of families that can live largely self-sustaining lives on the land with a high standard of living; second, the number of families or individuals required for those concentrations of industry, trade, education and government that may be necessary to supply the mass products, the skills, the services and security appropriate to a high standard of living in city and country both. There is little doubt that a system determined by these objectives would have a much larger proportion of families living in the rural districts and small towns and fewer living in the urban districts. What that proportion would be is difficult to suggest, in the present state of research in these fields. Probably sixty to eighty percent of the population could live fairly close to the land, with forty to twenty percent in the larger cities.

The trend of population, however, is in the opposite direction. Though the hard times of 1930 to 1936 were the occasion for 6,000,000 people to return from the cities to the land, with about 2,000,000 of those people still remaining there in 1937, the general trend of population has been away from the rural districts towards the great metropolitan areas and certain other classes of cities. Sixty percent of the population was rural in 1900. Less than forty-four percent was rural in 1930.

This migration to the cities has several causes. Agricultural production has become more efficient. With modern machinery and methods fewer men are needed to produce agricultural products. Accompanying this technological change has been a change in agricultural economy. Farmers depend more on cash from the sale of crops, less on what they produce for their own use, with the result that the market becomes their only link to the soil. This market has changed. The foreign market is less stable. The home market and the consumption of agricultural products has been reduced in some fields by substitutions such as gasoline for oats and hay. So long as agriculture moves towards a more commercial basis this is likely to continue.

The demand for agricultural products is, furthermore, comparatively inflexible. It does not increase in proportion to the increased consumption of other goods. It does not increase in proportion to the improvement in standards of living, or to the absorption of new products such as the automobile or radio. A person, after all, eats only so much. His salary may be tripled but he will not eat three times as much food. In consequence, the demand for agricultural products does not increase very much more than the increase in population. But the rate of increase of population in America is declining and probably will continue to do so. The consumption of food and fibers by the average person is also probably somewhat less because of his more sedentary, steam-heated life. For these and many other reasons the rural population declines. On the present cash crop basis the security of life in the rural districts may be no greater than in the city.

The cities were increasing by 14,600,000 people during the decade from 1920 to 1930 while the rural population was increasing by 2,400,000. It is a differential that already has resulted in an unbalanced population. Declines of more than 50,000 in rural population, according to Thompson and Whelpton in the President's report on Recent Social Trends, occurred in New York, Pennsylvania, Ohio, Indiana, Illinois, Michigan, Missouri, Virginia, South Carolina, Georgia, Kentucky, and Tennessee during the decade.

The growth of urban populations was further accentuated within the cities. Between 1900 and 1930 the proportion of persons living in cities over 500,000 increased from 10.7 percent to 17.0 percent, or three-fifths. In cities of 100,000 to 500,000 the proportion rose from 8.1 percent to 12.6 percent, or about one-half. In cities of 10,000 to 100,000 the proportion rose from 13 to 17.9 percent, or about two-fifths. In cities of less than 10,000 the proportion rose only from 8.3 percent to 8.6 percent, while in rural areas it declined from 60 percent to 43.8 percent. The population of America is not only leaving the rural districts; it is progressively being concentrated in the great metropolitan areas.

This drift to the cities is a result of commercial and cultural advantages that the cities offer, or seem to offer; it is not due to a shortage of land on which to live. Though the days of free land are gone, to be sure, there are still vast areas unused for the support of human life. About one billion acres of land in America are physically capable of agricultural use. In 1929 a little more than a third of this land was in crop production. Another third, according to O. E. Baker, needed only plowing to be put into production. Another third was forest, cut-over or undrained land. Although much of this billion-acre parcel of land in the United States is marginal and unsuited for a cash crop or a high standard of self-sustaining life, there is no doubt that America has land enough, nevertheless, to support a much larger number of her families on the soil. There would be some twenty acres or more of useful land for each family in America. And a reserve for forests, conservation projects and the like would still be left.

In the ten years between 1919 and 1929 there was a total net migration from the rural districts to the cities amounting to nearly 6,000,000 persons. During the same period land in harvested crops was abandoned for that purpose to the amount of 32,000,000 acres. Much of this, to be sure, was hilly land, eroded land, or land otherwise poorly adapted to commercial farming. It is doubtful, however, whether the millions moving to the city were greatly benefited in the long run. With modern methods in technology and agricultural work and, above

220

all, with a desire to live a self-sustaining life on the land in a measure independent of the cash crop, many or most of them probably would have been more secure and better off in the country than hunting jobs or relief in the urban districts.

For the great cities, attractive as they are, have not been able to provide jobs. They have not provided decent living conditions even for persons with jobs. The majority of workers there are poorly housed, poorly educated. Often they are mis-educated. Life there for the millions of workers has neither security nor fundamental significance. Studies by O. E. Baker in some of the poorer crop regions of Kentucky, where self-sustaining farming is still largely practiced, show that the people have better living and more security than corresponding folk both in the city and in the richer cash crop lands of Alabama. The city and the cash crop system, in a word, do not necessarily provide better living for the people dependent on them.

The trend towards urban concentration continues, however, at an increasing cost in human value, in living standards, and in some respects at a cost even of efficiency. This concentration is not only towards cities but within cities. Between 1921 and 1928, in 257 cities over 25,000 in population, the percentage of one-family dwellings given building permits dropped from 58.3 to 35. 2, while the percentage of multi-family dwellings rose from 24.4 to 53.7. This, according to R. D. McKenzie, is a characteristic of metropolitanism that is not borne out in smaller, independent cities.

In most kinds of building, indeed, the size of the structural unit increases in metropolitan areas. Office buildings, hotels, department stores, apartment houses, schools, and in many cases industrial buildings are larger in size and more specialized or more segregated in function. Height increases. The number of power elevators in the country increased from 138,756 in 1920 to 220,608 in 1929. The ratio between land area and rentable floor space increases at the same time. In the Empire State building, according to McKenzie, the rentable floor space is twenty-five times its ground area. It is 85 stories tall. In the Chrysler building the ratio is twenty to one; in the Woolworth building, about sixteen to one. The ratio does not increase in direct proportion to the height, however; this is because of additional elevators and other services required in higher buildings. This is a limiting factor on the height. Quite possibly the economic limit has been reached. Certainly it has been reached from the general point of view until better horizontal transportation on the streets around the building, and better vertical transportation within the building, is made possible.

From the point of view of general social good as well as architectural serviceability there is little doubt, indeed, that the entire concentrative movement of population into the great urban regions has reached a point of over-balance. It has gone too far. It has become predominantly destructive of our social and cultural integrity, of our economic security and our general sense of significance in life.

The balance, or over-balance, of urban and rural populations is a problem on which social and political policy may

222

have some effect. Taxation and tariff policies are influential, and in the past have had a large part in creating the present situation. Loan and credit arrangements, new services and resettlement plans, tenant farmer legislation are important. Technological advances, electrification and measures to insure cheap power are of great significance. In many ways the balance between urban and rural population may be deliberately shifted in one way or another. The problem belongs in the field of social policy. Those who assert that the trends are inevitable are ignoring, I think, not only the possible effect of our policy in the future, but the very definite effect of our policies in the past.

In other parts of the problem of population balance, however, the question of social choice seems more doubtful. The balance between young and old in population is changing rapidly, but how much this can be effected by a deliberately directed plan is hard to say. This problem is involved with the size of the population in America. Due to many reasons, of which the urbanization of life is one, the rate of population increase in America, as well as in much of the rest of the world, is declining.

Beginning in 1776 with about 2,500,000, the United States had a population in 1930 of 122,775,046. In 1920 the population was 105,710,620. In 1910 it was about 92,000,000. In 1900 it was about 76,000,000. Though the increase between 1920 and 1930 was 15.7 percent the rate of increase has begun to decline. The census of 1940 will probably find the rate of increase below ten percent, and the census of 1960, according to Thompson and Whelpton, below five percent. In 1950 the population will be around 145,000,000, and in 1980, not more than 170,000,000. Other and later estimates indicate a maximum population in about 1950, with a more or less rapid decline in population thereafter.

This decline in the rate of increase is due to several influences. The higher standard of living and the ways of life that go with it have retarded the birth rate. Changed family patterns have resulted from these standards. Marriage acquires a different relationship to the entire structure of life. Children become more of an economic responsibility, or even a liability, and contribute less and less to the family sustenance. Old people, particularly in the cities, have little or no function. Many other factors such as these contribute to the change in family significance and to the decline in the birth rate.

The effect of medical science on the population, though mixed, includes important influences towards cessation of growth and eventual decline. By increasing the expectancy of life some twenty years, medical science and a more protected form of life have been instrumental in a large increase of the number of people living in America. On the other hand much of this increase is in persons beyond the age of child bearing, with the result that, in respect to them, the birth rate is not increased in proportion to the increase in numbers.

The wide-spread knowledge of reliable methods of contraception or birth control has been an additional influence of importance in reducing the birth rate. This voluntary birth control is gradually reaching all economic levels of people and all

224

regions. The decline in birth rate follows. Largely because of this it is now predicted that the population of America will reach its maximum in 1950.

Another influence on the size of population is immigration restriction. The large immigrations to America from Europe before and immediately after the world war brought not only many additional millions of people, but many millions of people in the productive period of life who did not have American family standards nor a desire for only a limited number of children. These immigrations were checked and probably will stay checked.

Probably the most important influence towards the decline of population, however, is the increasing tendency towards urban life. In the city the young and the old are usually useless. They have no functional part. They are not integrated significantly in the social structure. They are carried, rather, as a superfluous burden on the backs of persons of productive age. In consequence, a large number of children or elderly dependents in the city family may make the difference between success and a good standard of living for the family and failure. Where there is knowledge of contraceptive methods it is only natural that the number of children in families will be small. As for the old people, more and more institutional agencies, pension systems, social security projects and the like are developed to take them from individual care and put them on society in general.

The primary cause of the declining birth rate and the imminent decline in population is really the kind of social system in which we live. Agencies such as voluntary birth control are only agencies. They express deeper conditions.

The city does not reproduce itself. It probably never has and never will. With the rural districts declining in population to a remnant of their former number there is reason to believe that they cannot much longer supply the urban deficiency with their surplus. The urban system has the elements of self-destruction in it. That destruction may not be postponed much longer.

But the size of America's population is hardly a matter of public policy. Thus far, at least, natural forces have been allowed to take their course. What the country's population should be to provide a proper balance between food supply, resources, power and protection, labor supply, high standards of living and other desiderata cannot be estimated accurately. The optimum population may be 170,000,000 as some suggest. It may be 200,000,000. It may be 150,000,000. The optimum size of population will depend, at least in some measure, on the age constitution and age balance of the population.

The size of population, in other words, is closely related to the ages of the people in that population. Rapid changes in the age groups of Americans raise a problem of first importance. The balance between age groups is shifting in favor of older people. This ageing of America has been going on for a long time, according to statisticians. But the rate of ageing of population today is faster. The median age in 1820 was 16.7 years. In 1930 it was 26.4 years. Although the total population increased between 1920 and 1930 more than 17,000,000 the

226

number of children under five years old in 1930 was 128,840 less than in 1920. And in 1930 for the first time the number of persons in a younger group, namely children under five years, was less than the next older group.

While the children under five years were declining in number, however, the number of persons between 65 and 74 was increasing by one-third, and the number of persons between 45 and 64 was increasing by one-fourth. By 1950 the proportion of people more than sixty-five years of age will probably have increased by one-half. This is a change from 5.4 percent to about 8 percent of the population. And by 1950 the proportion of people more than forty-five years old will have increased from 22.8 percent to about 30 percent. With this ageing of the population will come inevitable changes in the character and culture of society. Those changes, in my opinion, will not be entirely welcome.

Since these changes are taking place under conditions that are increasingly urban, we may assume that not only will there be a large increase in people beyond the age of greatest productivity, but that these people in increasing numbers will find themselves without work or social function. The urban system tends more and more to use the labor only of men in their most productive years and to carry children, elders, and many women as excess baggage. This excess baggage will increase by a considerable proportion. The burden of production, of taxes, of economic and social responsibility will be borne by a relatively smaller group.

Though it may be argued that technological advances will

make this burden easier to carry, it remains true that an unbalanced distribution of burden and responsibility makes for an unstable and precarious system. It withdraws significance from the lives of the elders and the women who cannot carry their load in modern urban society. It makes children a liability and a handicap to their parents. It withdraws from men in their productive years the opportunity for creative leisure and significant art. It tends to create a situation in which the state, or community as a whole, must take over more and more of the functions of life. It disintegrates human character and personality.

The increasing lack of balance among the age groups of our population, accompanied by the increasing tendency to segregate productive work in one age group, has far-reaching consequences in society and in art. Most of those consequences are bad. The disposition to turn matters of art, taste, and formal expression over to otherwise unoccupied women and elderly people will bring about decline and failure in the fields of expression. This is not the fault of the women or the elders. It is the fault of a system that withdraws integral significance from their lives. Art becomes a merely decorative possession. It is acquired or purchased. Because it is no longer identified with the significant and responsible activities of life, it becomes essentially frivolous. House building for homes and families that are no longer productive but merely consuming units shows this decay. It becomes sentimental, merely decorative, without significant function.

Whether this lack of balance between age groups is a mat-
228

ter in which social planning can be effective is doubtful. Policy that promotes a higher birth rate and a higher percentage of children and young people would have at least a temporary effect. A policy to distribute significant activity over a broader basis of age groups would have more importance. But that means an emphasis on a rural or small-town system of family units, no doubt, rather than the present urban type of development. In the functional family persons of all ages, from little Bobbie to grandmother, have at least some part. Such a family is almost impossible under modern conditions of wage labor and division of labor in the cities and of commercial farming auxiliary to the cities.

The sex balance in population, even more than the age balance, is a matter that, for the present at least, nature takes care of without artificial interference. If science finds a way to pre-determine the sex of children a problem will no doubt arise. At present only a few social factors, such as the immigration of males into America and the check of that immigration, the migration of males to the west, the lower death rate of women under modern conditions, the somewhat higher infant mortality of boys, affect the situation. These are social influences, except perhaps the last, that somewhat affect the balance of the sexes. In 1910 there were 106 males to 100 females in America. This was due to immigration of more men from Europe and to the normal excess of male births. It was counterbalanced by the higher death rate of males in all age groups. In 1930 there were 102.5 males to 100 females in the United States. The tendency is towards equalization.

Regional balance of population has proceeded with the growth of the country. Due to the accident of settlement and the east-to-west flow of folk migration, the eastern states have had a great predominance in population. This is slowly giving way to a more equal distribution. California and Florida, on the western and southern periphery of the country, grew most rapidly during the decade between 1920 and 1930. The center of population for the United States has moved westward until now it is in Indiana.

A balanced society depends in great measure on regional balance in population. In this respect the United States is naturally fortunate. The regions in it most capable of supporting a large population are widely distributed. With great resources in soil, coal, and iron, the Middle West can and probably will in time support the greater part of our population. With many diversified soils, beautiful climate, with water power and mineral resources the Far West will become no doubt another region of large population. The Southeast is a third great region capable of supporting a large population. Any policies that will tend to aid this kind of life and population in the Middle West, the Far West and the South will contribute to the balance of our society.

All of these regions are adapted to agrarian and self-sustaining life in small towns and the country. They are not by nature dependent on urban organization. The East, on the other hand, particularly the Central and Northeast, is more urban in character now, and presumably will remain so. It also has the greater mass of population.

230

The social problem in this respect is to prevent the urban East from exploiting other regions as a hinterland, draining wealth and youth from the South and the West without corresponding return. Though economists may consider such a one-way drainage of wealth a fallacy, not a fact, there are some indications that it does take place. On the other hand there already is a tendency by urban centers in the West towards greater financial and economic independence from New York. When—and if—the West and South find their security in their native soil and culture, without too much centralization even in their own cities, they will have reached a kind of stabilization that will give significance and endurance to civilization in America. This will depend, in great measure, on further balance in regional populations.

But the actual trend of population in recent years does not entirely bear out this thesis. Of nine states which gained more than twenty percent between 1920 and 1930, four were a part of the industrial, urban East, namely, New York, New Jersey, North Carolina, Michigan. Of the eighteen states that grew less than ten percent, according to Thompson and Whelpton, fourteen were agricultural western or southern states, namely, Virginia, South Carolina, Georgia, Kentucky, Arkansas, Minnesota, Iowa, Missouri, North Dakota, South Dakota, Nebraska, Kansas, Montana, and Idaho. The tide clearly has not yet turned. A regional balance is not assured.

The occupational balance of population is another problem of great importance. In a society where the centrifugal forces are of great power and things move with increasing speed

231

towards an unbalanced and disintegrative situation, the balance of occupations and of occupational ideologies becomes critically important. Human occupations may be integrative and stabilizing in nature, or they may be specialized and disintegrative in their human effect. To the first group belong those occupations that include a cycle of living, the beginning, the middle and the end of a significant activity, a completeness of action that is identified with a completeness of life. To the second group belong specialized activities, fragmentary parts of an impersonal organization of activities that is planned with a view to efficient mass production rather than with a view to a human cycle of action.

In the first group of occupations is self-sustaining agricultural life as contrasted with commercial or cash crop agriculture. Home industries and crafts, small town industries and services within the neighborhood for the market also belong here. Food production and processing, textiles and clothing, furniture and much building, live stock, forestry, the small town newspaper, the school, the machine shop, the miller, the music teacher—all activities of this sort can be integrated rather fully with the life of the individual and the community.

In the second group of occupations are specialized jobs in the factory, specialized jobs in sales and business organizations, sales managers, shipping clerks, production managers, advertising copy writers, authorities on Chaucer, authorities on colloids, tea tasters, tomato can labelers and so on ad infinitum. Such jobs are usually associated with mass production methods and extreme division of labor. They make for greater production in quantity. They belong to urban civilization but they cannot be integrated either with the individual's whole life or with that of his community. Usually his individual life, so far as he has one, and his neighborhood community, so far as there is one, are sharply segregated from his work.

In America there has been a rapid change in occupational population from the first group to the second. In 1920 about 40,800,000 persons were gainfully occupied in the United States. In 1930, more than 48,100,000 were gainfully occupied. During that decade the number of housewives, not gainfully employed, numbered about 23,000,000, with a slight decline in percentage. The number of persons at school, about 24,000,000, gained some two percent. Of all the persons gainfully occupied, according to Hurlin and Givens, those in agriculture and allied occupations numbered in 1910 more than 10,800,000 while in 1930 they numbered less than 10,300,000, a decline from 30.3 percent to 21.3 percent. Persons in the manufacturing and mechanical industries in 1910 numbered 10,250,000 and in 1930 numbered 13,790,000. This in both 1910 and 1930 was 28.6 percent of the total number of persons gainfully occupied. Persons in trade and transportation in 1910 numbered 6,223,000 and in 1930 numbered 9,963,000. This was a gain from 17.4 percent to 20.7 percent. Persons in clerical occupations in 1910 numbered 1,635,000 and in 1930 numbered 3,935,000. This was a gain from 4.6 percent to 8.2 percent. Persons in domestic and personal service in 1910 numbered 3,805,000 and in 1930 numbered 5,448,000. This was a gain from 10.6 percent to 11.3 percent. Persons in professional service in 1910 numbered 1,727,000 and in 1930 numbered 3,110,000. This was a gain from 4.8 percent to 6.3 percent.

It is clear from these statistics that specialized, urban types of occupations are gaining relatively to the more integral and completely sustaining kind of occupations. Due to greater efficiency and labor saving machinery the percentage of persons in the manufacturing industries has not increased, though the actual number has increased, but this is more than made up by the large percentage increase in clerical work, personal services and professional work. Meanwhile, the total number of those occupied in agriculture has declined. The percentage in agriculture has declined nearly one-third.

Though the number of persons in household industries, not gainfully employed, has remained statistically about the same for a number of years, it is clear that the content and amount of actual production in household industry—such as canning, baking, laundry, serving, cooking, care of children, education —has declined greatly. In the two great fields of decentralized production, agriculture and household arts, the decline of production for use has been very great.

The occupational balance of our population has changed rapidly in recent decades in favor of the urban type and pattern of work. It is a change that in my opinion again makes for insecurity and social precariousness. The lack of balance in this field is a matter in which policy and social planning can be effective. By focusing on the problem through technological, legislative, and educational agencies, a great deal can be done, if we desire it, towards bringing about a better and more stable occupational balance.

Cheap electrical power is one way towards this end. Within certain limits it is not improbable that even free electrical power, to be furnished by cooperative or federal ownership of mines and water power facilities and power plants, would be economically justified in the effect that it would have in populating and building up the countryside, and in increasing home and small community production. Cheap electrical equipment, such as small power machines, pumps, refrigerators, heaters, separators, washers, ironers, mixers and other household and small shop fixtures, is another way to bring about occupational decentralization. Cooperative or federal help in producing, financing, and marketing equipment of this sort would probably be necessary. In the Tennessee Valley Authority region, electric power that was brought cheaply into one small rural area, namely Colbert and Lauderdale counties in Alabama, was followed in a few months, says T. Levron Howard, by six new grist mills, five small cotton gins, one small abattoir, and numerous dairy coolers, electric churns, tool grinders, refrigerators, electric ranges, pumps, and other devices. In a north Alabama county seven percent of the homes to which electricity was brought for the first time were thoroughly remodeled, or entirely new homes constructed.

"Some farmers," says Dr. Howard, "have taken electricity when it has been a pinch for them to find room for it in their limited budgets. But the presence of power on their farms has led them at once to devise ways and means of using that power for the increase of their cash income. Already there have sprung up small manufacturing operations which the farmer and one or two helpers can carry on small scale, semi-industrial operations, sometimes carried on in the farmer's woodshed."

Other technological methods such as soil conservation devices, crop improvement devices, labor-saving devices on the farm, and new forestry methods are possible. Cooperative tractors and refrigerators, cooperative techniques and machinery in small towns: all of these, with intelligent planning and promotion, can enter into a planned policy of decentralization.

Legislative aids to occupational decentralization are more familiar. Much of Secretary Wallace's efforts to balance the legislative advantage that urban industry now has in respect to commercial agriculture, could also apply in respect to distributive or decentralized industry both on the farm and in the small town. So far as legislation encourages soil conservation, crop diversification, production for use as well as production for sale, and a permanent family tenure of the land, it is an agency towards the balance of our occupational population. Tenant farmer legislation and tax programs favoring home owners have also been mentioned.

An educational policy designed to encourage a better balance in occupations would involve a change in educational emphases that turns away from specialization and the training for the so-called white collar vocations, and turns towards an integrative and self-reliant point of view towards life. In some

236

respects the educational failure in this respect is greater than our economic and political failures. A falsely "cultural" or pseudo-cultural education on the one hand, or a rigidly specialized training on the other, is about all that American institutions offer. Both are based on an acquisitive attitude towards education. Imported cultures, superimposed eclectic tastes derived from alien sources, are plastered on our youth. The plaster soon scales off. Only a bleached and sunless mind is left. The failure in education deeply underlies the false attitudes, ambitious urbanism, and precarious economics of modern America. It is a failure particularly of that aspect of education that is called "philosophy."

The modern desuetude of philosophy and of most philosophers in the universities is indicative of this educational failure. Philosophy is defeated, or thinks it is. It drifts without purpose, without courage, manned by mediocre men who can neither teach, think, nor write; it goes with the tides, back and forth across the harbor of academicism, too weak to dare the sea. Other men have deserted it for specialties and semiscientific efforts to probe particular problems of knowledge. Only a few—such as John Dewey, T. V. Smith, Bertrand Russell, A. N. Whitehead or youngsters such as Charner Perry, Norman Bradish, Paul Schilpp—have realized the significance of philosophy as a creative integration in modern thought and modern action, and have gone out with it to meet reality. It is noteworthy that much of the work of these men and others like them has been done outside of the universities.

I have discussed balance in population in respect to rural and urban groups, age groups, sex groups, regional populations and occupational groups. Three of these—namely, rural and urban groups, regional populations, and occupational groups—are to a great extent matters of public policy. That there is not balance in these three fields seems obvious.

The effects of this disastrous lack of balance may be seen in many places. Two of the most serious effects are in land wastage and in cultural and folk wastage due to the differential decline in birth rates. The recent soil survey of the United States shows that some 50,000,000 acres of formerly cultivated land have been ruined for cultivation by erosion. This removes from use an area equal to all the farms of the thirteen original states. Fifty million acres more have been so damaged by erosion that they should be used only for hay and pasture or forest. Another 100,000,000 acres have been considerably eroded. Still another 100,000,000 acres have suffered somewhat. Nearly half of the arable land of this country has been damaged. The loss in soil resources, according to O. E. Baker, amounts probably to 25 percent. Were such a loss suffered in terms of conquered territory, Americans would consider it a catastrophe of terrible consequence. When we pour an empire equal to one-fourth of all our farm land down the Mississippi and other rivers, however, the soil-laden streams hardly gain our comment. It is an example of a failure in balance that arises from our way of living; our urban, exploitative attitudes; our commercial, cash profit farming;

238

our unwillingness to think of life and the land as a naturally balanced, cyclical system.

A second effect characteristic of our modern lack of balance is in the declining birth rates in different groups. There are now fewer children in the United States than there were a third of a century ago. The decline in birthrate is about 35 percent. If present trends continue, says Dr. Baker, there will be a rapid decline in population in a few decades. In 1930, for example, the number of children under five years of age of American stock in cities of over 100,000 population was some 40 percent below the number required to maintain the population of these cities. In all cities of more than 100,000 the deficit was 22 percent. In smaller towns it was 7 percent. In rural non-farm population there was a surplus of 30 percent, and in rural farm population a surplus of 50 percent. In 1930, according to Dr. Baker, the urban deficit and rural surplus about balanced. It would keep the population of the nation permanently stationary. But the birthrate has fallen another 10 per cent since 1930.

Among the occupational groups the unskilled laborers in the cities are still reproducing themselves. Among skilled and semi-skilled laborers there is a deficit in birth rate of about 10 percent. Among business and clerical groups there is a deficit of 25 per cent. Among professional groups there is a deficit of 30 to 40 percent. This, again, is an example of lack of balance. Farm laborers have more children than farm owners. Urban laborers have more children than business and professional men. It is a situation that requires the continual re-education of cultural groups. And those least able to give their children an education and to inculcate complex traditions have the most children. The result, of course, is that educational and cultural responsibility falls more and more on the government. Great standardized centers of education are established. An intimate and integrated education becomes well-nigh impossible.

Balance in population is a complex and difficult problem, so far as it enters the realm of conscious problems at all, that must be met courageously in order to prevent dynamic disorders and collapse. Balance in industry is a second aspect of the problem of a balanced society. I shall discuss that next.

Industrial balance and lack of balance have many obvious coordinations with balance in population. I shall consider three industrial patterns and their balance in respect to each other. They are centralized industrial production, cooperative industrial production, and decentralized industrial production.

Industrial production has been moving towards greater centralization for many years. The trend of invention and of the increasing mechanization of power has in general accelerated this centralization. The machine age has seen the displacement of unskilled labor by machines operated by fewer skilled men. The power age has seen the displacement of much skilled labor and individual machines by larger, more automatic and more integrated machines and a few semi-skilled laborers. Seven men in 1935 could produce the same amount of industrial goods that ten men produced in 1920. Thus the tendency, in some important fields at least, is to centralize industrial production around greater unit use of power and machinery but with fewer men. In terms of horsepower the increase in scale of production is evident.

Between 1914 and 1927, according to Willard L. Thorp in "The President's Committee Report on Recent Economic Changes," the average number of wage earners per manufacturing establishment in the United States increased 12 percent, the horsepower establishment increased 63 percent, the value of products per establishment increased 141 percent. During about the same time, namely from 1914 to 1923, the number of establishments employing from six to 20 men increased slightly more than one percent, while the number of establishments employing more than 1,000 men increased more than fifty percent. The number of intermediary establishments showed proportional increases.

In terms of industrial mergers this increasing concentration is also shown. Between 1919 and 1928 there were 124 mergers in the oil industry with 641 concerns disappearing. In coal there were 58 mergers with 238 concerns disappearing. In iron and steel there were 270 mergers with 1,094 concerns disappearing. In textiles there were 104 mergers with 401 firms disappearing. In motor vehicles there were 67 mergers with 300 concerns disappearing. In foodstuffs there

241

were 128 mergers with 835 concerns disappearing. In lumber and paper there were 91 mergers with 419 concerns disappearing. There are many other examples. In 1926, 1,029 public utility concerns disappeared through merger and acquisition. In 1927, 911 disappeared.

Financial concentration of industrial control naturally accompanied, where it did not cause, this process. In 1930 there were 300,000 non-financial corporations in the United States. Forty-nine percent of the corporate wealth of these was controlled by 200 corporations. These 200 corporations, according to Berle and Means, controlled at least 39 percent of all business wealth in the United States. The 24 partners of J. P. Morgan and Co. in 1933 were also directors of 89 other corporations with assets more than 20 billion dollars.

Facts such as these, and there are many more, indicate the extent of industrial concentration in America. It shows incidentally the correlated concentration of financial and property control.

Public ownership of industrial establishments is advocated by many persons, not as a way to eliminate concentration, but of getting it under control. It is assumed by them that the evils of industrial concentration are in their private ownership and management. Usually they neither recognize nor make protest against serious evils in the fact of concentration itself. They are, of course, partially right. Though private management also has some social advantages, it is true that many of the evils in centralized industrial systems as we now know them arise from the anti-social tendencies that inhere in the

242

profit system under these conditions. In some fields in industry, transportation, and public utilities, government ownership and control is probably the most feasible method of correction of those evils. The mails, the highways, the electric utilities, the railroads, the telegraph and telephone systems, the coal mines, probably should be government-owned.

But to grant this extension of governmental function does not mean that centralization is itself an ideal for industrial and other systems, nor does it mean that there should be increasing centralization in all fields. We can grant centralization in those fields where the economic function requires great extension and at the same time operative unity, but we need not grant centralization elsewhere. The socialist assumption that centralization in all fields is itself the natural and best pattern of economic and social life is by no means justified. It probably is a practical necessity in some fields, and it is only that.

Opposed to the thesis of extreme concentration and governmental ownership is the cooperative method. The cooperatives differ from state socialism chiefly in keeping their different functions and operations separate from and independent of each other in operation, and in refusing to organize them together under the politically authoritative state. Political and economic functions for them remain distinct. They are, as it were, a form of economic democracy that differs from state socialism in being more decentralized and more democratic. Their philosophy, says Wade Crawford Barclay, is a "society regulated by voluntary agreement in which every man has equal voice with every other man. Their collectivism is a concert of action in the determination of which every individual has an equal share."

Governments which own or regulate industries and utilities are often captured for the advantage of private interests, as Dr. Barclay points out, but the cooperatives by their democratic structure and method of operation avoid this danger. By returning their profits to their own members they furthermore prevent the drainage of wealth out of the rural districts and out of the hands of the poorer people whence it is sluiced to the great cities and the rich. Their economic consequence is definitely towards decentralization and regional equality, though their method involves centralization of purchasing power and management.

Some students of the subject, such as Ralph Borsodi, would go so far as to say that cooperation rather than government should be used for social insurance, for public utilities and railroads, for credit and money systems, for schools. Whether the cooperative should replace private and governmental functions to this extent is doubtful. But in any case the cooperative should have a larger part in our system than it now has.

The cooperatives, both producer and consumer cooperatives and the credit cooperatives, are indeed a most important technique in maintaining democratic decentralization and in preventing the increasing domination of the city. They can be a powerful balance against the increasing concentration of industrial production, of wealth and of population in the ur-

244

ban districts. In America, however, they have not developed as yet to a size and power where they can exert much balancing effect. Sweden has broken private monopoly by the cooperative method. In Switzerland, Finland, Denmark, and England they have become major factors in the economic life. In the United States they are successful local phenomena in some regions, such as Minnesota, Ohio, and Idaho, and in some fields such as gas and oil; but they are not yet in large-scale operation sufficient to alter the economic character of the country to any great degree.

Some 3,000 gas and oil societies sold their members in 1936 more than $48,000,000 worth of petroleum products and returned patronage dividends to their members amounting to $6,000,000. In Dillonville, Ohio, in an impoverished mining section, the cooperative during a period of 27 years has had total sales of $3,005,747, has a reserve of $112,-359, assets of $206,946, and has paid its members in rebates, thus increasing local purchasing power, $241,803. These are examples of what can be done.

One important reason why the ownership of farm lands has been considerably centralized, it has been pointed out, is because farmers have permitted the marketing of farm products and the supplying of farm consumer needs to pass into hands other than their own. Farmers' unions and cooperatives have been organized to meet this problem. So far as the farmer must turn to commercial or cash crop agriculture, the cooperative becomes a most important instrument for his protection.

245

The cooperative is a method of utilizing collective methods without accepting many of its evils. Though the cooperatives alone will not solve the American problem they should have a far larger part than they now have in any balanced pattern of industry and economic life. Whether they can flourish greatly under American conditions is hard to say. They are, in any case, potentially an instrument of first importance, not yet realized.

A third pattern of industrial and economic life is decentralized industry. In America this issues in two separate phenomena. There is, first, what may be called vestigial decentralization. The old agrarian, the household, homemaking industries and the craft industries of our fathers still hold on in some regions and among some groups. Though these are more and more scattered and broken as the years pass, they remain in our tradition rather firmly. The "South," meaning the Southeast, is probably most devoted to this ideal. But the farms and crafts of New England, the rich acres of Pennsylvania, the transplanted agrarians and craftsmen of the mountains and the far west, the Indian Pueblos of the Southwest, the religious communities of Iowa, Virginia, Pennsylvania and elsewhere show the vitality and sweetness of the older life in America.

The second phenomenon in America having to do with decentralized economic and industrial life is the later and more deliberate return to decentralization on the part of many industries, and by families and individuals leaving the urban districts. Part of this movement towards decentralization is for the sake of industrial efficiency and saving. Part of it is for social, human, educational, and cultural purposes of prime importance.

This more deliberate movement is not large enough, thus far, to change the general character of the industrial and economic pattern. It is an important tendency, however, that may in time alter the balance or over-balance of industry as it is now. There is a tendency on the part of large industries to move from metropolitan centers to cities of somewhat smaller size. In 1927, for example, 94 industrial plants left cities of more than 500,000, while only 23 entered them. Thirteen plants left cities of 300,000 to 500,000, while nine entered them. Sixteen left cities of 100,000 to 200,000, while 38 entered them. Twenty plants left cities of 10,000 to 25,000, while 40 entered them. Forty-six plants left cities under 10,-000, while 44 entered them. There is also a tendency for concerns to break up their plants and distribute them among smaller towns. Mr. Ford has done this in an enlightened manner by making provision for the laborer to have a garden, a home, and part-time occupations outside of his factory work, and at the same time retain good wages. Other concerns have decentralized in this way in order to drive down wages and to break their workmen's solidarity. Other abuses of this sort, such as piece-work at home in the sewing industries, are well known.

There has been considerable success in the establishment of small, well-managed shops and factories owned and often operated by a family and a few helpers. These produce for the

247

local market. Sometimes they have a regular market in some larger concern or store at a distance. Cabinet making, machine shops, industrialized arts, agricultural specialties, jam making, and textile crafts are illustrations of this kind of decentralization. Small industries, if well managed, often save in overhead and distribution costs more than the larger concerns can save through purchasing power and through other advantages that lie in large organization. There is a point, which varies in different fields, where larger organization costs more than it saves. Some industries are finding this out. Plants in large cities, says Thorp, are decreasing in size.

These industrial tendencies are ameliorative. They do not meet the central evil of over-centralization. They are all to the good but such changes in industrial organization alone will not produce a stable balance of economic life. This balance can be brought about only when larger numbers of families and workers live under conditions in which they themselves produce and consume most of the things necessary to a good life.

Agriculture, home making, and local craft work naturally become the industrial foci of such a movement. All of them are capable of adjustment to a self-sustaining system. It is the misfortune of the modern world that they have become, in the minds of many people, only quaint and futile relics of old times. This ironic sentiment, however, is both ignorant and false. It is the product, no doubt, of the same kind of urban advertising and "sophistication" that labels all persons "hicks" who do not clamor for the urban kind of thing and the smartness of Broadway.

There is no good reason why the benefits of science, invention, and flexible power cannot be turned to the self-sustaining integral life. Modern invention and progress are not necessarily identified with the centralized organization of life. Only a confusion as to the real nature of applied science and of large organization makes them identical. The essential instability in personal and social life that marks urban organization, furthermore, will bring even urban values to early disaster. Decentralization in modern terms may require some radical readjustments, even social invention, but that is preferable, even from the point of view of urban psychology, to collapse.

Great numbers of people, indeed, are finding the conditions of life imposed by highly centralized, unbalanced industrial production intolerable. These are not only the millions of jobless folk who have no security aside from public relief, but many young, well-educated persons who see no satisfactory future for themselves in the intricate and impersonal organization of the cities.

Many of these people have returned to the rural regions, or are planning to, and under great handicaps are trying to live the cycle of the soil. With little training, and against the odds of a system not set for that kind of endeavor, it is surprising that any number at all succeed. Few figures are available as to that number. The two million who remain of the six million persons who migrated from the cities to the rural districts during the depression of 1930–36 are no doubt in part members of that group. There are many others scattered over the country on small farms and homesteads who approximate the self-sustaining cycle of life. There will be more.

Balance in property in America is partly a question of balance between those who have property and those who do not have property, and partly a question of balance between those who have one kind of property and those who have another kind of property. The problem of property has been made the center of many efforts towards economic and social reform. The socialists and revolutionary communists start their dialectic journey towards Utopia from that problem. The distributists, represented by Hilaire Belloc, Chesterton and others, also make the property question central in their attacks on both the capitalistic and collectivist forms of organization. Though I doubt whether the problem of property so overwhelmingly dominates the modern situation as these groups would make out, I of course recognize it as of major importance.

The meaning of the word "property" has long been debated by the specialists. I shall discuss for the most part that aspect of it which relates to the means and instruments of the production of wealth. As Belloc says, "The name for a control of the Means of Production is 'Property.'" It is in respect to this aspect of property that the question of balance in America is critically important. Though goods—such as candy and cigarettes, pleasure automobiles and dinner coats, grapefruit and silk stockings, which are used primarily for consumption—are rather widely distributed in the United States, a balance of consumption goods, or a balance among those who possess consumption goods, does not greatly affect the control of life or a just distribution of freedom and power. It is, on the other hand, the balance among those who control goods, such as shoe-making machines, steel mills, land, mines, tractors, printing presses, which are used primarily for the production of other goods, that determines the character not only of economic life but, to a great extent, of life in general.

In property of this latter sort, namely production property, or just "property," there is a great lack of balance in America. Both in land and in industrial property this lack of balance has been growing greater and greater as the years go by.

The technological evolution of industrial production in the last century or so has moved towards the production of goods in larger and larger units. This has been accompanied by the use of great power in machines of larger and larger capacity, and the production of goods by those machines in greater quantities or masses of standardized articles. This is the cycle of modern mass production. Coal power, or the power of some other natural resource, is concentrated in huge engines or power plants. These in turn drive great machines near by which produce in huge quantities certain standardized goods.

On the structure of property rights this technological evolution has had a great effect. In the old days of the hand crafts a weaver, for example, very likely owned his own hand loom and operated it in his own house. The blacksmith probably owned his own forge and used it in his own shop in the village. The miller probably owned his own mill, with a few sons or paid workers from the neighborhood to help him. The dyer and the fletcher probably owned their own tools. The wright, the fisher, the baker, the tanner, the hunter, the butcher, the carter, the chandler, the howard, the tailor, the barber, the potter, the thrasher—all these and many more probably owned whatever instruments were necessary to produce the goods appropriate to them. The ownership of productive property was widely distributed, and the balance of property in this sense was equalized in great measure among many elements of the population.

This kind of balance gave a considerable economic stability. It gave stability because the control of the means of industrial production was on a wide base. A man controlled in great measure his means of livelihood without dependence on the decisions and disciplines of many persons more or less remote from him. This stability was limited by his meager resources and his meager power, with hand or horse, to produce. It was stability limited by scarcity in contrast to the modern system of great power and resources, mass production, and abundance limited by the instability of a highly centralized machine. Such a machine stops when any one of a number of persons fails; or it stops perhaps of its own glut. In the one case there was stability with scarcity. In the other case there is instabil-

252

ity with abundance. The ideal situation, if ever it can be attained, is obviously stability with abundance.

In the modern world the instruments of industrial production are likely to be highly complicated; costly machines, housed in huge buildings, fed by great quantities of coal, oil, raw materials. They cannot well be owned by the individual worker. They now are less often owned even by the individual manager or manufacturer. They become the property of groups of financiers, pools, banks. They are remotely controlled. Their stopping and starting, and the hiring and firing that go with them, the wages and the conditions of labor, the amount and quality of their product, the buying and selling, the borrowing and building—all these are parts of a great impersonal organization in which the individual workman has little influence, and no security beyond whatever security his job may have. He has no property right—in 1937—either in the instruments of production or in his job.

By this well-known process, partly technological, partly economic, financial, and social, industrial property in America, as well as in most of the Occident, has become highly concentrated. The means to life are not in the hands of those who live.

This is illustrated by the distribution of income in the United States according to segments of the population. In 1929 four-fifths of the wage-earning population had only two-fifths of the national income. The individual incomes of these forty million wage earners were less than two thousand dollars a year. In 1929 less than three-tenths of one percent of the population gainfully occupied had more than seventeen percent of the national income. In other words, 141,523 people had an income of $15,591,000,000 while 39,612,300 people had an income of $40,282,000,000. The other ratios show corresponding inequality.

In 1929, according to Doane, some 99 percent of the people in the United States had incomes not greater than $5000, but 83 percent of the liquid wealth of the country was in the hands of the one percent of the people whose incomes were greater than $5000. Again, it has been shown by the Brookings Institution that in 1929 about 6,000,000 families, or 21 percent, had annual incomes of less than $1000. It was also shown that about 36,000 families at the top of the income scale received as much income as 11,500,000 families at the bottom of the scale. So it goes. Property is more and more concentrated as the modern economic system matures and drifts off into senility. Security grows less.

In agriculture, the growth of tenancy marks the increasing alienation of productive property from those who operate it. This is accompanied, in many regions, by increasing concentration of farm ownership. In any case the farm under these conditions becomes ever to a greater degree a property used only for the production of cash income both by tenants and owners, and the old agrarian security to that extent declines.

The results are disastrous to agrarian life and its people, and to the soil that supports them. Said O. E. Baker at the conference on Integral Society at Northwestern University:

254

"The farmers in most parts of the United States are slowly losing the ownership of the land. The equity of farm operators in farm real estate, that is, the amount left after the value of real estate operated by tenants and mortgage debts on real estate operated by owners is subtracted from the total value of farm real estate, constituted about 63 percent of the total value in 1880. In 1890 the figure was 58 percent, in 1900 about 55 percent, in 1910 just 50 percent, in 1920 only 46 percent. In 1930 the proportion has fallen to 42 percent, and in 1935, although the mortgage debt returns from the census are not yet fully tabulated, it appears likely that it is below 40 percent. In 55 years the proportion of the farm lands and buildings in the nation really owned by the farm operator has fallen from nearly two-thirds to only two-fifths. In prosperity, as well as in depression, the decline has been about four points each ten years. Should this decline continue for another 55 years, the farm operators would own only one-fifth of the farm real estate of the nation. Four-fifths will belong to persons other than farmers.

"This proportion is being rapidly approached in the Corn Belt. In Illinois, Iowa, and South Dakota in 1930 the farm operators really owned less than 30 percent of the land, and it is probable that now they own little more than a quarter. Corporations, mostly insurance companies and banks, owned 10 percent of the farm real estate of Iowa, on January 1, 1935. In the wheat regions the equity of farm operators in farm real estate ranged from 38 percent in Montana to 28 percent in South Dakota. In the Cotton Belt, the proportion varied between 30 and 40 percent but owing to the system of land tenure by croppers, who really are laborers paid with a portion of the crop, this figure exaggerates the real situation. On the other hand, a cropper is much lower down the economic and social scale than a tenant in the Corn Belt, and as most of the plantation owner-operators live in the towns and cities their interests more and more tend to build up the towns and cities rather than the open country. In the Dairy Belt from Maine to Maryland and Minnesota, and in the Corn and Winter Wheat Belt, which extends from Virginia to Southern Missouri and

Southeastern Kansas, where agriculture is less commercialized and the tradition of the farm as a home as well as a business persist strongly, the farmers have been more successful in retaining the ownership of the land. Indeed, in Pennsylvania, the equity of farm operators constituted over 60 percent of the total value of farm land in 1930, and there has been little change in this percentage for at least a half century.

"Migration of youth from the farms has been, in my opinion, the most important force inducing this loss of land ownership by farmers. This migration of rural youth to the cities has been the inevitable result of the invention of agricultural machinery, the increasing use of power in farming and other advances in agricultural technique associated with a birth rate in the farm population still 50 percent higher than that needed to maintain the farm population permanently stationary. During the decade 1920–1929 it is estimated by the U. S. Bureau of Agricultural Economics that over 19,000,000 people left the farms for the cities and that about 13,000,000 returned, leaving a net migration of over 6,000,000. About 60 percent of this migration was from the south."

This alienation of farm property from those who operate the farms is coordinated usually with a corresponding alienation of property from the agricultural regions in favor of the city. And with it the drift of population cityward goes on. On this Dr. Baker continues:

"Viewing the United States as a whole, will urban prosperity promote rapid migration of youth from the farms to the cities, particularly from farms on poor land, and thus tend toward a commercial production on a smaller land area? Or will urban unemployment, particularly a diminishing need for unskilled labor, prevent this migration and compel a backing up of rural youth on farms in the less fertile areas especially, such as occurred during the depression? This

256

would almost inevitably induce a less commercial agriculture. In other words, will agricultural production tend to concentrate on the better land, notably the Corn Belt, the more fertile portions of the Dairy Belt, the river bottom lands of the South, and the irrigated valleys of the West, as the commercial demand for farm products diminishes, with the less productive soils and hilly lands slowly reverting to pasture, and then to brush and forest, as the farmers in such districts grow old and die? This was the trend in many of the Eastern States for several decades prior to the depression. Or will agriculture expand and perhaps intensify in the poorer regions with the establishment of many new farms, particularly part-time farms, some clearly of forest and some subdivisions of farms, as occurred during the depression?

"No one can forecast with confidence which course American agriculture will follow in the years to come. But in my opinion the last course is more probable, though its development doubtless will be retarded until after the next depression, perhaps even longer. And it is my opinion, further, that the agencies for the promotion of agriculture, in particular the experiment stations and extension services, must study the situation and be prepared to help effectively self-sufficing and part-time farmers as well as commercial farmers.

"Nor is this all. When the farmer and his wife grow old and die, the estate is divided among the children. During the decade 1920–29 about one-fifth of the farmers and their wives died, and their estates were distributed among the children. One-third or more of the children had moved to town, and those children who remained on the farm had to mortgage the farm in many cases to pay the brothers and sisters who lived in the cities their share of the estate. A rough estimate indicates that between $3,000,000,000 and $4,000,000,000 was transferred from the farms to the cities and villages during the decade 1920–29 incident to the settlement of estates.

"Although it is not intended to draw up a balance sheet of rural-urban contributions, it is worthy of note, in passing, that there are great movements of farm wealth to the cities in addition to those incident to migration. Interest on debt paid to persons other than farm operators amounted to about $10,500,000,000. These payments are of a different character from the movement of wealth incident to migration, but there can be little doubt that portions of these payments were for the use of capital that had been previously transferred to the cities in the settlement of estates. The total amount from these four sources appears to have been about $33,000,000,000 during the decade, or $3,500,000,000 a year, which was about one-third of the average annual gross income of all farmers during the decade and roughly over half of their net income.

"During the economic depression migration from the farms was greatly retarded. Many farm youth found it impossible to obtain work in the cities. About 2,000,000 youth were backed up on farms who would under pre-depression conditions have migrated to the cities. But migration to farms continued during 1930–33 in pre-depression numbers, the movement to farms totaling about 6,000,000 during the five years 1930–34, of whom 2,000,000 are still on farms. Nevertheless, only in one year, 1932, did the movement to farms exceed that from farms in the nation as a whole.

"Despite this net movement from farms, considering the nation as a whole, the pressure of population on the land in many poorer farming areas has become intolerable. Most of this increase in farm population occurred in the Appalachian Mountain region, extending from New England to eastern Ohio and northern Georgia, in the Ozarks and in other poor farming areas. The decrease in farm population was notable in many cotton and tobacco districts and may be attributable in part to the low price of cotton and credit stringencies."

The tragic loss in soil and soil resources in the United States is a part of this picture. Already, as I have said, an area of soil equal to the crop area of the thirteen original states has been destroyed. Already one-fourth of our soil resources are gone. This soil loss is clearly a consequence to a great extent of our

258

social and ecomonic policy in respect to agrarian life. When family units with some sense of continuity and of value in farm life can sustain themselves successfully on the land, live on it and from it, with the necessity for a cash income reduced to a tolerable minimum, there will be a strong impulse to maintain the soil, to diversify crops, to prevent erosion, and to live in an enduring cycle with the soil.

Our present land policy, our social attitudes, our subservience to urban standards and ideas makes this at best difficult. It is a situation that is no doubt critical in the life of America and its institutions. Once more I quote from Dr. Baker, perhaps the foremost authority in this field:

"Prosperity cannot preserve our democratic American agriculture. Only the preservation of the rural home and family and the maintenance of rural institutions can do so, in my opinion. A continuity of family proprietorship in farming is essential. And continuity of family proprietorship is dependent on a philosophy of life. A philosophy of life is dependent on an ideal and gradually assumes the character, if it has any strength, of a religious conviction. Among these ideals is that of the home and the family farm and the preservation of the family line from generation to generation. This is the ideal that our parents and grandparents lived and labored for.

"Unless the farmers and farm women of the Nation think about these things and how they can aid their children to love the farm and the farming people, they will continue in all likelihood to lose the ownership of the land. Indeed, they may lose even more than this. They may lose the family as an institution for the protection and education of children and youth and for the provision of security in illness and old age. In fact, they have been gradually losing these functions of the family during many years. Otherwise, much of this

259

government relief would have been unnecessary. They may lose also the church as a social institution; they are losing it now. They may lose even the democratic organization of the state. Not that any dictator will destroy the constitution, rather that as the family fails to function the government must step in and assume the load to prevent the disintegration of society. The responsibility of the family decreases, the responsibility of the government increases, and eventually the spirit of democracy declines.

"It is becoming clear that the land is the foundation of the family, and that the family is the foundation of the democratic state."

Productive property, both urban and agricultural, is becoming more and more concentrated in the hands of those who do not directly use or operate it. In Chicago, for example, more than one-half of the real estate in the city was foreclosed by mortgage proceedings between 1929 and 1933, according to Hoyt. It is probably true that, if the period from 1929 to 1937 be considered, more than half of the home owners of Chicago have lost their equity. Such alienation of property is characteristic. Clearly there is not a stable balance of ownership of property in Chicago, in other cities, or in the rural regions.

In America a balanced property system would no doubt include five types or groups of ownership: (1) government ownership and operation of certain properties; (2) centralized private or corporate control and operation of certain industrial and commercial properties; (3) decentralized private ownership and operation of other industrial and commercial properties; (4) cooperative ownership and operation of some property; (5) decentralized ownership and operation of most agricultural properties. Already these five types of ownership

260

are parts of our economy. The lack of balance among them is due mainly to the inordinate growth and power of the second type, namely centralized private control of industrial and commercial property. So great has been its growth and its encroachment on the other types of ownership, that only the government seems to hold its own, even in a measure, against it. This is further aggravated by the fact that, in these days of finance-capitalism, the control, by bankers, is often divorced from the operation of the business. The bankers, in short, are doing to the managers what the managers once did to the individual craftsmen.

The centralization of property, so far as it is focused in the corporation, is not the natural and inevitable destiny of the economic system, as many assume. Legislation in many ways has been favorable to the corporations and indirectly unfavorable to other forms of ownership. Tax legislation, tariff legislation, the very definition in law of the corporation as a kind of deathless person, are all artificial supports of corporation control. There are many other ways in which corporation control is given artificial advantage. In the same way, absentee ownership of land becomes more easy and more usual as our land policy matures. Abstract control, or control by paper, of this primary means of production becomes more and more a burden that the actual operators and workers on the land must carry. An effort to balance the advantages, now held by corporation ownership in industry and by absentee ownership of farms, by corresponding advantages to other and more distributed forms of ownership is no doubt the main

261

necessity in this field. It will also require the abrogation of some of the advantages now held by the corporations.

Political balance has long been recognized as a problem within a democracy as well as a problem in maintaining a democracy. It is almost solely in this field, indeed, that the problem of balance in American life has been considered at all. From the days when the Constitution was written and adopted with its various checks and balances, political life in America has been a shifting set of balances, an equilibrium more or less precarious which has established the doctrine of "liberalism" in our politics and has given it character.

The balances are of various sorts. There is the balance between the people of property and those without property. In earlier days, when a larger proportion of people owned productive property, this was a matter of deliberate policy. Today, with property more concentrated, it no longer is openly recognized as a matter of political policy. Suffrage has been extended progressively while the distribution of productive property has declined. More people have a political vote, as it were, but relatively fewer people have an economic vote.

A balance between regions and population masses, as well as an inner balance of regions against regions, was contemplated in the formation of a bi-cameral legislature. The regional representation in the Senate, as contrasted with the populational representation in the House, though seemingly unfair, has been, as a fact, one of the most wholesome influences in the American political situation. There was also the functional balance between the executive, the legislative, and the judicial branches of government; the balance between the military and the civil in the control of national defense and of instruments designed to enforce internal order; the balance of local, state, and national powers.

This system of balances has worked fairly well. So far as these balances apply, the government of the United States has probably been more successful than any corresponding government during the same period. It has failed where the balance has broken down due to uncompensated forces—such as those that resulted in the war between the states—that were not fully faced and resolved in the formative years of the nation, or to new forces growing at unequal rates that have appeared as new factors in recent decades. Chief of these new forces is, of course, the growth of industrial power and property, in contrast to agriculture, and the formation of the great cities.

The great growth of cities in every region of the country, and the relative increase of industrial and commercial power and population, could hardly be contemplated by the fathers of the country. Though cities, to be sure, had been great in other lands and had contributed their characteristic problem to statesmanship, the industrial concentration that developed around the new use of power and machine did not exist. This is a new factor that has upset our political balance. For it there is no adequate provision in our present form of government.

The growth of large cities in every region of the country also tends to destroy the natural occupational balance that found representation in our early government. Human occupations have increased greatly in number. Division of labor and specialization have gone on apace. A man's occupation is increasingly likely to be entirely divorced from the ownership of appropriate productive property. These factors, combined with the fact that most of the people with new and diverse occupations are in the cities, overwhelming in numbers the rural populations near by, have brought about a lack of balance in political representation in reference to occupation that could hardly be contemplated in an early day. The socialists like to call the people in propertyless occupations the proletariat. As a fact, these people in America are much diversified, with greatly different skills and educations and with very different ideological patterns. But the problem of occupational representation and balance in our political system is nevertheless pertinent.

It is clear of course that the modern problem of political balance is closely associated with the corresponding problems of balance in industry, property, and population. Hitherto, political balance has been treated as the primary problem. In the future it should probably be secondary to the problems of balance in these other fields.

In the fields of art, religion, education and, indeed, human life the problem of balance is less obvious. The exertion of

264

power, the influence of quantity, is not characteristic of them. Balance, if there be balance, is clearly another sort of thing. This does not mean, however, that these interests are unrelated to other aspects of balanced life. Though fields of interest such as education, religion, and art are concerned with values that in themselves are not commensurate with energies, quantities of goods and their physical control and operation, they are nevertheless influenced in method and, we fear, in aim by the prevailing economic and industrial pattern. They, too, move towards standardization, division of labor, specialization, mass production. Their ends are the acquisition of cultural goods. They become matters of possession rather than of participation.

Modern education, particularly in the colleges, can hardly be said to have any important contact with intellectual or artistic life or with productive effort of any significance. The purpose for which colleges presumably were founded—namely, to develop the better capacities of youth and to give expression to the intellectual and spiritual life of a people—has been in effect abandoned. While the faculties are buried in the sterile dust of "scholarship" the students are absorbed in campus politics and in social and athletic competitions. Not all the teaching staff nor all of the students accept this cultural impotence, to be sure, but most of them do and seem, indeed, to prefer it. "Scholarship" has become an arrogant word in most institutions of higher learning. The word bears all the orthodoxy of its monastic source. It is now used to cloak mean minds or dull ones with formal robes of academic prestige.

This educational situation, this sterility and arrogance of scholarship, is a result mainly of our efforts to handle students in masses, to fix external rewards, to standardize by external, quantitative measures, and above all to specialize the intellectual and cultural life in numerous, mutually exclusive departments. It is no wonder that there is so little intellectual initiative and courage in the colleges when their methods are so similar to those in economic life that have well-nigh destroyed the free, self-sustaining person.

In the arts the situation is somewhat similar. Art is set off from the rest of living activities as a specialized mode of experience and, like education, is treated as something that one acquires rather than what one does. It, too, has become purchasable and, because purchasable, highly specialized. Though initiative and genius in the arts is more usual than in education, it is likely to be a lonely initiative and a but partly expressed genius in a world where standardization and specialization are the dominant modes of attainment. The imaginative faculty is quantitatively incompatible with such standardization and specialization.

In religion we find many of those official vehicles of the spirit called the churches turning with considerable courage to meet the modern social problem. This movement is by no means unanimous, for many churches and churchmen are supporting the system and the forces on which they most depend, namely, money and moneyed men; but other churchmen in spite of handicaps and pressures try to apply the simple

266

principles of Jesus to the modern world. It is not easy. The modern highly centralized society makes of Christianity an irrelevance. This is because the Christian doctrine of good neighbors and love cannot apply to the principles of our impersonal social and economic system. The great horizontal organization of the modern industrial life is dehumanizing in its very principles; it creates an anonymous society in which the personal and humane attitudes of Jesus simply have no where to take hold. Jesus thought in terms of men and of relationships between men. In a society where patterns of action replace patterns of men, and where men lose value or are not considered, in the sense of an integrated human life, Christian doctrines have few points of application.

Some churchmen, nevertheless, have made brave work of attacking the specific injustices and failures of modern society. They have tried to bring Jesus in. They do not realize, perhaps, that he cannot, indeed would not, enter such a house.

If we think of religion in a more fundamental way, not as church doctrine, nor as doctrine at all, but as the mystic integrity of life itself, it is clear that the main tendencies of the modern social world are destructive of religion. It is the loss of this religious integrity of life, this deeply appreciative moment of value in our being, that has turned so many of the better churchmen towards outward social reform and so many other churchmen towards pretense, front and hypocrisy.

On education, on art, on religion the impact of the modern social system has been disintegrative. They have lost focus.

267

They have lost self-containment. They do not belong intimately to the world around us or they are trying desperately to prevent the loss of that belonging.

Balance in these matters, if it be balance, will lie in removing education, art and religion, so far as possible, from the formal types of institutions which now house them. To native life they belong. In folk art, folk religion and even folk education the better future of America will lie.

To find agencies and instruments for a greater development in this way, without building again those disastrous fatalities of the highly complicated, formal institutions that now encumber our culture, is not easy. A greater measure of decentralization in religious life and thinking, in artistic creation and criticism, and even in education, is a principle that will be basic in any balanced cultural life. In other words a greater measure of self-reliance is necessary.

The difficulties in the way of such a culture, which really is the good life, may be well-nigh insuperable, so far as deliberate effort is concerned. Perhaps deliberate effort is not relevant, perhaps even harmful in such fields. There remain, however, questions of standards, namely deliberate standards, particularly in education and in art, that we seem hardly prepared to forego in their entirety. External though they may be and dangerous to the inner spirit of the thing, a world which must remain socially organized on a large scale to a certain minimum degree, so that abundance and order may be had, will necessarily resort to external standards to some extent. It is here that the problem of balance lies. A balance

268

between the discipline that comes from having standards and the folk initiative that comes from freedom from institutional control will result in a great culture and a good life.

I have discussed balance in population, in industry, in property, in politics, in art, religion, education and, indeed, in human life. Such a balance seems to be necessary, so far as we may hope for a self-sustaining cycle of life and society. That our world now is out of balance in most important things is clear. In some fields there is reason to hope that balance is not impossible. In others the prognosis is less favorable.

This book on architecture and modern life has discussed, first, the nature of architecture in its relation to social life. Architecture interprets the structure of society. Architecture prophesies the structure of society. Architecture also is the structure, in a mystical sense, of the social world.

The book discussed, second, the dominant characteristics of architecture in the past and present world. A brief interpretation of the great historical, prehistorical and "nature" architectures was made. The Mayan, the Egyptian, Greek, Byzantine, Persian, Gothic, Indian, Chinese, and Japanese architectures were briefly discussed.

The derivative architecture of the present and its failure either to interpret or express that present was considered. The promiscuity of the present-day eclectic styles, their hack work and facile smartness, their insincerity and impoverished imagination was pointed out. The brutal up-thrust of new styles through older styles, where steel at last asserts itself, where new materials and new functions no longer can be concealed was then discussed. The new forms, present before society knows it, the new significances in some modern work that by virtue of necessity are thrust amid the clutter of older favorite cultures and styles of the period, were considered.

In the third chapter was discussed the characteristics of the modern social world so far as they influence expression. These characteristics are, roughly, the horizontal structure of modern economic society as contrasted with the older vertical structures. This term "horizontal" refers in this case only to the economic type of organization. It is quite the opposite of horizontalism or earth sense, in architectural design. A second characteristic is the pluralism of personal life in the modern world as contrasted with the more unitary, monistic personality of an older day. Modern personal life is more explicit and external and less implicit than the life of our grandfathers. A third characteristic of the modern world that greatly influences expression is the sharp cleavage between productive activities and consuming activities in contrast with the more integrated activities of our ancestors. These characteristics find one sort of expression in the great power and mobility of the modern world. Power and mobility, indeed, are the outstanding phenomena of this age.

In the fourth chapter was discussed the architecture of the

270

future. The nature of organic architecture was considered and its essential characteristics, its plasticity, its relation to form in respect to function, were illustrated in terms of modern machine design, functional building design, utility design, so far as these point the way to the future. A discussion of the new sense of space was followed by a consideration of the modern meaning of pattern. The relationship of form in building to the means by which building is produced was studied. These all were illustrated in the story of the building of the Imperial Hotel, Tokyo. An evaluation of the architecture of the future was made.

In the fifth chapter was discussed the future of society and expression. This future was considered as a part, an additional dimension indeed that art and imagination add to the present. The future in this sense was discussed in terms of three great conflicts or contrasts in the ideology of the modern world. On the outcome of these conflicts the future depends. They are, first, the contrast between modern urbanism and agrarian life; second, the contrast between security and opportunity in the modern world; third, the contrast between human integrity and specialization in personal life. The conflicting tendencies of these different ideologies and their predictions, as it were, in artistic expression were considered. Last, the nature of expression as a function of society—the imaginative dimension of society, or the future—was discussed.

In the sixth chapter the nature of a balanced society was examined. Balance in population, in industry, in property, in politics, in art, religion, education were discussed. What is the balance now, what should it be, what can it be, were questions answered to some extent in each case.

The next part of the book, and the last, will be a discussion, in dialogue form, of the philosophy of structure in society and in architecture. The meaning of architecture in relation to social life will emerge, I hope, with greater clarity and significance.—B. B.

VII. Dialogue

Wright: We have nearly finished this book, Baker Brownell, and our points of view have been too much in accord. Can't we turn up some features of this subject on which we might find ourselves in interesting disagreement?

Brownell: I have always had the impression that we agree on major things but disagree on all minor ones. But there are at least two things left to examine. One is the nature of structure in society and architecture, and the other is a study of ideal structure as it would be in existence, as, for instance, in Broadacre City. Our book has moved along from one aspect of structure to another in society and architecture. Now what is structure?

Wright: Well, since we have been talking about architecture and structure, it might be interesting to examine an example of structure where it is really an interpretation of a social condition—democratic, of course. It is the ideal we profess, isn't it? So let us consider this example of democratic structure.

Brownell: Before we do that, I wish to ask this question: What is structure? Is it here in the room? Is it out there in the hills and pastures? Your room here, due to some structure that you have given it, moves out among the cedars and birches on the slope. It is part of them. As I look out of the window at the hills of the Wisconsin River across the way from Taliesin, they seem to me to have structure. So does that Ming jar standing on the stone pier of your terrace. The ideas that we are now discussing also have structure—at least I hope so. But what is structure?

Wright: It is pretty hard to take the word "structure" apart. Webster makes a failure of it. The word itself stands as a necessary symbol of a factual condition.

Brownell: I admit that structure in things is a fact, but that does not tell much about its nature, it seems to me.

Wright: When we say "structure" we speak of the nature and character of an organism, do we not?

Brownell: The character of an organism . . . there is something in your phrase that reveals a great deal about structure. But doesn't it reveal something that you see rather than something that you think or make conceptually clear? Can't we simplify and sharpen it? It seems to me that when we speak of structure we are speaking of the composition of parts to make a whole.

Wright: The word composition can hardly be used in connection with structure in the organic sense. Its features, parts, fibers, tissues become a constitution in a genuinely creative sense.

Brownell: Do you mean by constitution, the relationship of

274

the parts to each other? Or do you mean something more integral, more spiritually one than that? Do you mean, perhaps, form?

Wright: Yes, that, but more. Form is the inevitable result of structure. There is no structure without form, no form without structure.

Brownell: Then is structure an abstraction of form?

Wright: What do you mean by "abstraction"?

Brownell: An abstraction, I suppose, is taking a part out of something and treating it as if it were a whole. Abstraction of form is the pure design of the relationships of the parts to a whole without the concrete body or matter. If you carry it far enough, it usually tends to become mathematical.

Wright: But to me abstraction—to make anything in the abstract—is to make clear in some pattern the spirit of the thing.

Brownell: Is that spirit mathematical? I mean spirit in some pattern.

Wright: Spirit perhaps is always what you might call mathematical. But certainly in abstraction it is the structure or pattern of the thing that comes clear, stripped of all realistic effects, divested of any realism whatever. Abstraction is stark form, we might say.

Brownell: Yes, but I would say further that structure is the very simple thing that we mean when we say that it is the arrangement of the parts in a whole.

Wright: That, of course, it is. But the definition I think we are seeking must go deeper than that.

Brownell: You are giving structure a metaphysical kind of reality which it may or may not have. What is stock form?

Wright: I am endeavoring to give it reality, which is always metaphysical, as well as sub- and super-physical. There is no division into parts where reality is concerned.

Brownell: I think that you are spiritualizing it. I don't mind your doing that, but structure in the broadest sense is a much simpler thing.

Wright: But your assumption is only a part of structure.

Brownell: What is the other part?

Wright: The other part is the necessity for it and the actual substances of which the correlation of parts is made. Even more important are the inter-relationships that are the "in between" of Lao Tze.

Brownell: There, I think, you have changed to another conception of structure—namely, not merely the pattern but the force and support of an organization. In fact, structure seems to be becoming a great many things.

Wright: Well, I am speaking of structure with an "interior" sense of the whole.

Brownell: You mean, then, that the structure is not only the bones but the flesh of the body, and now also the inner system of it?

Wright: And not only the inner system of it but the reason for it as well—the each in all and all in all making them necessary to each other. Let's throw that in, too.

Brownell: That sounds like a kind of cross between Plato and Gertrude Stein. It has wonderful possibilities. And back

276

of that, if I may go on collecting your definitions of structure, it seems to me you have identified structure with the total concrete reality of the body. Surely, that is no longer structure. Do you mean, for example, that the structure of the blue Ming jar is the whole jar?

Wright: You continue to talk of construction. To me structure is the very basis of what I call reality. When I speak of structure I have in mind reality, the essential constitution of whatever may be constructed. Something intrinsic, not merely extrinsic. Perhaps that word "constitution" more than any other single word comes close to my meaning. The *constitution* of the thing is *how* the thing is made integral. It is the fashion. We speak of our constitutions, and when we so speak we mean the way we are made, do we not? And when we speak of our constitutions we are speaking of something integral, that which characterizes the fashioning. It is structure that enables us to be what we are, how we are, for what we are.

Brownell: Constitution is good, it is perhaps what you have called the character of an organism. But we are puttering around the word "structure" too much. Shouldn't we be more concerned about structure in architecture, in society and in other concrete things? I, for my part, have moved away from Plato since my youth. I would be inclined to say that neither structure nor form has reality, as you call it, except in concrete, complete things.

Wright: Well, Baker Brownell, you started this with a request for some analysis of the word structure. And Plato's eternal "idea of the thing" is still valid, so far as I can see. I should say structure is what Plato meant by "Eternal Idea"— the essential framework of reality.

Brownell: All right then, I did start it; but now I want to end it. Our "structure" thus far has been so abstract and evanescent that it can't even be seen. Why not try to consider structure as we always must find it in experience, namely, in concrete objects and individual things? Take the big Ming jar again. It stands on the pier of your terrace. It is a plastic flowing blue. The sun behind it glints around the edges. The jar is cylindrical in shape, tapered at the two ends, with an abstract design of some sort in relief around the sides. I suppose it was made to be a tea jar. Now it is standing here above the Wisconsin River, aristocratically alone, and more precious, seemingly, because it is alone. What is the structure of the Ming vase? Is it the elements which constitute it? If so, what do those elements include?

Wright: First they include the idea of a serviceable jar for storing tea, then the forces put to work upon materials to shape them to the desired end. There must first be this ideal of function and of purpose. In this case the function is storing tea, a jar from which tea may be sold, and so a jar that can be man-handled. Before clay is touched there is in mind this definite concept as to what is to be achieved. Now how? By way of the potter's clay and the potter. This beginning is a feature of structure. We call it concept. To me it is an element of structure because structure begins there. If we are to speak of structure as organic structure it is essential to include conception. So far as reality is concerned it is the most "real" or es-

278

sential feature of the whole creative process. Structure is, of course, the product of this process.

Brownell: We can and perhaps should think of the universe as a set of dynamic relationships or processes. Pragmatists, I think, would do that in contrast to the Platonists and the Rationalists. They would make structure an order of activities and would think of pattern and static design only as metaphors, so to speak, or translations of the order of the making process.

Wright: Nature could not have static structure first if she would. Structure does not come into the world ready-made. There must have been a concept and then a process or development of structure accordingly.

Brownell: That sounds like Platonism again, with the form or concept prior to the process. But perhaps you think of the "concept" as the process of a person's thought. I myself would not personalize nature in that way. Nevertheless we do think of the physical universe as having two great aspects. One is its structure and the other is its process. Probably they, too, are relics of Platonism. In any case, the process is determined by the character of the structure.

Wright: Physicists may prefer that order for convenience, but structure where character is concerned is not first.

Brownell: Would you say that the automobile begins to run before it is made? Isn't the running of the automobile based on the prior fact that the automobile has a structure of parts patterned to each other?

Wright: If we were talking of the function of the car,

279

yes. But we are talking about the making of the car, not its functioning. Then, certainly it must begin to run before it is made. The making process in regard to the automobile is really a kind of extension of the past into the present of this process of the running of the automobile.

Brownell: In that case you may be stepping out of the field of discourse—namely, the automobile. The physicist in his conception of the world as a whole probably has no right to step out of the field of discourse, however, nor is it possible for him to do so. It is true that for him action or proceeding cannot be secondary to design and plan. They are one.

Wright: They are one. That is my own contention. So here we are again and once more. We have the plan. Then we proceed to include within that plan the nature of materials and the shaping of the parts. We proceed definitely within certain limitations, towards a conceived end, part to part, as parts are to the whole.

Brownell: By "plan" I suppose you mean, as I think Plato would, that there is a difference between the becoming or the process in a structure and the design or form. I hope you will pardon me for bringing in these old academic references, but Plato, I think, would say that design or form can be abstracted from the becoming or process of action, and that the universal form only is the real whereas the action in time is not.

Wright: No, I do not mean to say, nor do I think, that a difference can really exist between the process of making the structure and the design or form. Otherwise how could I assert, as I do, that form and function are one? I say that structure is not only involved as much with procedure as with any other elemental scheme of action, but defines and limits action, as it is in turn defined and limited by it. Structure is integral to action as action is to structure.

Brownell: There still is the difference, however, at least the difference that physicists talk about, between structure and process. The automobile has a structure such as the chassis, the wheels, the engine. But it also has a process—it goes.

Wright: No. Physicists must have separate pigeon-holes and separate labels—the more the better. I am not talking about process as the subsequent functioning of some form. I mean that initial process that proceeds to make a thing what and how it is, as it functions. The subsequent process that makes it go is inevitably bound up in the nature of the whole structure. But it is not this proceeding to which I refer. All structure has its process, before it can have any proceeding as entity. First the concept, then the process, finally the ultimate proceeding or functioning.

Brownell: Let us return to the Ming tea jar on your terrace. The structure of the designs in relief on its surface is not a process.

Wright: But it is. That feature proceeds from generals to particulars. It has definite motivation and the motivation eventuates into appropriate pattern.

Brownell: But the pattern, when we have it, is not getting anywhere. It does not do anything.

Wright: It does. It is alive. It is a realized form expressing the purpose of the jar while it reenforces the walls. It is a rhythmical expression of this jar maker's joy in his job.

Brownell: Do you mean that it is rhythmical as a process, a cumulative kind of activity? Is rhythm always a time rhythm—namely, doing something, going somewhere?

Wright: I don't know just what you mean by "time rhythm." But time is as surely involved in all rhythm as interval is essential to emphasis. I cannot conceive of rhythm which would be essentially timeless—that is, without intervals or emphasis. Once you say "interval" we have the image of time at once, a space between something. The moment we fix points we imagine time. It is an unfortunate matter of fact, I believe, that it is impossible for our finite minds to conceive of anything except as this element of time in some form enters into it, nor any sense of space except as we fix limits.

Brownell: Then you would say, perhaps, that these buildings of yours are not "frozen music," they are music, music that never was frozen, never can be. But it seems to me that there are timeless elements in our experience.

Wright: If there are timeless elements in our experience, Baker B., we could not be conscious of them. We might have a feeling that they were so, but we could not mentally grasp them as such. We could make no image of them.

Brownell: Perhaps we could not express them or perhaps we could. The whole purpose of the arts is to express those timeless moments.

Wright: Not consciously, I think. The whole purpose of
282

art is to objectify those subjective elements and feelings which all people may have, but which many people cannot express for themselves. An intuitive nature might perceive them and yet only an artist nature be able to objectify them. Perhaps it is a matter of horizon. One man's is wider than another's. And what is one man's today is not his tomorrow. Within this horizon creative art must take place, whatever may lie outside, in which you call the timeless. What is it to be an artist? Simply to make objective in form what was subjective in idea. It is to make things within and yet beyond the power of the ordinary man. The artist may feel no deeper, may see no further but has the gift that enables him to put that insight into form in whatever medium he uses. Without this specific power he is not an artist but merely a man of feeling and of appreciation unable to create.

Brownell: It is not a matter of seeing further or feeling deeper, nor is it only the power to make those discriminations articulate. A dog gives form to his feelings and insights, such as they are, when he barks. But this formulation of experience, at least natural experience, is not enough for art. It is expressive, but art is the expression of more than he expresses. The ability to see and feel and to be sensitive to experience is a gift of great importance, but the artist is not primarily an extremely sensitive photographer's plate able to catch impressions beyond ordinary human susceptibility, and his function is not merely the natural expression of those impressions. He may do that, but he does more. The artist—and I mean the artist in everybody as well as the great man of art—reaches beyond the rela-

283

tivities and the incompleteness of life that we call "time" and things temporal; he creates or finds what nature does not give and what the world of fact cannot record; he finds what is not relative or incomplete but is final. He gives to reality a final timeless significance that nature alone cannot give. Art tries to make articulate the timeless elements in our experience. It is action, yes; it is creative action; but it creates something that is not given in anyone's natural experience, however sensitive that experience may be. The artist creates something beyond natural experience. I rather think structure, as I mean it here, is that timeless synthesis. Only the artist, or the artistic or religious spirit in every man, can do those things. Only he can create those timeless forms.

Wright: Whether the forms created are timeless or not is of little consequence to the artist himself. He is that thing which he does. He does not try to lift himself by his own boot straps, if he is wise.

Brownell: Of course he is that which he does. That is the point, the very agency of his timelessness. The whole meaning of art is to transcend the time order.

Wright: Transcending the time order—that, indeed, he does. But his effort is to get order here and now. In other words, to make it actual in *the present.* That is the important thing to him. He dips into the universe probably without being self-consciously aware of it. He is in tune with it because he is of it, if indeed he is not it himself. He comes with something for the here and now. He has made of the "universal," as you call it, the very thing we should call the "here and

284

now." That is his function, his "business," as we might and do say.

Brownell: We have come to the same place by different roads. The here and now, which I would call the wholeness of the concrete experience, is the important thing. In that here and now he integrates all the future and all the past. That is what I mean by the timeless moment of artistic experience.

Wright: But my point is that that is not so important to him, if he is truly an artist, because he *is* that thing. He does not have to think much, if at all, about it. If he consciously thought and thought about it when he wanted to do some work, if he deliberately tried to be in tune with infinity, he would never create anything at all. He would be an actor playing to the gallery. No, the creative artist just wants to make these things, with which he is working, the best and most beautiful things that can be made in his medium for his purpose, and he wants to do that because it is a joy to him. He likes to be useful, too, in his way if he is an architect. But more likely he will use rather than be useful.

Brownell: I think that is not so much in disagreement with what I have said as you may imagine. I mean precisely that the immediate significance of it is the important thing to the artist. That is what I mean when I say that he abandons the past and the future, or rather carries them into the living present.

Wright: Oh yes. He *does* carry the past and future into the living present. But it is for others to come along and pick up the concrete object, find the significance of it, realize the

285

critical interpretations of it, and eulogize it, perhaps. But the artist does not care very much about that, although the man himself—there is one in every artist—might be pleased.

Brownell: No, that is not quite what I mean by significance. I mean by significance here its relation to itself and its completeness of value in its own field of reference. It may be nothing more than a splotch of red color or the blue glisten of the sun on the Ming tea jar. He finds it directly and immediately important to him.

Wright: I don't think that would be very intelligent on the part of any artist. The only significance the splotch of red or the blue glisten has for him lies in this interrelationship which alone can give it any significance at all.

Brownell: It is the immediacy of it that counts. Intelligence for him is secondary.

Wright: Intellect is his tool box, but intelligence is never secondary. Perhaps you mean intellect.

Brownell: The words are not very different, nor important. You may take intelligence either as the perception of relations or as the process of reason; in either case it is secondary in the artist to the immediacy of experience. Knowing about things, to the artist, is secondary to participation in them.

But it is late in the morning now. The hours that we have been talking about have gone through the cedars and the birches on the hillside in their usual order. The future hours are no doubt marching on us also in their regular procession. You have returned from Dodgeville where you visited Gene Masselink who was hurt last night. But the sun is blue-green

286

on the side of the Ming jar on your terrace. A mourning dove in the trees below is calling. The stony pasture on the hill across the way has turned bright under the sun. It is bright now. And this moment is this moment. All past and future is here, and only here.

Wright: Perception is only a property of intelligence and knowing about things is not enough. One must realize them. Participation in that sense only is action. I prefer to think of art as that integral action. What we call art, to be sure, is the means of making something, making sound, forms, giving fresh impressions of something. But primarily the artist is a maker, a free fashioner. A poet says it with words. A painter says it with color and line. The architect says it with stone or bricks and mortar, or steel and glass and an industrial system, usually to ennoble a utilitarian purpose or make the mundane a thing of beauty. But they are all of a stripe. All are of the same fiber. And they are pretty much of the same character, too. But rarely do they ever recognize the same quality of thought or the same inspiration in a different medium. This concerning them has often puzzled me.

Brownell: I think you are saying, and saying very well, that art is practice. You are saying that art is the action involved in creating beautiful structures. It is a dynamic conception of art. I rather think it can be called a plastic conception of art in the sense that plasticity means the flowing together of action in time. And I believe, strange as it may seem, that art is practice. Artistic action, however, has its value primarily in that magic ability to integrate the past and the fu-

287

ture in this burning present moment. Art is activity which has beauty and value in itself. In this respect the medium makes little difference since, through any medium that the artist may use, he gets something of the same final value.

Wright: Art is, as thought is, the highest form of action. But it does make a difference that artists should be blind except as they put their eyes to their own particular key-hole. If I were to put into a building a certain quality of feeling and thought, and if a musician were to put the same qualities into music, and a painter put them upon his canvas, the musician would come into my building and never recognize them there. The painter would do the same thing by either the building or the music. That looks like the dumb, halt, and blind to me. And then add to that disability the fact that to three-fourths of the people neither building, painting, nor music would have any significance at all—and you have something that looks tragic.

Brownell: I don't think that it makes so much difference whether they recognize each other's work. The important fact is that each one is getting the same thing out of his activity so far as he gets it at all.

Wright: Not the same. Too limited. Each is speaking a different language, understanding no universal language. Artists in different mediums seem to understand each other as a Frenchman would understand an African or an African a Chinaman. Any artist should be more interested in qualities than in any specific language in which they were expressed, even his own language. Qualities really worry him and delight

288

him most, and although qualities in the concrete are, after all, infinitely various and different from each other, to the artist mind they should be recognizable wherever they are.

Brownell: To get back to the question of structure. I wonder if structure does not mean something rather deeper than either one of us so far has actually said?

Wright: It begins to look as though it depended upon who uses the word.

Brownell: I mean that the artist in his approach to structure is breaking down those divisions to which we have been accustomed in Occidental philosophy or in religion.

Wright: He should be breaking down divisions but setting up new unities perpetually. But he can do so only if he has experience of the organic point of view.

Brownell: Structure in other words is the integration, not only of time but of those abstractions that we have called spirit and matter.

Wright: Do you think matter an abstraction?

Brownell: I think it is if you separate it from spirit.

Wright: How can the separation be effected or effective?

Brownell: It cannot be effective, but it has been effected ever since Plato made it long ago, or the Indic philosophers before him.

Wright: Isn't that separation the cause of what we call artificiality?

Brownell: I think it is, very definitely. It is intellectual artifice.

Wright: Yes, it is itself intellectual artifice but I think it

289

is the basis of our superficiality. Is not such artificiality the very characteristic feature of our present failure?

Brownell: Yes, I would agree that our present failure comes almost directly from the Platonic separation of spirit from matter, as we have seen it come down through the medium of the western church.

Wright: Education with a capital "E" seems to be based almost wholly upon Artificiality with a capital "A."

Brownell: That is true. Formal education is the machine producing a modern disaster.

Wright: Let's say *the* modern disaster.

Brownell: I would accept that, except that there are so many other modern disasters.

Wright: Name one comparable in extent and fatality!

Brownell: I would name this, the separation in economic life between the activity of production and the activity of enjoyment.

Wright: But that separation is only the consequence of the initial separation.

Brownell: I believe they are concomitant. They both came out of the same parent. I think we can see our entire living process not as a series of preparations and sacrifices for something not present, but as a living and immediate value in the process itself.

Wright: You speak of value. You believe in "values" then?

Brownell: Well, values are another thing. They are nearest to us, but hardest to explain. We don't know them, we find

290

them. We find them in concrete things, in that Japanese print tacked on your draughtsman's board, in the color of glass of the window pane, in the design of this room and the fire deep in its place in the wall.

Wright: But do you really believe in "values" so called?

Brownell: All human beings must believe in values.

Wright: I doubt that. I think our concept of values devastating.

Brownell: Perhaps our concept of it, because we usually think of value in terms of postponed values.

Wright: Don't you think that when we assume values we evaluate—simply pronounce judgment and really establish nothing?

Brownell: Quite true, we often do.

Wright: Is it not another kind of price system in the wrong realm?

Brownell: Possibly, but the fact remains that if value means interest in things, which I think fundamentally it does mean, we cannot escape values in life.

Wright: Well, one may use the word value in different senses—to value is to cherish—but to value in the sense that I think you are using the word, is a determination of relative position or of desirability.

Brownell: No, I would disagree there. I think you mean the act of evaluating, which involves a critical attitude, and that I don't mean in this case.

Wright: Both are worthless, of course. But what do you mean?

Brownell: I mean simply that we take attitudes toward things of like and dislike, of love and hate, funny and sorry, good and bad, and the like.

Wright: All of those "values," if so they are, are as likely to be matters of ignorance as of enlightenment.

Brownell: I think they are neither matters of ignorance nor enlightment, but matters of human attitude. They are deep in our fiber and we cannot escape them and don't want to.

Wright: I want to escape attitudes, my own and those of others. I often do escape them. Mine as well as others.

Brownell: Then you agree with Santayana when he says that the spiritual life is the disintoxication from values?

Wright: No, I seldom agree with Santayana and do not now.

Brownell: I thought so. Yet I think your whole life is characterized by tremendous drives in terms of values.

Wright: You are using the word values in another language now, probably your own.

Brownell: No, I mean you love things and you hate them. You find things that are beautiful and things that are not beautiful.

Wright: Beautiful or not beautiful to you—certainly. But how can a man love without hating, and hate without loving, if beauty is in question?

Brownell: You do both.

Wright: Yes. Love and hate are each one side of the same shield.

Brownell: That is a matter I shall not touch now.

292

Wright: Where now are "values" in this connection?

Brownell: Values are the fact that you are not indifferent to these things.

Wright: I do not see how "values" come in or come into being in that connection.

Brownell: This seems to me what values are.

Wright: You mean loves and hates? Acceptances and rejections, in other words?

Brownell: Just that.

Wright: Well, I think I would not use the word values in that connection—desirabilities you mean.

Brownell: That is all right; desirabilities and undesirabilities, if you will. It does not make much difference.

Wright: When I think of values I think of something that I have weighed and found wanting, or weighed and found satisfactory. They are estimations for what they are worth today and they will change tomorrow. They are temporal and never anything but tentative.

Brownell: I would say that is the classical standard of values so far as you refer to the weighing process. So far as you think of them as temporal and tentative, it seems to me that you perhaps mean personal taste. But I doubt if either one is the essential nature of value. They are single points of view toward value.

Wright: Values as the word is used must imply appraisal. It must be some estimate by some one to some end?

Brownell: No, I would say not to some end necessarily— simply the fact that you like something or you don't like it.

Wright: You are dissociating it, then, from "judgment" and making it an entirely personal matter?

Brownell: Unquestionably. I think the economic system is based on one type of value, which I think is a bad one, namely the idea of postponed values and postponed rewards. Whether it is personal is another question that depends on what is meant by personality.

Wright: Value then becomes not only an idiosyncrasy but a personal idiosyncrasy. Somehow I fail to get your idea as to what constitutes value—in other words, the *structure* of value, otherwise.

Brownell: Possibly because what I am talking about is so simple.

Wright: Yes, but the word, as you use it, is of a language that you have become accustomed to using. Have you not given the word a significance which is perhaps uncommon?

Brownell: That may be true. I don't insist on the word *value*. I merely insist that deep in all our lives is the fact that we take to some things and we don't take to others. Some things are beautiful and some things are not. We like some things. We don't like others.

Wright: So you are only using the word *value* then in the sense of to prize or cherish, or to prefer, or to accept or reject, and to denote your own acceptances and rejections. A matter then purely relative.

Brownell: I will not argue over the word. But I am not sure that value is relative, in the deeper sense. Otherwise, the

294

word *taste* would do. I say that I am not sure. As for the word, I would just as soon give it up, but whatever word we—

Wright: I have learned that to proceed in life upon the basis of such idiosyncratic—pardon the word—conventions as "values" is to step from one wobbly stepping stone to another wobbly stepping stone, eventually to find yourself where you didn't want to be.

Brownell: I quite agree with you.

Wright: "Value" can only mean something we have established as for us or against us, and every such establishment is subject to the law of change. Inevitably all our "valuations" are nine-tenths worthless because they are being continually altered by experiences. Our own and that of others. It is so much safer to have as few so-called "values" as possible because values soon become baggage. I prefer to travel light with as little baggage as possible. I don't know really how much baggage of the sort I am trailing along right now, in spite of myself. But as soon as I can make it clear to myself that I have committed an "evaluation" and by way of "judgment" considered a matter settled for myself, I, like the man in the nursery rhyme who jumped into the bramble bush and scratched out both his eyes, jump into another bush and scratch them in again.

Brownell: You mean, I think, that one must always be creating afresh in terms of his likes and dislikes.

Wright: What I mean is that one must never sit in judgment. Our judgments are dangerous. Yet the educational

295

and economic order dotes upon them and trusts them. Jesus went to "Judgment," but, in the sense we use the word, did Jesus judge? One of his sayings that I remember is—"Judge not that ye be not judged." Nevertheless "judging"—in other words evaluating—creating "values" became, notwithstanding his wisdom, the basis of all these institutions of ours which crucify life today instead of liberating it, and which seem to have formed a crust upon life which life is now struggling to break through. Therefore, I am inclined to be suspicious of so-called "values," yours and mine, too, unless you mean something by the term which goes deeper than I am wading.

Brownell: You cannot quarrel with me on that. I am quite willing to give up the word "value" if you wish. And I shan't quarrel with what you say in regard to the disastrous effect of so-called academic scholarship.

Wright: No, I did not say "academic scholarship." I was thinking of our entire modern philosophy of modern education when I spoke of the *crust* which life is trying to break through.

Brownell: And still I make no protest.

Wright: Yes, but it has economic phases. It is not called "academic" then. Nevertheless it goes all through the fiber of society owing to this mistaken idea of need of evaluation which then becomes just another name for institution. Extrinsic instead of intrinsic.

Brownell: I think that what you really are saying is something that I agree with thoroughly, namely, that values

296

are often used second-hand and are fixed and are not fresh and new.

Wright: It is always dangerous to make them except first-hand. Even then the *attitude*, it seems to me, is wrong. Why sit in judgment? Why not humbly enter into action for the sake of experience, and by way of that experience enter into another action and another and another? Why attempt to formulate, reduce, catechize and arrange something that, in its very nature, is best fluid and inevitably remains in a state of change?

Brownell: You have said that beautifully. But I am not going to permit you to set me up as a straw man to attack when the meaning of what you are saying is what I am trying to say. We simply happen to be using different words. I have said that I would give up the use of the word.

Wright: Well, here we are again right where we have been all along. Now let's start and try to disagree about something. Let's start fresh and see if we cannot come out with disagreement.

Brownell: I am not sure that agreement is so deplorable. There can be adventures in agreement too.

But one more word on structure. I think that we are groping for something deep in the idea of structure. Doesn't it lie below these artificial, rational distinctions between subject and object, inner and outer, form and matter, flesh and spirit, and similar ideological divisions?

Wright: I am afraid structure will have the last word after all.

297

Brownell: It always does. Isn't the structure that we are talking about the integrity of concrete things? Our actual experience of those concrete things has none of those ideological divisions.

Wright: Well, yes. Certainly the integrity of common things. Whenever we start we seem to slide into deep water, at least as deep as that. Let's say the concrete integrity of things and let it go at that for the moment. This afternoon the thing will be further along.

Brownell: Now, Frank, you are an architect. You have insight into the forms of building and of living. You create designs for living and you mould brick and glass and stone, wood, air, concrete and light, steel, space and plaster into organic forms and plastic structures that are pertinent to life and are beautiful. You think in stone and glass, with a little contempt, I imagine, for these strange, shifting things that we call words. We have used many of them in this book, restless, undisciplined, disordered words, for that is their nature.

Now we want a few words more, such as they are, on structure in architecture and society, and particularly on your project, or dream, Broadacre City. You have done things in glass and steel. Now tell us what you are doing. You will find it harder, I think, to tell the things that you are doing, than to do them.

Wright: I'll try. But accuse me of no dream, please. You have heard of the little boy, have you not, who, curious, cut out the head of his drum to find out where the sound came from, and had neither sound nor drum? You don't want to place me in a similar position, I am sure. But nevertheless the little boy did find out a very important thing, and that was that the sound was not in the drum.

Brownell: And that analysis destroys it.

Wright: Yes, but sometimes we destroy that we may build. The danger does not prevent our human desire to poke around in this scrap heap we call our minds to see what curious and pretty things we can fish out. For one, I feel that, cerebration aside, thinking about things, considering them in their relationships quite sincerely for what one may be searching for—if we are searching for this thing we call reality—is worth a man's time. It is because mere cerebration, in the form of association of ideas, has passed for thought, that architecture is in a pretty hard case and that a Broadacre City is necessary.

Taste, association of ideas, is insufficient. A man, to build, must know. And I believe he may know the direction at least. He may learn to reach the center line of movement by way of thought and progress in line with what we call growth. So, in this state of becoming in which we all find ourselves, we may take the course, not of least resistance perhaps as things go and yet, yes, as a seed in the soil warmed by the sun reaches upward to the light, so it *is* natural for the man to take this course rather than any other. Therefore, why not the line of least resistance? We shall call it truth, come what may.

Brownell: I love this great house of yours, these limestone fireplaces in each large room, these long slopes of the house and the hill. And when I am here I sense somehow that not only have you made the house in the way you live, but that you live in the way that you have made the house. It seems to me that so simple a sort of thing as that, the relationship between the structure of architecture and the structure of social life, or of human life in general, has a deep meaning.

Wright: *Organic* structure, of course, has that integrity, whether social or architectural or what we call life.

Brownell: And isn't it the same structure, both of the house and of your life?

Wright: Yes, it is the life I have put in the house that really is the house. And in any building, which may be called architecture, you will find life put into it, interpreted as we have said. Your social structure will be made articulate, manifest in the terms of building we have been calling Architecture, if you have a civilization that is on speaking terms with culture. What we call a house, or place of worship, or a place to work in, or a place to dance in or sing in, well—such places cannot exist at all as any form of life unless they are interpretations of human life. They express and bless human beings.

Brownell: Do you mean that the house is a manifestation of the activities of life? If the activities are broken, scattered, disintegrated, the houses of men will be broken, scattered,

300

disintegrated. If the activities of life are whole and wholesome, if they are significantly one in structure and meaning,
the buildings that house those activities—

Wright: Yes, I mean that. I mean that whatever a social
or individual life may be, architecture will express that and
something more.

Brownell: But it is not only the individual house for the
individual man or family. We are living in a crowded and
complex world. We must think of housing not merely individuals and families, but housing many individuals and many
families who must live in relationship to each other. I think
that your Broadacre City project has been largely an endeavor to synthesize building with the modern social problem. Let me ask several questions about Broadacre City. I
think that the idea is based on the relationship of buildings
and people to the land. Am I right?

Wright: Yes, as a matter of course. Intrinsic relationship, not extrinsic. Life has drifted by way of artificialities,
"values," false abstraction, and by way of resultant academic
standards into an urbanism that has gone or is going sterile.
Man cannot be taken, still less can he take himself, away from
his birthright, the ground, and remain sane any more than he
can take himself away from the air he breathes, the food he
eats, the water he drinks. His spirit is conditioned completely
upon normal relationship of his life to what we call the life of
nature. Being natural he is fruitful, happy, safe. The moment he attempts the unnatural he is punished. He has taken
awful punishment. He must yet take worse punishment. Per-

301

haps whole civilizations, this one in particular, must disappear because of the fatal artifice which humanity seems to consider to be civilization. Humanity even speaks of its digression in this respect as culture.

Brownell: And civilization, that high-powered and supposedly high-valued word, really means in its derivation, *citification.*

Wright: No, let us use again the word "disaster." When I say man's birthright, I mean his right to a place in the sun certainly. But he can have no place in the sun except as he has his feet on his own ground. Now, by his own ground I don't mean some plot, two by twice, that he has bought and paid for somewhere. I mean as much ground as he can utilize in his share of making life fruitful and beautiful as a whole.

Brownell: As to the size, the ground area, and number of people in your Broadacre City project, what about that?

Wright: Because we are in the United States of America I laid out Broadacre City on the assumption that an acre of ground for every individual was minimum. Meanwhile, certain sections were set aside to be used for the growing of preferred trees as crops: these areas to come into use as population expanded or increased. Were a man properly educated, that is to say, were he brought up in the gospel of work rather than the prevailing gospel of as much as possible of something for as little as possible, he could, with his feet on his own ground, become an independent unit in a society completely capitalistic. Youth would be brought up to be not as the millions of citizens who are merely potential capitalists, frus-

302

trated now, and who, were they to realize their actual position, would find the game and the cards all stacked against them by the winners. No, he would be brought up in a new recognition of the principles of sanity and coveting its effects.

Brownell: That doctrine of work, which you speak of, is much misunderstood. I think even you too may misunderstand it. Carlyle, for example, thought of work as a sacrificial necessity. How tragically wrong he was; and Carlyle was my boyhood favorite! A man, from Carlyle's point of view, who found pleasure in his work was not a good workman. On the other hand, I think your use of the word "work" may not be Carlyle's use. It seems to me that our western doctrine of work, which descends from the old separation between the preparation for heaven and the enjoyment of the reward after death or at the end of a long life of work, is a most disastrous doctrine. It underlies, psychologically at least, many of the disasters of our modern times. Work, I think, should be redefined as activity which includes consumption as well as production, which is enjoyable and significant in itself as well as significant for the results that it brings about after the work is performed. Until we have a life in which work has both kinds of value, namely, instrumental value and final value, until then we shall not have a life that is worth while. As I see it, your idea of Broadacre City involves an idea of work which is both productive and significant in itself as well.

Wright: Work. Significant, yes, because productive. And because productive or fruitful work, joyful. Carlyle was unfortunate. Such an opinion of work as you mention was his perhaps because he was sick, or because he was a Scotch Presbyterian, or because of an untoward domestic situation. At any rate he was an old scold; he was not only unhappy, but proud of it. But we must admit, however, that he was a tremendous worker. Didn't he rewrite *The French Revolution* completely from beginning to end when a servant had thrown the original away?

Brownell: Yes, we admire Carlyle's nobility, but his doctrine of work is nevertheless the expression of a bad point of view.

Wright: Yes, and yet I wonder if Carlyle would call the writing of his *Sartor Resartus* and his essays in *Past and Present* work?

Brownell: I don't see how he could.

Wright: He might call the rewriting of *The French Revolution* work. I think Carlyle means drudgery by his use of the word *work*. Drudgery and work are not synonymous terms.

Brownell: Sacrificial drudgery.

Wright: Sacrificial, yes; by that I think you mean work chiefly a penance for the good of the soul or a disagreeable duty. And work *has* gone wrong for us in our day because of that; but more, I believe, because it has been made a speculative commodity. Work is and must be done in exchange for money. And money has become more than ever that thing by means of which, alone, every man is enabled to get that in which any man may take pleasure or whatever he desires.

Brownell: In the same way our idea of freedom today,

304

even when expressed by men as liberal as George Bernard Shaw, is of purchased freedom at the price of sacrificial work. It makes freedom the same as leisure, in other words an insignificant freedom.

Wright: Right. Or it is only a license, by way of earnings, to do as one wishes, which is seldom if ever freedom.

Brownell: Freedom seems to me to be the ability to work productively and enjoyably and at the same time to control, so far as possible, the conditions under which one works.

Wright: Or, let us say, as we are speaking of art, to find one's self in what one does.

Brownell: Shaw said not long ago in an article on democracy, "The practical form of freedom is leisure." Then he went on to say something like this, "Genuine democracy can exist only when the necessary slavery to nature—that is, the task of productive work, without which we would all perish, is equally shared, and the leisure left when that is done equally shared in consequence."

That is a perfect example of the kind of fallacy that I think permeates our Occidental ideology. It is the main trouble with our life. It is a common misconception of freedom and of work. Of course, I don't want to dispute Mr. Shaw's statement that unpleasant work as well as pleasant leisure should be more equally shared. None of us would dispute that very much. I do wish, however, to dispute the idea that the practical form of freedom is leisure and that productive work is a necessary slavery to nature. The idea has a long history of error.

305

Wright: It has. Go ahead, dispute the idea. It is not only fallacious. It is the popular error that will put an end to our own history.

Brownell: The Occidental ideology—and Plato started this thing—is based on the sharp cleavage between production and consumption. It is based on the idea that production is a sacrificial, though menial, effort put forth in order that consumption or aristocratic enjoyment may take place later. Work was Adam's punishment. Our Christian heaven is based on much the same conception. This world is a preparation for something that comes later, postponed to the future. "Success" has the same theory. It is a theory of postponed rewards. We must have a future, but—

Wright: My turn to agree and applaud. And yet isn't anticipation nine-tenths of enjoyment? Anticipation is tied up with this deadly charm of gambling. Every man, woman, and child in the United States is born and bred a potential gambler. We have fostered the gambling spirit. It is a form of anticipation but an abuse of it.

Brownell: You can have your anticipation. I shall take the immediate or direct reality.

Wright: Is reality then also divisible into Past, Immediate, and Future? If so, I should say that anticipation is very much the better part because out of the past it stands in the present because of the future.

Brownell: I think you are suffering from the cleavage of which I spoke. The immediate, or the direct, is just that timeless synthesis of art that I urged on you this morning. But as

306

I move about in your buildings and see your work and listen to some, but not all, of your words, I feel sure that you are not really suffering from that fatal cleavage, at that. But Mr. Shaw is. This beautiful design of space in your room, reaching through the open walls into the sun, denies my charge against you, though some of your words seem to say otherwise. But to return to "work" and "freedom":

It seems to me that the real problem of both society and art is not to give leisure or unoccupied time, but to make human activity significant. If activity is significant, it must be both free and functional. If it is functional without freedom it is likely to be some form of slavery. If it is free without function it can be little more than frivolous. Mr. Shaw bounces from slavery to frivolity. One is about as bad as the other.

Wright: And what, then, is this bouncing of Mr. Shaw? Activity without art?

Brownell: What he says would indicate that as his philosophy. Contrary to Mr. Shaw, I suggest that art and society must come together in the ideal of human activity. When human activity is significant and is well directed we may say, I think, that social ideals and artistic ideals both are attained. That is a pretty broad definition and you probably would force me to qualify it, if you had a chance.

Wright: Yes, go on. Are you not giving me that good chance?

Brownell: This significant activity, or art, is possible only in a society where work can have functional significance and also appreciative significance. It is, namely, a society where

307

the activity of producing is also in part the activity of consuming or enjoying. A society in which productive work is sharply separated from enjoyment by means of techniques such as mass production, centralization, specialization, standardization, will fail in terms of human values although it may produce a great deal of cheap goods. A society of this sort is marked not only by the decline of self-sustaining industry but by the decline of native, self-sustaining art, of folk art, or amateur art in the best sense of the word. Extreme professionalism, expertism or virtuosity in the arts takes the place of generally distributed and diffused artistic production. The great mass of people take their art, their sport, their enjoyment in general as a spectacle to be purchased rather than an activity to be lived.

Wright: More approval. And let me say that architecture is in a basic strategic position in this integrity of production and enjoyment, of art and of life of which you speak. It is itself an expression of that very integrity, as in Broadacre City, or architecture is only a liability.

Brownell: Now tell me about Broadacre City. How many people will there be in each city? What will they do for a living? How will they live? The afternoon is moving on. The cattle on the hill over there are lying bunched up under the ridge. They are chewing their cuds, no doubt. What philosophers they are! Probably they too think it's time to hear about Broadacre City.

Wright: Before we proceed with the details of Broadacre

308

City, let us get a little clearer the basis upon which it was conceived. Broadacre City is no city at all in the sense that you are using the word. Broadacre City is everywhere or nowhere. It is the country itself come alive as a truly great city. It is out of the ground into the light by way of man's sense of himself in his work. With his feet on his own ground each man is not only a potential but an actual capitalist. So you see, while the present condition under which he lives is money-bound first and is everything else afterward, in Broadacre City a man's own capabilities in his work become his wealth and by means of that wealth he obtains, more directly than is possible now, those things of which he dreams and that he desires. He is not and never can be unemployed or a slave in any sense. The true wealth of our nation would be increased enormously instead of funneled down to the little drip that we are in the habit of calling our financial resources.

Brownell: Does that mean that he lives in a comparatively self-sustaining system?

Wright: Not comparatively self-sustaining. Absolutely self-sustaining, if he is a true self. A true self still lives in most men notwithstanding the ravages of such libertine individualism as the once famous Liberty League called upon in the name of freedom.

Brownell: Still he must buy tools, automobiles, power, with money, must be not?

Wright: Not with money as a speculative commodity, but by some simple social medium of exchange which enables the fruits of his labor in connection with natural resources to be exchanged for the fruits of another man's labor in that connection.

Brownell: That means that we must know more about the actual structure of this Broadacre City. How do the people live?

Wright: Wait a little. Let's proceed from generals to particulars. Let's discuss *why* they must live there, first. To understand why, we must know more about the actual nature of this thing we call money, for one thing. A simplification of our entire economic concept is essential, beginning with that abstraction as well as with the use of the ground. Simplification is not so difficult as it seems because a natural economic order is yet possible to us in America, and possible, I believe, without bloodshed or any greater suffering on the part of any one except those who would unjustly and unfairly try to prevent a just measure of life for other men. They suffer in that attempt anyway, dying a thousand deaths where they need die but once.

Brownell: Do you mean that we may have a local revolution in respect to Broadacre City and ignore the course of economic life outside?

Wright: No revolution local or outside. There is no need of revolution nor of isolation. I think Broadacre City is really in process of arriving right now as an organic necessity of our times. I believe the recent depression—let's call it by its right name, break-down—of the past seven years has produced the revolution quietly beneath the surface of things. This revolution will eventuate in what I am calling, for lack of a better term, Broadacre City. He can see that the present impositions upon life have gone almost as far as they can go. These impositions have given us, in general, a factory worker's and an industrialist's and, in particular, a *speculator's* view of a universe. Acting on these views has resulted in the exaggerated urbanism we suffer from. This urbanism has increasingly crucified life in the name of "service" and "freedom." Efficiencies we have worshiped we are finding to be extravagant exploitations of the very life we—some of us—sincerely enough expected them to serve.

Brownell: But admitting that that has failed in human terms, do you think that Broadacre City will come as a natural consequence?

Wright: All that Broadacre City needs, in order to come into existence, is the application of the principles of an organic architecture to the life of our people, and the interpretation of that life in terms of Architecture. We need structure in the sense we have used the word where we now have only a badly planned set-up. We cannot say we have a system.

Brownell: That seems rather indefinite. If, for example, every person is to have an acre or so of land, how can you provide for his keeping his land?

Wright: I do not know by what method except that his work upon and improvements will hold it. He will not be allowed to alienate his land. He may designate his successor. But other things are even more important. Perhaps first and foremost we need to begin with a new success ideal.

Brownell: True.

Wright: And this different sense of life which insures that new ideal, I believe, is coming. We, as a people, have lately been "behind the scenes." As I now occasionally go about among young people, talking to them in these universities of ours, I think I see that new ideal coming. Every man I meet and talk to, from the intelligent workman to the richest of the rich men, feels dissatisfied, more or less uneasy, uncertain. In short, not happy.

Brownell: I think most of them would like to have what you say, but they think that the inevitable evolution of economic life is towards greater concentration and away from what you say.

Wright: They did think so up to this time. But I believe now the majority of our thinking people have gone deeper and are beginning to think and feel otherwise.

Brownell: But it is time that we know more of the picture of Broadacre City. How do they live? How many people are there? What is it like?

Wright: No picture please. Not yet anyway. Let us first see where we are now.

We are now in a society built like some badly planned factory, run like a factory, systematically turning out herd-struck humans as machinery turns out shoes. Our society is a cultural weed of a dangerous kind: dangerous to ourselves and to others. When life itself becomes a restless tenant, as it has become on our farms no less than in big cities, the citizen must lose sight of the true aims of human existence and voluntarily

312

accept substitutes. His life, now unnaturally gregarious, tends towards the blind adventure of a crafty animal. To live, or "get by," is some form of graft, coupled with some febrile pursuit of sex. Only in these does he find or see relief from the factual routine in this mechanical uproar of mechanical conflicts of this mechanical life of his—conflicts that seem to hypnotize him while they crucify him.

Brownell: That is what I mean by the separation of enjoyment from significant production.

Wright: A citizen pays as he is paid. He is bought as he buys. As he buys and sells so he is bought and sold. He is struggling to maintain a heartless, worthless artificiality. His faculties, his vital sap, meantime ebb. The citizen's entire life, for lack of some basis natural to him—therefore organic—is exaggerated and sterilized by way of machinery instead of blessed. American life itself has now become some form of anxious rent. The citizen's own life is rented, his family evicted if he is in arrears. This stricture is what we please to call a system; God knows it has no structure. It is a stricture that is no system but is only an adventitious circumstance. Should this anxious lockstep of man fall out with the landlord, the money lord, the machine lord, man is a total loss. The "system" goes to smash, and he perpetually fears the smash.

Brownell: Still, the people in Broadacre City would use machines, would they not?

Wright: Yes, all the powerful modern machines at work upon the resources are the premium paid to human greed. Machines and resources would be naturally his. Both are now turned against him and involuntarily are turning against him in the city. They could be his own now, by way of no revolution, but by way of a simple understanding of the nature of what he is, what he does, and where he is. They could go now to work for him in the circumstances if the right structure could be found, the right pattern that would not soon again become another stricture.

Brownell: How would the necessary machines be produced and how would the citizen of Broadacre City purchase them?

Wright: They would be produced much as they are produced now, except under happier circumstances, produced by such people as those who use them. I think it unnecessary to change radically any of the methods and processes which have given us our great advantages except to make them more radical and humane. But we must arrive at some understanding as to a beneficial and natural human basis on which to make use of them. That means a rational social structure in place of the adventitious stricture.

Brownell: But doesn't efficient production of big machines involve the big factory and the big industrial city?

Wright: No longer. The big factory and the big city were the inevitable consequence of the present exploitation we call centralization. Such as this was "the great efficiency." It was to bring to all human beings everything which they desired. It has brought them to the beginning of the end.

Brownell: But isn't centralization involved with division

314

of labor and specialization, which are necessary to efficient production of cheap machines?

Wright: Yes, centralization is dependent on men as cogs, or in the elimination of them as factors in production so far as possible and their increase in consumption. But what do you mean by "cheap"? If you mean machines that cost an exploiter the least money, if you mean getting ten machines for the price of one, then "cheap" we clearly have at a pretty stiff price.

Brownell: I mean by "cheap" machines those which the average person in the average community can buy if he needs them.

Wright: The "average person" in the community in Broadacre City could have all the machinery that was profitable to him as a human being to use as one. And we must use the word "profitable" here in a little broader sense than the mere money sense of a price system has given it.

Brownell: How would he get the machines?

Wright: He would make them, as he makes them now, but he would make them under circumstances and in a situation where there would be pleasure in the making and true profit to him in the making as well as in the using.

Brownell: Would he make them through methods of industrial organization?

Wright: Probably, if cooperation is organization. And it is a form of it. I see nothing wrong with organization if it is organic. I see everything wrong with the exaggeration of or-

315

ganization, and with inorganic organization which is only aggregation or organization run to seed. Some forms of organization are primitive impulses and valuable instruments of any social life.

Brownell: What do you think of the influence of new technological methods such as the use of electrical power in place of steam?

Wright: I think that these new facilities and extended powers together with our other advantages, mobilization, glass and steel, are what make Broadacre City possible.

Brownell: Would this city be a large city?

Wright: As I have said, this city would be everywhere and nowhere.

Brownell: It would be a decentralized city?

Wright: Certainly. Decentralization of all those interests in which individuality is concerned is a basic condition fundamental to Broadacre City. But centralization of all that does not involve individuality would be a matter of what we now call government.

Brownell: Can you produce U. S. Steel by decentralized methods?

Wright: Yes, of course; more effectively, so far as human life is concerned and the benefit that it derives from steel, than steel is produced now.

Brownell: There would still be the Garys and the Pittsburghs, would there not?

Wright: No, there would not be. The Garys and the Pittsburghs have served their term. We do not need them now. Together with other crude scaffolding and hardships by way of which we have reached this crisis they would disappear.

Brownell: Do we return to the home forge and the village smithy?

Wright: No, indeed. We keep all the advantages which concentration upon making money has unwittingly pushed to over-development. We've got them. Why not keep them? I see no reason why we should throw one of them away. By means of them we could have many more. But the test of achievement in any civilization is not the amount of money that some men make because of it, but what the eventual result that civilization is found to yield where a human life is concerned. These results are human if at all valid. Or, instead of valid, let us again say intrinsic.

Brownell: What would the average citizen do in Broadacre City? What would be his pattern of work and enjoyment?

Wright: As a matter of fact there would be no "average citizen" in Broadacre City. Broadacre City aims to eliminate the "average citizen."

Brownell: What would the "unaverage citizen" do?

Wright: Let us understand, first, that we are concerned here with a future for individuality in organic sense. I believe individuality to be the prime integrity of the human being as integer of the race. Without such integrity I believe there can be no real culture whatsoever, no matter what we may choose to call civilization. I have called this city Broadacre City because it is a broad freedom for the individual, honestly democratic, based upon the ground—the minimum of one acre to

317

the person. To date our capitalism has miscalled personality individuality. Our eclecticism, which must be called mere personality instead of true individuality, has, by way of what we call taste—we have used taste as a substitute for culture—obstructed where it has not obscured the integrity of individuality. And we, on account of that vicious, fundamental misunderstanding, have become the prey of our captains turned playboys, our kept universities, our high-powered culture-mongers (such as the arch-salesmen, Sir Joseph Duveen, et al.) and we—the people, yes—stand in danger of losing our chance at this free life. Nevertheless, our charter of liberty originally held it out to us. And now I see a pattern for that free life in Broadacre City. It is a life that reckons with the law of change as a desirable circumstance, not as fatality.

Brownell: That is a good statement of the ideal of life in Broadacre City. But is there anything in your plan that explains how it will come into existence?

Wright: First the ideal, which, thanks to your pretended dumbness, I have now outlined somewhat. Now, then, we come to the plan.

Brownell: Not all of it was either pretense or dumbness: I am trying to see the thing in the concrete. What is the plan? Will there be shops, roads, hydrants?

Wright: Ask me rather, first, "What is the nature of this plan?" And I will say it is a free pattern. It is of the ground and with the ground. Wherever this free pattern is applied it varies with the ground and as the conditions of climate

318

and life vary. The ground may happen to lie suited to one kind of life or to many kinds. The common spirit of the people involved is disciplined automatically from within by means and methods and materials which are all organic.

It is a great unity in diversity I have sought.

The changes that Broadacre sees and accepts as natural and desirable have already made the big city no longer efficient or endurable. But the city struggles, as it must, against the change. For example, let's say that the present city spacing was based fairly enough on the human being on his feet or sitting in some trap behind a horse or two. So all now is too small, too mean for the automobile. And originally the city was a group life of powerful individualities true to life, conveniently enough spaced. But by way of instantaneous communications and easy mobilization this better life has already left the modern city. Not only such genius as the city has known for many a day is recruited from the country, but success in the city means life in the country. What, then, is the overgrown city for? Almost all necessities that once chained the individual to city life are dying away and the present citizens must die there as these needs die. It is only as life has been taken from him and he has meekly accepted substitutes offered to placate or fleece him that any citizen voluntarily remains in the city. The fundamental unit of space-measurement has so radically changed that the man now bulks ten to one in space, and a thousand to one in speed, when seated in his motor car. Mobilization is rapidly becoming universal.

319

This circumstance alone would render the present form of our cities obsolete. Like some dead dwelling the city is inhabited only because we have it. We feel that we must use it and cannot afford to throw it away to build the new one we now know we need. But compulsion is here. I imagine we'll soon be willing to give all we have, to get this new freedom that might so easily be ours. We will give what we have left to get it for our posterity, even if we may not have it ourselves. Devouring human individuality invariably ends in desolation, some kind of desertion such as is under way. Invariably, as history records, greed ends in destruction of the devourer. The city is in this case the devourer, and the impulses that exaggerated the mechanical forces that built it are senile in nearly every phase.

Brownell: Now what of the new Broadacre City?

Wright: The principles underlying the free pattern called Broadacre City are simply those of an organic architecture. Organic architecture now comes with a demand for finer integrity in order to unite modern improvements with natural resources in the service of men. Integration is here, as set dead against centralization. By the natural working of organic forces and ideas man is now to be brought forward to his inheritance, the ground, that he may become a whole man again. There is no longer much excuse for him to remain the parasite that spasmodic centralization has succeeded, almost, in making of him. The practical solution is this matter of social structure or free pattern. And definitely it is a matter of what we call or-

320

ganic architecture. So we must begin to learn to see life as organic architecture and begin to learn to see organic architecture as life. Broadacre City is not only the only democratic city; it is the only possible city looking towards any future for these United States.

Brownell: The big bell has rung three o'clock. The sun has moved around and is now a spot of silver foil on the side of your Ming tea jar. I grant that the big city has the seeds of death for itself and for people in it. But until we know the actual structure of Broadacre City, we have not yet made articulate in materials the new structure of society that you suggest. I suppose that you mean a Broadacre City type of community to be perhaps not more than 5,000 or 10,000 people.

Wright: No, any number of people, so long as the ground holds out, and our states insure that there is no danger of its running out. On the plan of Broadacre City nearly all of the inhabitants of the United States today could be accommodated today in the State of Texas alone.

Brownell: Do you assume that commercial farming will give way to self-sustaining farming?

Wright: Commercial farming is certainly a failure. It must give way to something. Why not natural farming, if you can imagine such a thing? Such farming would be self-sustaining farming.

Brownell: What would that be?

Wright: The answer to that question cannot be yet. We are getting too far into minor details before we clean up the

321

big ones. The general scheme we have not yet finished in outline.

Brownell:　But it is hard to understand principles unless we can see them in concrete experience.

Wright:　Well, let us proceed then to concrete experience. We have spoken of the new scale. We have spoken of the new simplicity : spoken too of the new space consciousness. Organic architecture in relation to organic living has been the real theme of this book, although well concealed by too many words. What, then, is all this to be like in terms of people, of town organization, of buildings and materials? What, then, will Broadacre buildings be like?

Brownell:　That is the question.

Wright:　The answer cannot be complete in words. That is why I have made plans and models. But something may be said.

Let us first take the problem of the poor. That means the housing problem receiving so much philanthropic attention from higher up at the moment. Beneficent though it is, it can only result in putting off by mitigation the day of regeneration for the poor. The majority of the poor are those damaged most by this growth of unearned increment as it piles up into vast fortunes by way of some kind of rent. Where is the place of the poor in this city now built by triple rent, that is to say rent within rent upon rent for rent? A vicious circle. There is always some dignity in freedom, even though one's own way may sink to license or filth. But what dignity can there be in

322

the cell of a soulless economic repetition? What dignity is there in spiritual poverty, even though some posy be stuck in a flower box, like a gratuity, for each poor man by those who, having bested him, would now better him?

Why not make more free to the poor the land they were born to inherit as they were born to inherit air to breathe and daylight to see by and water to drink? Else why are they born? I am aware of the academic economist's reaction to any land question. Nevertheless, Henry George clearly enough showed us the basis of poverty in human society. Some organic solution of this land problem is not only needed, it is imperative. Broadacre City proposes one and it is not the Single Tax.

What hope is there for a great or even a good architecture while land holds the improvements instead of the improvements made by the man holding the land? For any organic economic structure this is the wrong end about. Our architecture in the circumstances can only be for some landlord. But by some form of exemption and subsequent sharing of the increase in land values, we can now make his acre available to each so-called poor man, or rather make more than an acre available according to his ability to use the land. And let us begin to call his "education" that training which makes him competent in respect to this birthright of his—the ground. He has been industrialized to the limit. Now agrarianize him. Somewhat. Stop "classicizing" his progeny.

Brownell: And then what house for him? And where and how may he go to work to build it?

323

Wright: Having ground—what house? See the plans. They are truly ground plans. And where? Well, you will see in the models that mobilization is already his by way of a mobilized traffic lane that used to be the railroad, or some bus or perhaps a second-hand Ford, or perhaps a new one of his own, as the prices for Fords and other cars are going now. Emancipated from the rent that he must now pay in the city in order to work at all (everything he earns he must spend to keep him on the job), the machine worker goes back by way of this machine to his birthright in the ground. Ten miles or twenty is now easy for him. So where? Anywhere almost. He may go to work, perhaps, for some manufacturing employer in some decentralized factory unit near by. Fifteen miles is near by now by any modern standard of space or of time.

Now as to "how." Let us say that the poor man—the man at the machine is usually the poor man—buys the modern, civilized, standardized privy (it is a duplicate or even triplicate bathroom) manufactured and delivered complete in a single unit, even as his car or bathtub is manufactured and ready to use when connected to a standard tile septic tank or a cesspool. These costly civic improvements that cost so much are growing less necessary every day. Pass the hat, please, for Mr. Insull! The free man plants this first unit on his free ground as a focal point to which a standardized complete kitchen unit appropriate to the general plan of Broadacres may be added. As the months go by, the rent saved may buy other standardized units, harmonizing with the first. He earns them by work he has been trained to do on his own ground or trained

324

also to do in the factory units scattered about within, say, fifteen to thirty miles. Near by. The units would be suited in general scheme of design to assemby either on flat land or on hillside and be so designed as to make a well planned whole when put together. These various organic units cheaply become the machine worker's by way of his labor either in the factory unit near by or on his own ground or the ground of others. The benefits of standardization thus become his, just as the automobile has become his by the cheapening power of a mass production that serves him. Serves him now as a man and not as a machine. Such is the pre-fabricated house in Broadacres.

Being no longer intimidated by starvation—he can eat— he may say "yes" or "no" without fear. His ménage may grow as his devotion and labor grow. His family joins in this life on and of the ground in new circumstances—a new freedom altogether. He buys each building unit as he needs it in a group scheme that has had the benefit of expert study, in design and production, by the world's best minds. Not only may this group of units be variegated and so harmonized by design as to do no outrage to the landscape, but even now it may be so cheap that his rent for three months in the present city in order to "keep on the job" would buy him the first units needed for life in Broadacre City.

Brownell: Who do you think will do these things—will produce these units? The government? Or will you leave it to private industry?

Wright: Either by private or cooperative industry or by

governmental cooperation general manufacturing might be done. I see no reason why in Broadacre City there should be any discrimination one way or the other. The organic nature of the circumstances would determine "how."

In a year or two any man could own a house scientifically modern and aesthetically complete along any one of an infinite variety of lines and plan schemes, and his house would never become a regimentation. It would always be good to look at and at the same time be his own house. All could be hooked up in his own way with such a garden as he might make, out-buildings harmoniously added as he would need them.

Brownell: Will there be any way of controlling his own bad taste in selecting house design?

Wright: His own bad taste in selecting house design would be controlled by the fact that there would be no bad designs and that he would no longer be educated in bad taste. Even if he wanted bad ones he could find only good ones because in an organic architecture, that is to say architecture based upon organic ideals, bad design would be unthinkable. Impossible. With some proper aid in the way of tax exemption, here within reach of the poor man is a natural home of his own. In quality, so far as it went, his own home would be no inferior associate of the house of the man better off or further along next door. His devotion to work as a man would bring home comforts and graces to him as a free man. And the machine could give him this freedom in a five hundred dollar house, say, as it gives him his hundred and fifty dollar

326

automobile now standing in his forty dollar garage. This could all be his on a higher level of quality than ever before if the benefits of mass production were made available to him by voluntary cooperation.

Brownell: It seems to me you are thinking at one time of organic architecture as an ideal and at another time as a compulsion.

Wright: I am thinking of it as both. Is not any ideal a very real compulsion?

Brownell: Only ideally, I am afraid.

Wright: Do you mean by "ideally," fancifully? Some personal fancy? The only discipline that can ever characterize any democratic society, I believe, is discipline from within, and that can only be what I call the discipline of an ideal.

Brownell: But I am wondering if there is here an adequate instrumentation of the ideal. What will make it actual? And for that matter, how can you save people from their own bad taste?

Wright: Two questions at once. I will answer the latter. Save people from bad taste? By allowing them to grow up more naturally, cultured as well as "educated" (perhaps instead)—providing meantime designs for manufacture that are organic designs. They may be had even now. Where then would be bad things that a man could buy to outrage the sensibilities of others? Where could he get inferior designs? You may ask where he would get superior designs. In the changed circumstances, he would probably make them himself. Or, if not, he would have a wide range of choice in designs made by those who could. He would himself, however, determine various relationships that would still give individuality to the whole arrangement. In any case, bad units he could not find. Nor could he assemble those he could find in any way to do violence to the unity of the whole. Because the scheme, I would remind you, is organic in character.

Brownell: I think your ideal is noble, but I cannot help but feel you are ignoring the kind of human animals we are, with our bad taste and our commercial architects. Still it is true, I suppose, that today it is impossible to buy an ugly automobile, and so tomorrow it may be impossible to buy an ugly house. I wait with hope.

Wright: I do not take our present bad taste and commercial architects to Broadacres. As for nobility—what is it? As for commercial architects, commercial architecture would have no place in Broadacre City, nor anything else purely commercial. So that unnatural type of animal would not be there. I referred at the outset to a new success ideal. I don't think Broadacre City would be fit for humans that have been more or less degraded by the circumstances in which they now live. Something would have to be done for them while they last. Some preparation for their end. Time for development is essential for the betterment of anything human. Betterment cannot be imposed. Seldom ever is it a gift. Broadacres sets up preparation first and foremost, as you may see by studying the plan.

Brownell: That development is very important. I am

328

doubtful, however, whether education can do much more than make articulate the standards and values already practiced in a society.

Wright: As education stands at present, you might be right. But culture remains. Let us turn the job over to culture. From generation to generation is organic growth: and that growth is culture.

Brownell: You mean culture as a verb, I take it, a kind of action, not a noun.

Wright: I have no concern with culture as verb or noun. It is an act. It would be folly to take a man away as he is, take him from tending a machine which his whole thought, all the cultural life he had experienced, and put him onto ground which he did not understand and with which, to begin with, he could do nothing. I repeat, organic growth is slow growth. There is no short cut. The quick turnover is cut out. But, only growth is safe. Broadacre City is a safe city.

Brownell: An illustration of your Broadacre City occurs to me which you will probably not accept, but which seems to me a good example of a functional relationship of land to life in towns. In early New England they built their villages with a limited amount of lar 1 to each person, and when there was no more land available, they allowed no more people to settle in the village. They started a new village somewhere else. Their building and their land were functional in respect to their lives.

Wright: So far as they went—so good. They did well in the circumstances. But that they were really functional in the

329

organic sense I do not believe. It was the same building they were accustomed to and wanted, by habit only; furthermore, it was probably the only one they could get, and they borrowed money to buy their ground. They did their best with it. But their life was destined to pass away because it had no genuine organic basis in relation to the whole.

Brownell: It was good within their limits because there was nothing else they could do.

Wright: It was good within its limits, but not good enough today according to present possibilities in the light of an organic architecture.

Brownell: I see Father Menifer with his twenty protégés marching upon you. They have left their big bus down the hill and have come to see Taliesin. Everyone has a camera, it seems. I can't see who is conducting them. It looks like Jim Thompson. Now he has detoured them. They are going towards the play-house. That will give us a few minutes more. It is nearly four o'clock.

Your big Ming jar has turned greenish in the afternoon sunlight. It is a Ming jar, I hope, after all I have said about it.

Wright: You are safe. Yes, it is a Ming tea jar. I brought eight back with me from Pekin (now Peiping) but four have been destroyed by weather, or the fire of 1925 . . . they are gone.

Brownell: But this one is left. It has changed color in the different sun. On the hill across the way the shadows of the rocks and trees have disappeared, so far as I can see, withered

360

quite away on the steep slope. And our efforts to find the nature of structure and of structure made manifest in the social and architectural pattern of Broadacre City have also matured, though not, I hope, withered away. Perhaps the simplest conclusion we can make, in view of what we have said many times throughout the book, is that we cannot hope for a good architecture until we have a good society.

Wright: The discussion may have matured somewhat. But I doubt the maturity. As for the hope for a good architecture, we can have a good architecture meantime by way of good architects working for good individuals. We may have valuable exemplars without waiting for the entire mass to come along and make them a mass product.

Brownell: They can act as lights for the way.

Wright: Naturally such creative exemplars so act. If we ever do have an organic social order worthy of an organic architecture, it will come to us with the other because of the perception, devotion, and better understanding of such appreciative people as are ours. As for creative work we call the results works of art—I cannot see that thing coming from the bottom up.

Brownell: Nor from the top down.

Wright: Why not?

Brownell: I think one is as vicious as the other.

Wright: Why? Why should the top of a society be vicious, if that top is not artificially top, therefore sterile? Unable to go to seed? Nature produces her seeds at the top unless

331

we are speaking of pumpkins and then they are well inside.

Brownell: I don't mean that the top is vicious. I mean the method of coming from the top down.

Wright: But the blossom at the top or tip has preceded the fruit. It is organic. Better things could not come from any other source or from any other direction than from the genuinely best or bravest of our people.

Brownell: There are many instances where great movements have been created by the changing conditions. The best and bravest are many, many people awaiting only those conditions to call them forth.

Wright: True enough. The few in the many, as the many are in the few. Just as you will find all great movements motivated by great individuals. Great individuals expressing the many.

Brownell: The great individual reflects the implicit ideals of the many who are unable to express them.

Wright: Yes, but I think the ideals of the few creative intellects, which are really the minds of the body politic, are reflected no less by that body. Perhaps greatly more. What I refer to is again from the top down, but the organic top of a bottom from which it proceeded or was produced.

Brownell: But isn't that the same as "from the bottom up," which is something that you repudiated a moment ago? Then you were about to go Platonic again—aristocratic segregation. But now, when you say "the organic top of a bottom from which it was produced," it is hard to tell which way you are going. Perhaps you are going both ways.

332

Yet I think that your attitude is probably consistent after all. If you discriminate between the great artist's self-confident isolation from herd standards in the process and method of his work, and the artist's necessary integration with his people in function, ideal, and the deep expression of their lives, and if you give the greater emphasis to the latter, then I am sure that you are consistent. The artist is the instrument of a people's expression. But I wouldn't call that "from the top down."

Wright: Perhaps we are involved with the immortal "which came first, the hen or the egg?" I don't mean that top which is top by virtue of adventitious circumstance. I don't mean the top by way of an artificial aristocracy, one of birth and of privileged place. Nor do I mean those advantaged by money who have their place by virtue of something not their own. When I speak of "the top" I mean the organic top. I mean humanity's best and bravest minds, natures, and characters produced out of itself by way of itself, in the course of events to come down by way of itself that others may become top in due course. There can be no other interpretation of life as organic.

Brownell: That's better. I would answer what you were saying a moment ago by quoting your own fine doctrine of art, namely, that art is making manifest the implicit character of the materials of which it is created. I think the great individual is simply making manifest the characteristics of the people from which he comes.

Wright: I don't think you should use the word "simply"

363

in that connection if you mean by simply "only." Growth cannot come by way of any interpretation and expression of the stupidities, limitations, inferiorities of a people. It comes down to all that find the best and the highest of which they, the people, are capable, leading them, reacting upon them. And the matter goes still further: things of which the people themselves are frequently unaware until they see them, ideas which exist for them only as potentialities, are laid out for them by somebody a little further along than they, a little more articulate and certainly vastly deeper in the experience of life. The great artist lays it out for them where they can see it, touch it, apprehend it as life itself.

Brownell: Just as a beautiful carving in wood is determined by the limitations of the nature of wood, so the great individual is determined by the limitations of the people from which he comes.

Wright: But my point is that he is not limited by the determinations of his people. The limitations of his own human nature and the characteristics of the people of whom he is a part are as much the artist as themselves, but they are to him no limitation. However, if he is too far from the nature of the people he cannot serve them; if he is too much of them he cannot serve them; only if he is to them as your head is to your body or your mind is to your corporeality, can he do anything at all for them as artist. They see in parts. He must see and grasp the whole. His work is the flower of his race proceeding from that race as seed from the soil, dropping down into it again to germinate and produce other flowering.

334

Brownell: Again we come to the same point of view, but by different roads, and I think that perhaps is our conclusion.

Wright: A conclusion proper enough, although Broadacre City still remains to be seen as an architect's model, not coming much nearer because of words, notwithstanding all your skill. As for the artist, I might add that until the artist is more the society he serves than the society is itself, he is not a great artist.

THE END

Afterword

THOUGH the foregoing pages were written after much conversation between the two authors, who were not, to begin with, very far apart in fundamental points of view, there remain a good many minor inconsistencies in the book if not, perhaps, contradictions. We have made no great effort to get rid of them. Many of them are due to different interpretations of words. Others refer to minor prejudices and predispositions in the authors which we do not care to compromise. After all, strict consistency is only a lesser virtue in a book such as this.

The most serious of these inconsistencies is probably in the use of the word "horizontal." It is used in two senses: first, as the earth-sense or the long line of the house lying on the land; second, as a type of industrial, economic, and social organization which in effect is in conflict with the earth-sense represented by the word in its other meaning. The use of the word in the respective contexts is so important in each case that we did not try to change it.

Chicago and Taliesin, May 22, 1937.

BAKER BROWNELL

FRANK LLOYD WRIGHT

Index

338